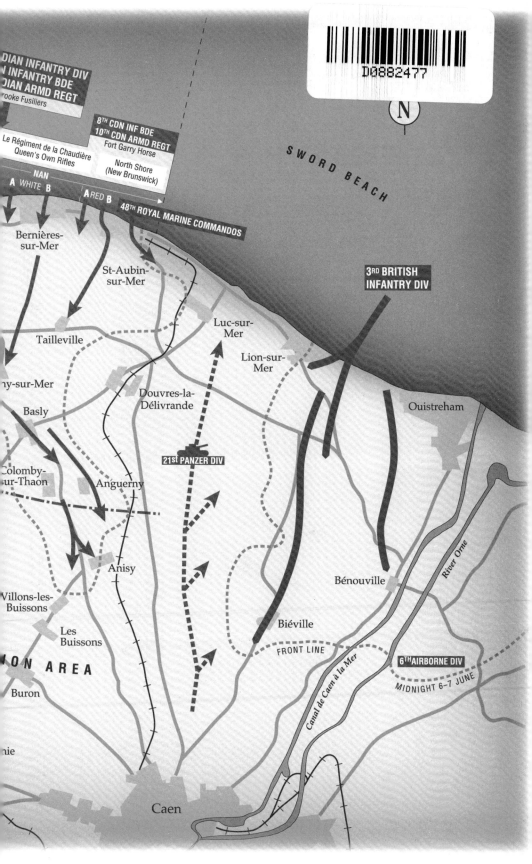

DIAN INFANTRY DIV
N INFANTRY BDE
DIAN ARMD REGT
rooke Fusiliers

8TH CDN INF BDE
10TH CDN ARMD REGT
Fort Garry Horse

Le Régiment de la Chaudière
Queen's Own Rifles

North Shore
(New Brunswick)

NAN
A WHITE B   A RED B
48TH ROYAL MARINE COMMANDOS

S W O R D   B E A C H

N

3RD BRITISH
INFANTRY DIV

Bernières-
sur-Mer

St-Aubin-
sur-Mer

Luc-sur-
Mer

Lion-sur-
Mer

Ouistreham

Tailleville

ny-sur-Mer

Douvres-la-
Délivrande

Basly

21st PANZER DIV

Colomby-
sur-Thaon

Anguerny

Bénouville

River Orme

Anisy

Villons-les-
Buissons

Biéville

6TH AIRBORNE DIV

Les
Buissons

FRONT LINE

MIDNIGHT 6–7 JUNE

ON AREA

Buron

Canal de Caen à la Mer

nie

Caen

Books of Merit

JUNO

ALSO BY TED BARRIS

MILITARY HISTORY

Behind the Glory: The Plan That Won the Allied Air War

Days of Victory: Canadians Remember, 1939–1945
  (with Alex Barris)

Deadlock in Korea: Canadians at War, 1950–1953

Canada and Korea: Perspectives 2000 (contributor)

OTHER NON-FICTION

Fire Canoe: Prairie Steamboat Days Revisited

Rodeo Cowboys: The Last Heroes

Positive Power: The Story of the Edmonton Oilers Hockey Club

Spirit of the West: The Beginnings, the Land, the Life

Playing Overtime: A Celebration of Oldtimers' Hockey

Carved in Granite: 125 Years of Granite Club History

Making Music: Profiles from a Century of Canadian Music
  (with Alex Barris)

JUNO

CANADIANS AT D-DAY
JUNE 6, 1944

Ted Barris

Foreword by John Keegan

Thomas Allen Publishers
Toronto

National Library of Canada Cataloguing in Publication

Barris, Ted
    Juno : Canadians at D-Day, June 6, 1944 / Ted Barris.

Includes bibliographical references and index.
ISBN 0-88762-133-3

1. World War, 1939–1945—Campaigns—France—Normandy.
2. Canada. Canadian Army—History—World War, 1939–1945.
I. Title.

D756.5.N6B36 2004   940.54'21422   C2003-905514-0

Editor: Jim Gifford
Jacket design: Gordon Robertson
Jacket image: Bill Grant / courtesy the Royal Canadian Military Institute

Every reasonable effort has been made to locate the copyright holders of material found in this book. In the event that any material has not been correctly sourced, the publisher will gladly receive correspondence in efforts to rectify the citation in future printings.

Published by Thomas Allen Publishers,
a division of Thomas Allen & Son Limited,
145 Front Street East, Suite 209,
Toronto, Ontario M5A 1E3 Canada

www.thomas-allen.com

  **Canada Council
for the Arts**

ONTARIO ARTS COUNCIL
CONSEIL DES ARTS DE L'ONTARIO

The publisher gratefully acknowledges the support of the Ontario Arts Council for its publishing program.

We acknowledge the support of the Canada Council for the Arts, which last year invested $21.7 million in writing and publishing throughout Canada.

We acknowledge the Government of Ontario through the Ontario Media Development Corporation's Ontario Book Initiative.

08 07 06 05 04   3 4 5

Printed and bound in Canada

To Alex Barris, who's written a million words in recognition of others, but who never spoke a word about his service as a U.S. Army medic in 1944–45, when his "unselfish devotion to duty" earned him the Bronze Star.

CONTENTS

List of Maps and Illustrations

Foreword by John Keegan

In May 1994, as the fiftieth anniversary of D-Day approached, I was invited to dinner with President Clinton in the White House. He was about to depart for Europe to help celebrate the Continent's liberation and he was seeking the advice of historians as to what he should say. The other five historians present were American; I was the only Commonwealth representative. Carlo D'Este urged the president to praise the French Resistance. Stephen Ambrose stressed the importance of the airborne operations. Forrest Pogue, who had interviewed men who made the landing on the evening of D-Day itself, spoke movingly of his fellow countrymen. When my turn came, I said, "Don't forget the Canadians." I explained that, of the five D-Day beaches, two had been British, two American, and one Canadian, Juno. I said that it had been an extraordinary achievement for a country of Canada's modest population to provide a force large enough to assault so large a sector, to take it and to advance inland, and that the achievement was a source of enormous Canadian national pride. The president nodded, noticed my advice, and, when in France, paid generous tribute.

The Canadian Army's exploits on Juno Beach were indeed extraordinary; so were those of the Royal Canadian Air Force in the skies and the Royal Canadian Navy offshore. The story of all three services is told here by Ted Barris, largely through the personal testimony of participants who left a record or whom the author has interviewed. By a skilful interweaving, he takes the readers through reconnaissance and preliminary bombardment with the RCAF, the Channel crossing with the RCN, and then the first landing, by paratroopers of the 1st Canadian Parachute Battalion, which jumped as part of the British 6th Airborne Division. It was a party from that battalion which secured and then blew the Robehomme bridge over the River Dives, on the eastern flank of the bridgehead, a key task since it would turn the river into a water obstacle preventing a German counterattack against the open end of the landing beaches.

The main Canadian effort, on Juno itself, was mounted by ten battalions of Canadian infantry supported by three armoured regiments. The Canadians of the First World War had fought in units that bore numbers only, a system that denied them easily memorable identity. For the Second World War the units had resumed their old militia titles, giving the Canadian order of battle a splendid roll call of place name and history: Queen's Own Rifles, Régiment de la Chaudière, North Shore (New Brunswick) Regiment, Stormont, Dundas and Glengarry Highlanders. The armoured regiments were the 1st Hussars, the Fort Garry Horse, and the Sherbrooke Fusiliers.

The Queen's Own Rifles of Canada was to leave, entirely through the hazard of war, one of the most memorable of all D-Day images. Inside one of its landing craft was a film cameraman, Sergeant Bill Grant. There were several other photographers with the assault troops, but all lost their equipment in the frenzy of the approach. Grant did not, set his camera rolling, and so caught the drama of touchdown and beach crossing. So the viewer sees the infantrymen readying themselves in the last seconds of the run-in—one pats the man ahead of him on the back to receive a "don't bother me now" glance—the ramp goes down, the seawall and beachfront houses appear, and then the riflemen sprint down the ramp, across the sand, into the defenders' fire. The footage is one of the most graphic depictions of combat ever recorded.

By the end of D-Day, many Canadians had left the beach behind and were battling deep inland in the Normandy countryside. Of the 15,000 who had landed, 960 had been killed or badly wounded. The Royal Winnipeg Rifles were at Creully, one of the deepest points of penetration anywhere in the landing area.

The battle of Normandy was only beginning. Weeks of hard fighting lay ahead before the Allies could break out and begin the great encirclement that would drive the Germans to the Seine and eventually out of France altogether. It is still possible, however, to detect on the ground where and how the Canadians fought, by reading the dates of death on the headstones in the Commonwealth War Graves cemeteries that mark the progress inland. Hundreds are Canadian and many, many of them are marked June 6, 1944. Ted Barris fittingly tells their brave story.

— John Keegan

Acknowledgments

Just after 5 a.m. on June 6, 1969, I finished the last newscast of an overnight radio shift in Lindsay, Ontario. Those awake that Friday morning heard my report on the major stories of the day: the crash of a Mexican airliner, the countdown to the launch of Apollo 11 and plans for the first moonwalk, Richard Nixon announcing the withdrawal of 25,000 troops from Vietnam, Joe Namath quitting football and observance of the twenty-fifth anniversary of D-Day.

Within minutes of my sign-off there was a knock at the front door of the radio station. As I was alone in the building at that hour, I answered the door myself. Standing in the bright sunshine, saluting me, was a middle-aged man in full Canadian military uniform. He greeted me curtly but politely and informed me that the invasion had begun: Canadians had landed on Juno Beach.

Events of June 6, 1944, had so affected the man he seemed to be reliving the moment.

Out of respect, I listened and said nothing. From the ribbons and medals across his chest I realized he was a Second World War veteran and could well have dashed onto the beaches of Normandy a quarter century earlier. I'm sorry now that I didn't invite him in to recount his wartime experiences. In the years since, as I have grown into middle age myself, I have listened to many veterans like him. This is the first time, however, I've had the opportunity to thank that unknown soldier for sparking my interest in the Canadian D-Day story.

D-Day veterans themselves form the nucleus of this work.

In the 35 years since my first encounter with that uniformed veteran on the front step of CKLY in Lindsay, hundreds more have fielded my questions about the Canadian contribution to Operation Overlord. Those who have provided unique inspiration through their personal memoirs include Fred Barnard, Eugene Bell, Stephen Bell, Ella Binns, Gordon Clarke, Charles Cline, Bob Dale, Jan de Vries, Gordon Drodge, Bruce Evans, Kathleen Evans, Ken Ewart, Walter Filbrandt, Jack Foote, Charley Fox, Hector Gaudet, Pierre Gauthier, John Gorsline, Tom Guy, Laurette Hilborn, Noel Horan, Ernie Jeans, Don Kerr, Dave Kingston, Sam Levine, Bill Little, Mark Lockyer, John MacCormack, John McDonald, Ray Mecoy, Joe Oggy, Cliff Perry, Osborne Perry, Desmond Piers, Richard Rohmer, Chuck Ross, Fred Sampson, Walter Schierer, Alan Skaife, Hubert Thistle, John Turnbull, Frank Vines, Fred Walden, Garth Webb, Reg Weeks, Hal Whitten, Jimmy Wilson, and Scott Young, to name only some of the principal figures.

Among those Canadian veterans who recorded their first-hand memoirs in written form and allowed me full access are Wesley Alkenbrack, Edward Baker, Richard Brown, Tony Burns, Bob Cameron, George Devonshire, Ren Henderson, Richard Hilborn, Bill Ross, Dr. Paul G. Schwager, William Stewart and Bill Warshick.

French civilians Jacques Martin, Bernard Martin and Roger Alexandre, among others, gave me a unique perspective of the D-Day invasion from ashore in Normandy as they witnessed it.

Special thanks to Rosalie Hartigan for her assistance in giving me access to Dan Hartigan's published memoir *A Rising of Courage*. Appreciation too, to Murray Peden, author of *A Thousand Shall Fall*; Monty Berger, *Invasions Without Tears*; Ralph Campbell, *We Flew by Moonlight*; Russell McKay, *One of the Many*; Richard Rohmer, *Patton's Gap*; and the Greater Vancouver Branch of the Aircrew Association, *Critical Moments*. I owe special thanks to journalist and author Jean E. Portugal for her inspiration and assistance via her published series *We Were There*.

For their help in procuring correspondence and photographs exchanged between D-Day troops and their families, I thank Cecil Pittman for the Meakin family letters; Penny Adair and Beverly Vasey for the letters and memoirs of Donald James; Gene More for memorabilia of his father, Charlie More; Joanne de Vries for personal photographs; Mary Lea Bell for photographs from the Ken Bell collection; Edna A. Baker for the letters of Edward Baker; brother and sister Bill and Roberta Lockyer for stories of their father's return to Juno Beach; and Carol Phillips for correspondence with Brian O'Regan.

While a personal book collection has provided a steady diet of background on this story for years, other collectors— some private, some public—have offered valuable access for my research. In particular, I wish to thank librarian Arthur Manvell and museum curator Gregory Loughton at the Royal Canadian Military Institute in Toronto; Dave Zink, owner of Grenadier Militaria book store in Port Perry, Ontario; Leon J. Chamois, curator of the Stormont, Dundas and Glengarry Highlanders regimental museum in Cornwall, Ontario; Wes and Carole Libbey of Cornwall; and Sylvia and Clifford Robb in Uxbridge, Ontario.

Often I needed verification of historical detail data and from specialized authorities on print or photographic material.

Among those who ably assisted this project: author and archivist Dr. Jean-Pierre Bénamou, Bayeux Museum in France; Frank Marie, archivist of Le Mémorial de Caen in France; Martina Caspers at the Bundesarchiv in Germany; Katie Simpson at the *Illustrated London News* library in England; historian Ted Ross at the Juno Beach Centre (France); historian Mike Filey in Toronto; Michel Wyczynski, honorary archivist of the 1st Canadian Parachute Battalion Association; Dan Somers, archivist at the National Archives of Canada; Major Mathias Joost at the Directorate of History and Heritage in Ottawa; Janet Lacroix and Dennis J. Mah of the C.F. Photo Unit in Ottawa; Alastair Neely, curator, 1st Hussars Museum, London, Ontario; Gord Crossley at the Fort Garry Horse Museum and Archives in Winnipeg; Tom Bochsler and Terry Meginnis of Bochsler PhotoImaging in Burlington, Ontario; author Larry Milberry and publisher of Canav Books; Gary Hughes, curator, North Shore (New Brunswick) Regiment, Saint John, New Brunswick; Jan Roseneder, librarian, Museum of the Regiments, Calgary, Alberta; photographer Terry Paul; and Dan Black, managing editor of *Legion* magazine. Special thanks to Ken Wright for his enthusiasm and his eagle eye.

In the preparation of the manuscript, in particular the final chapter, which chronicles the creation of the Juno Beach Centre, I am most grateful to the committee and volunteers of the Centre, especially Garth Webb, Lise Cooper, Don Cooper, Don Kerr, Ted Davie, Bill Granger, Chick McGregor and Dennis Hopkins. For assistance and access at the Centre in Courseulles-sur-Mer, France, I am grateful to onsite director Natalie Worthington and her staff, including Katie McBride, Rachel St. John and Sylvia Wayne.

Since much of the book's raw material came from exclusive conversation on audio cassette or videotape, I could never have written a word were it not for assistance in transcribing the original interviews. Some recorded in French were ably translated by Dr. Francois Bessay, Nadia Torfs and Laura Senese; those who transcribed the bulk of the recordings were Marlene Lumley, Alex Barris, Kate Barris, Whitney and Quenby Barris, Jessica Bodger, but mostly Braunda Bodger.

At the CBC Radio archives, Gail Donald and Norbert Boily (in Toronto) and Marie-Claude Langlois (in Montreal) provided me with access to the original recorded transcripts of CBC and BBC war correspondents, principally the D-Day reports of Matthew Halton and Marcel Ouimet. Media librarian Lynda Barnett provided access and assistance at the CBC photo archives in Toronto. For access to the Dominion Institute's electronic data bank, I thank Jessica Humphreys, manager of the Memory Project, and Rudyard Griffiths, executive director of the Institute. Jennifer Parmelee provided additional videotaped interview content from talks given by Reg Weeks. For transcripts of interviews I conducted for a Wal-Mart sponsored veterans' archives, I thank Darri Beaulieu of Wal-Mart Canada corporate affairs and Robert White of White Hat Productions in Toronto.

I am grateful to military historian Sir John Keegan for his vivid introductory images and welcome analysis of the manuscript.

For their contributions in the assembly of this book, I express thanks to mapmaker John Lightfoot, copy editor Kathleen Richards, art director Gord Robertson, inputter Miriam Brown, proofreader Jeanette King, and Mark C. Luk for gathering bibliographic resources. I give heartfelt thanks to managing editor Jim Gifford and publisher Patrick Crean for their passion for this work, for their attention to details large and small, for their respect for the gift of veterans' recollections and their sustained zeal for our *Juno* to succeed the way our fathers' Juno Beach did.

I have often wondered, as I prepared these chapters, how very little the men who participated in the D-Day operation could have known about their futures that grey morning in 1944. To them, the day's activity was confined to a cockpit, a gun sight, a damp spot aboard a landing craft and ultimately an objective that remained secret until the very moment their planes and ships were launched that day. They could not have known that the massive deception plan against Hitler's armies would work almost to the last detail. They could not have known that neither the German air force nor its navy would challenge the invasion force to any large degree. They could not have known that by day's end nearly 175,000 Allied troops would have set foot safely in France. That 9,000 would die in the day's action. They could not have known that within eleven months they would bring an end to the war in Europe. That they would alter history. At best, their efforts on June 6, 1944, were viewed in the cold dawn of D-Day, as one colossal gamble, a well-laid plan with no guarantee of victory.

In that sense, their "longest day" and this book are similar. A good plan, much work, but a gamble with no guarantees.

"You are about to embark upon the Great Crusade," Dwight D. Eisenhower told the thousands who took off, set sail and prepared to dash ashore or parachute in France that June 6 morning in 1944.

No author has armies at the ready to carry out the foot soldiering that comprises a book such as this. I did find many who were able and willing, however, to contribute to, as the SHAEF commander described his military objective 59 years ago, a "great and noble undertaking."

— Ted Barris, 2004

JUNO

PRELUDE

N OTHING about this mission was what it seemed.

Since June 1941, Canadian tank crews had lived in tents on Salisbury Plain in the south of England. For six months straight they had trained inside troop carriers, pretending they were tanks. When a supply of Matilda tanks, whose earlier models were in service in the North African campaign, finally arrived on the scene, each troop of tank crews took turns practising amphibious landings and dryland tactics in them.

Then the crews had received squadrons of Churchill tanks. Thicker-skinned and often referred to as "having bugs in their guts," these were the fighting machines they would actually use in battle. Next, the Canadian corps men were told they were headed to the Isle of Wight for simulated assault practice. Then the rains came, washed out the training time, and sent them, soggy and dispirited, scurrying back to their south England barracks.

Even on this designated pre-dawn summer morning, commanding officers had told the tank-corps crews they were performing a demonstration run in front of King George and Queen Elizabeth. And though they told the crews not to take any extra baggage, just to load their vehicles with as much ammunition as they could carry, to the men the exercise still seemed like yet another rehearsal.

Even Trooper Stephen Bell was not what he appeared that morning. He was not actually the twenty-year-old that his enlistment attestation papers claimed he was. He had really been born in 1923 and was technically still a teenager.

Suddenly, none of that mattered any more. This morning, an underage Saskatchewan farm boy, who had originally signed up in Toronto with the 48th Highlanders, became Trooper Bell, a bona fide wireless radio operator seated inside a fully armed Churchill tank, aboard a landing craft for tanks (LCT) en route to the coast of France.

"Halfway across the Channel," Bell said, "I realized we weren't going on any demonstration."

Stephen Bell crossed the English Channel that day in a naval task force consisting of 237 vessels. In addition to Bell's tank crew, aboard the scores of infantry and tank landing craft, were more than 6,000 soldiers—4,963 Canadian, 1,075 British, 50 American, and 15 Free French—all part of a commando-type raid against Nazi-occupied France.

One of Bell's comrades, Archie Anderson, voiced a feeling common to all that morning: "We had a foreboding as we left England."

The first sign of trouble came as the carriers neared the task force's disembarkation point. In the darkness just before 4 a.m., any hope of surprising the enemy evaporated when twenty-three of the Allied landing craft and three armed escorts ran head on into a German convoy and its armed E-boats. The short engagement that followed scattered part of the landing fleet and, worse, alerted German shore batteries that the Allies were up to something.

H-hour was just before 5 a.m. Within thirty minutes, the tanks in Stephen Bell's assault group were supposed to land. According to the plan of attack, the four-inch guns of four Royal Navy destroyers would lay down a barrage from just off-shore and five squadrons of Royal Air Force Hurricane fighters would suppress enemy fire with air cover during the tanks' run-in. The tanks arrived fifteen minutes behind schedule. By then the air and naval bombardment was over and the German 37-mm anti-tank gunners began zeroing in on the approaching Canadian armour.

"With all the tracers coming at us, it was like the fourth of July," Bell said. "We were hit on the turret just coming down the [carrier's] ramp. The shell hit the top of the tank and blew the lid right off. All you could see up there was daylight. . . . It also blew out the radio, so I was useless."

A greater natural foe presented itself at the base of Bell's LCT ramp. Instead of finding the expected steady incline of sand breaking the surface of the salt water and rising gradually up to dry land, his tank debarked onto a seashore of fist-sized rocks, all loose and unstable. As soon as the track treads of his 44-ton Churchill tank touched this slippery chert, they churned up the stones like snow in a drift rather than planing over the top, and sank deeper and deeper on the spot.

"We got maybe fifteen or twenty feet up from the water's edge," Bell remembered, "and that was it. Engines ran, but the tank wouldn't move forwards or backwards. We got hit three or four times in that fifteen feet."

The 14th Canadian Army Tank Regiment (Calgary Regiment) landed on the beach in two waves. Two Churchills were swamped immediately and sank in the shallows, while half of the rest met the same fate as Stephen Bell's F2 tank. They all bogged down in the loose shingle on the beach. In addition, the

Churchill's main gun, primarily designed to deliver armour-piercing shot, was of little help in defending the troops of the Royal Hamilton Light Infantry, the Essex Scottish, and Les Fusiliers Mont-Royal against mortars and machine guns.

Undeterred, Bell and those left in his tank pressed on, eager to participate in the battle. He and crewmate Johnny Booker scrambled outside with a machine gun. Within minutes they had found shelter against the tracks of their disabled tank, scooped some loose stones into a parapet, set up their gun, and begun firing, Bell feeding the shells to Booker who fired them. Unable to use his radio and constrained to feeding the machine gun, Bell became frustrated.

"Let me fire for a while," Bell called to Booker. "I'm fed up doing nothing." They switched places and resumed the fight.

Minutes after Bell began shooting, the German defenders homed in on their position and another anti-tank shell slammed into the Churchill right over their heads. Tank-track debris came splintering down on the two of them. This time both were wounded, shrapnel striking Booker in the legs and Bell in the back; the latter discovered his ears were bleeding from the concussion of the shell explosions, so he stuffed field dressing into them. Nearby, the rest of Bell's tank crewmates were faltering too. Gunner Charlie Provost was shot in the head and died. Then driver Bill Willard was hit in the ankle, knee, and shoulder, and as he lay wounded, a mortar shell landed next to him.

"Willard got opened up from his breastbone down to his crotch," Bell said. "Earl Snider and I had this first-aid kit. We got a couple of safety pins, stuck everything back inside, and pinned him up."

By eleven o'clock the beleaguered Canadians began to retreat off the beach into returning landing craft. Orders to the crews were to pull back with their tanks, if possible; otherwise the men were to destroy them. Stephen Bell and his remaining crewmates had little choice. Their vehicle had been hit more than a dozen times. Booker and Bell joined the rush for the boats, trying to pull some of the wounded down to the landing craft with them, but before they could make it to the water's edge German troops poured over the promenade and the seawall.

"Down behind one of the [landing craft] they'd hoisted a white flag," he said, "because the tide was coming in and they knew that if they stayed they'd drown, and if they moved away they'd get shot. . . . Besides, every boat except one or two got blown up in the water.

"Talk to anybody on that beach and they'll tell you that water was like red ink. The blood. Bodies like cordwood rolling in the water. The water coming up on the beach was foaming red."

By midday, Bell faced German troops in the middle of the chaotic wreckage of tanks and landing craft and the groups of other huddling Canadian survivors. The Germans shouted at him to surrender and pointed at the revolver on his waist. He loosened his gun belt and let it drop to his feet. For Stephen Bell, the war was over.

The six-hour hit-and-run raid on the French seaport of Dieppe that morning, August 19, 1942, had ended with Bell's becoming a prisoner of war. He was one of 1,946 men the German defenders captured that day, more than the whole Canadian Army would lose in Western Europe in almost an entire year of action between D-Day on June 6, 1944, and VE Day on May 8, 1945. Altogether 3,367 of the nearly 5,000 Canadians who had embarked from England that day became casualties. More than 900 of those were killed in the bloodiest nine hours in Canadian military history.

The Germans triumphantly paraded the Canadians—the ones who could walk—through the streets of Dieppe in front of cameras. They force-marched their prisoners to a nearby cement factory, then to a prison camp near Paris, and eventually shipped them to POW camps in Poland. As punishment for their role in the Dieppe raid, many of the Canadians were shackled or bound for weeks and months at a time. Each received little more than a cup of tea, two potatoes, a slice of black bread, and soup as a daily food ration. Stephen Bell attempted to escape five times and was recaptured four times.

Bell had thirty-four months of imprisonment to think about why the Dieppe raid had failed and why any consideration of a large-scale Allied invasion of France needed a complete overhaul. While he would have nearly three years of captivity to mull over the mistakes at Dieppe, Bell's superiors had little time to come up with a strategy for invading France and establishing a true second front against the German army.

Plenty of evidence exists to demonstrate that there was little or no element of surprise at Dieppe. The August 19 raid had originally been planned for July 4, but was called off because of bad weather. The obvious danger in resurrecting an aborted raid was that the Germans might well be on the alert. Indeed, the day after the original raid was called off, Adolf Hitler himself issued a communiqué to his top commanders warning of the probability of an Allied raid on the French coast. The most likely area, he noted, was the Channel coast, somewhere between Dieppe and Le Havre. The Allies would have to keep airtight security around any future attempt to open a second front in northwestern Europe, and proceed without alteration or postponement once the plans were set.

Accidental encounters such as that of the landing craft with German E-boats on the run in to the Dieppe beaches vividly illustrated the importance of Allied superiority in the air over the Channel as well as in the water lanes of any invasion flotilla between Britain and the landing area in France. Backing up the assault's sea and landing forces with the firepower of a handful of Royal Navy destroyers hovering offshore and with air cover from a half-dozen squadrons of Hurricane fighters for a matter of minutes was clearly insufficient. To succeed against entrenched enemy defences, a sustained assault required an equally sustained neutralizing of those defences by naval and air bombardment preceding the landing. In other words, every invasion element, every detail, would need to be coordinated among the land, sea, and air forces.

Improperly constructed, difficult to navigate, and poorly defended Landing Craft Infantry (LCIs) would have to be vastly improved to deliver troops successfully to any beach in France. More efficient and ergonomic ways would have to be found to launch armoured vehicles from Landing Craft Tanks (LCTs) into the heart of a shoreline battlefield. The vulnerability of both craft—and the men and equipment they contained—would have to be eliminated or at least dramatically reduced before a frontal assault on an armed and entrenched enemy could succeed.

Dieppe also demonstrated that all members of the Allied Expeditionary Forces had to work from the same battle plan with the same purpose. The avowed goals of the Dieppe raid were at least threefold and motivated by the political agenda of each participating Allied force: the British wanted to engage in an exercise that would teach all the Allies how to invade Hitler's Fortress Europe; the Canadian command staff, after watching its troops become bored for two and a half years at training camps in England, wanted its forces to see some action; and the Americans wanted to satisfy, however minimally, the Russians' urgent plea that the Allies open a second, western front to back up their own attempts to repulse Hitler's forces on the eastern front.

Finally, the planners of any potential Allied invasion strategy might have done well to consider the words of those civilian war correspondents who witnessed and reported on the Dieppe raid itself. The first British and American reports glossed over the truth of the disaster. One correspondent who declined to join in the chorus of self-congratulation was Ross Munro of the Canadian Press. He covered the raid from the deck of an infantry landing craft and he veiled his despair over the debacle only enough to deflect the censors.

"Canadian shock troops had a rough time of it at several points," he wrote, "and losses probably will not be small." He had no qualms about admitting that he had just spent "the grimmest twenty minutes of my life . . . when a rain of German machine-gun fire wounded half the men in our boat, and only a miracle saved us from annihilation.

"By the time our boat touched the beach the din was at a crescendo," his first CP story noted. "I peered out at the slope lying just in front of us, and it was startling to discover it was dotted with the fallen forms of men in battle-dress. The Royals [Royal Regiment of Canada] ahead of us had been cut down as they stormed the slope. It came home to me only then that every one of those men had gone down under the bullets of the enemy at the top of the incline."

His integrity compelled him to praise the valour and spirit of the Canadians without ignoring the horror of their fate. The events of that awful day never receded in Munro's mind, and he wrote about it again, in 1945:

"Looking out the open bow [of the landing craft] I saw sixty or seventy bodies, men cut down before they could fire a shot. A dozen Canadians were running along the beach toward the twelve-foot-high seawall, one hundred yards long. Some fired as they ran. Some had no helmets. Some were wounded, their uniforms torn and bloody. One by one, they were hit and rolled down the slope to the sea."

Ralph Allen, war correspondent for the Toronto *Globe and Mail* newspaper, writing after the fact, in 1961, referred to "the magnificent fiasco of Dieppe." He analyzed the ways and means that the apparently defeated Allied Expeditionary Force in 1942 managed to right itself by the spring of 1944. He wrote that the Dieppe raid that "ended in a bloody and almost total failure . . . provided many of the lessons which made the full-scale invasion of Normandy in 1944 a decisive and unexpectedly inexpensive success. . . .

"The final verdict," he concluded, "may be that Dieppe was a tactical failure, but a strategic success."

On a day early in June 1944, former tank-trooper Stephen Bell, after his third escape attempt, was passed a note circulating among the POWs at Stalag 11D in Stargard, northwestern Poland. The scrap of paper contained shorthand transcribed from a broadcast heard in the camp on a hidden radio. It said the Allies had landed on the coast of France.

Stephen Bell knew about D-Day even as it happened. And though daily survival and other escape attempts were a greater priority for him at the time, knowing that his Dieppe experience had prepared others for a new and greater assault on occupied France gave Bell hope and perhaps some satisfaction that his two years of imprisonment and deprivation were not in vain.

The events of June 6, 1944, at a beach code-named Juno would bear that out.

WINDOW OF
OPPORTUNITY

He had anticipated the moment for half a lifetime.

Before dawn on D-Day morning, Flight Lieutenant Charley Fox slipped into the cockpit of Spitfire KLB. In his words, "You put a Spitfire on and you wore it." That morning, as he throttled the primed and loaded fighter aircraft down the runway and into the still darkened skies above RAF Station Tangmere, near the south coast of England, he felt his heartbeat quicken and noticed the palms of his hands were slightly damp. His excitement might well have begun the day he fell in love with flying, in 1934, when three silver-coloured RAF Hawker Fury fighter biplanes passed low and fast over his home in Guelph, Ontario. On that June 6, 1944, morning, his excitement might have come from a realization that after logging more than 1,500 hours of flying with the RCAF as a rookie pilot, then as a British Commonwealth Air Training Plan instructor, and finally, in February 1944, as tail-end Charlie, the new man on the squadron, Charley Fox, was flying what could be the biggest operation of his life, ordered to engage Luftwaffe fighters on their side of the Channel.

"Nervous? No," he said, "but I felt very much alive that morning."

Flight Lieutenant Fox flew with RCAF 412 Squadron on D-Day, in formation with a dozen other Spitfires. As laid out meticulously during the previous few days of briefings by everybody from the air marshal to the wing commander, the operation of the day boiled down to one simple command: "protect the beaches" on which the greatest amphibious invasion in military history was about to take place. Fighter pilots described it as "flying cover."

"We had been across to France on numerous operations," Fox said, "shooting up and dive-bombing rail lines, bridges, and sites that later turned out to be buzz-bomb launch pads. But this was different."

Moments out over the Channel, Fox began to appreciate the magnitude of the day's operation. For one thing, the view around him, through his cockpit canopy, was crowded with hundreds of other aircraft all headed south. When he peered through the brightening gloom over the surface of the Channel, he saw the once-in-a-lifetime sight "of ships streaming out, a solid mass of boats heading for Normandy." Then, just a hundred miles from his British fighter station, Fox and his 412 Squadron mates began to fly their sweeping patterns over the French beaches. With his left thumb poised over the gun button on his control column and craning his neck through what seemed 360 degrees, Fox scanned the skies for marauding Focke-Wulf 190s or dive-bombing Stukas.

"Those silk scarves fighter pilots wore weren't for show," Fox said. "They protected our necks, literally. If I went up with just the regular blue serge battle dress on, all that swivelling of the head looking to the rear and up and from side to side, I'd come back with my neck bleeding."

As frequently as Fox looked skyward, he could not resist looking down to the beaches as well where fire and smoke and the waves of men filled every view. And as loudly as his Spitfire's Merlin engine roared, the thunder of the naval and artillery shells exploding on the beachhead below echoed in his cockpit and leather headgear headset even louder. One other thought quickened F/L Charley Fox's pulse that

*morning. Despite being out of touch with him for months leading up
to D-Day, he knew his younger brother Ted, with the Royal Canadian
Artillery, was somewhere in that mass of humanity swarming below
him, either on the beach or on his way to it. He worried about that for
a moment, then focused again on the job at hand.*

*Charley Fox flew three operational flights over the beaches on
D-Day.*

*"Emotions, for some reason—everything—was so much more
intensified at that moment. Our sense of smell, sight, everything,"
Fox said. "We were living on the edge."*

2:30 p.m. June 4, 1944—East Riding, England

THE WEATHER at RAF Station Wyton had been miserable
during those first days of June.

The combination of fog and low cloud in the East
Riding region of central England, just inland from the North
Sea, was typical. For most of the aircraft on the station—two
squadrons of Lancaster heavy bombers and one squadron of
Mosquito fighter-bombers in 8 Group (Pathfinders)—the low
ceiling, strong winds, and limited visibility meant no-fly days.
No-fly for some, but not for Flight Lieutenant Robert Dale.

An RCAF navigator originally from Toronto, Dale had
already completed a full tour on Wellington bombers, thirty-
one missions over occupied Europe. When he had completed
that tour in January 1942, his RAF superiors had recognized
his operational service with the Distinguished Flying Cross. In
fact, as was the tradition, Dale had been invited to an investi-
ture at Buckingham Palace where the king, George VI, had
presented the DFC to him personally. As Dale remembers it,
he was the only Canadian at the ceremony and His Majesty
made a point of speaking to him about the many Canadian servicemen and -women on duty in England.

Following the award presentation, Dale's RAF commanders had posted him to a series of training courses, one in central England at RAF Cranage, then the Special Navigation course back in Canada at Port Albert, Ontario. He studied astro navigation, developments in new radar aids, and the latest techniques in weather observation and forecasting.

"Meteorological reconnaissance came into play a lot," Dale said, "because we learned the importance of plotting weather fronts. Before bombing raids it was absolutely vital to know where a weather system was, what speed it was going . . . because that determines cloud cover, visibility, and icing conditions."

Normally the "Spec N" course would have taken Dale two years to complete. He finished it in six months. At the end of 1942, he found out the air force had five postings in Canada open for the graduating officers. With his record, he figured he was home for good, that the brass would make him a navigational instructor in the British Commonwealth Air Training Plan somewhere in Canada. Instead, he was posted back overseas as No. 1 Group Navigation Officer at RAF Station Abingdon, in southern England.

A year later he volunteered to return to operations, trained on Mosquitoes and in January 1944 was posted to No. 1409 Flight, a small special unit of 8 Group (Pathfinders) conducting a variety of operations. Stationed at RAF Wyton, Dale began navigating aboard the latest Mk XVI Mosquitoes, which carried out such operations as master bombing, diversionary targets ("spoof" raids), photo-reconnaissance, and tactical weather-reconnaissance missions. During the next few months, the flights over Germany and occupied Europe seemed continuous. In one month alone, Dale chalked up thirty-six trips.

By May 1944, Bob Dale was nearing the end of his second full tour of operations. Air Vice Marshal Don Bennett, with

8 Group, called the Canadian into his office. The two were by now good friends as well as experienced airmen. Lying on Bennett's office desk was an opened letter from the Royal Canadian Air Force headquarters in London.

"You're to be repatriated," Bennett told him.

Dale acknowledged that the RCAF probably felt it was time to send him home.

"I hope you don't mind, but I've told them you're not available. . . ."

Dale waited for the other shoe to drop.

"You know as well as I do that big things are about to happen."

Dale admitted to Bennett that he did know something big was up and he would not want to miss it. No matter that this would be his third operational tour and that his odds of survival were consequently diminished; the two agreed that the repatriation request would be turned down. So the Canadian navigator began his third, and perhaps most important, tour on ops. And that's why, on another of those miserable rainy days in England, navigator Bob Dale and his Mosquito pilot partner, Nigel Bicknell, were ordered aloft for what seemed a routine trip.

It was the Sunday afternoon of June 4, 1944.

Just after 2:30, Dale and Bicknell met in the ops room of the station for a briefing on the day's solo operation. The duo would fly a weather-reconnaissance pattern, east from central England, out over the North Sea, inland over Holland, south and west across the northern coast of France, as far as Brest, then a final leg back across the English Channel home to RAF Wyton as quickly as possible. The route was routine for both the Mosquito crew and any German defenders who might observe the aircraft on their radar. Along the roughly thousand-mile flight path, the duo was directed to make standard weather recordings and report their findings in a debriefing when they landed later that day.

What Dale and Bicknell did not know right away was that a high-level intelligence meeting related to their mission was convening in Portsmouth on the south coast of England as they took off from Wyton. As they had throughout the month of May, RAF Group Captain J. M. Stagg of the Meteorological Office and his American counterpart, Colonel D. N. Yates, conferred at Southwick House in Hampshire, the Advance Command Post of the Supreme Headquarters of the Allied Expeditionary Force (SHAEF). Each week in May, the two meteorological specialists had been required to bring with them the forecast of the weather "for a dummy D-Day" and present it to the SHAEF Supreme Commander, U.S. General Dwight D. Eisenhower. Hearing their forecasts, the general would choose a projected date for a hypothetical D-Day and at the meeting the following week, discuss whether Stagg's and Yates's predictions had been accurate, and whether a "dummy" decision had been sound.

It was now June, however. The practice runs were over. The SHAEF brass had decided that on June 5 the greatest land, sea, and air invasion ever attempted, Operation Overlord, was to begin. The Allied armies would open a second front by breaking through Hitler's Atlantic Wall and invading the coast of France if weather conditions were right. Responsibility for the correct decision, therefore, rested with the British and American meteorological staffs, who had to provide accurate forecasts as well as identify the kind of weather conditions that each of the Allied invasion services needed. For the navy, winds in the Channel had to blow in a certain direction and below a certain velocity, at the same time providing enough visibility to enable naval gunners to sight targets along the French coast. Maximum visibility was equally vital for the air force bomber, fighter, and transport commands. Cloud and wind conditions would determine the accuracy of air-force bombing, the effectiveness of fighter cover, and the success or failure of dropping airborne troops and supplies inland from the French coast. Ultimately, the assault troops landing safely in France—Operation Neptune—depended on good weather.

The meteorological history of the region did not work in Stagg's favour. The chances of normal June weather patterns delivering on all those variables were 50-to-1 against. Added to those poor odds was the fact that uncharacteristically clement May conditions were suddenly deteriorating. Just before the weekend, on Friday, June 2, winds began blowing in the wrong direction and above permissible velocities. Obscuring stratus clouds and fog were predicted. Stagg reluctantly recorded in his diary that a high-pressure zone over the Azores had given way to a series of lows moving east across England and into the Channel. During the Friday SHAEF meeting at Southwick House, the atmosphere inside had been as gloomy as the forecast for outdoors.

"Isn't there a chance that you may be a bit more optimistic tomorrow?" Eisenhower had asked hopefully.

"No, sir," Stagg replied. Clearly upset, he explained further about the tip in the weather from favourable to unfavourable and left the room.

Conditions over the British Isles had not changed by the Sunday afternoon when airmen Bicknell and Dale directed their Mosquito out over the Channel towards Holland and then south across France. They climbed up through the heavy cloud cover, entering clear sky above 20,000 feet. All along the flight path they recorded the cloud thickness, winds, and the conditions below the ceiling of the weather system.

"We saw the front at its maximum intensity, low cloud and rain," Dale said. "We marked front stems on our chart. . . . They wanted to know the height of the cloud and the cloud base. So we went down and figured we were in solid cloud at 8,000 feet or so. Then down to the base at about 500 feet. . . . The weather was really bad."

After three hours' flying time, the Mosquito was back out over water, the Bay of Biscay off northwestern France, and heading home. However, instead of returning to RAF Wyton, the Mosquito from No. 1409 was diverted to RAF Ford, a fighter station on England's south coast. Immediately after landing, Dale was hustled into a room and plugged into a telephone conference call. There were a few pleasantries, then a short and to-the-point debriefing of the crew's findings. In a few short minutes the Canadian navigator had given his superiors all the details associated with the weather system.

"I got the feeling they already had the picture of things in their minds," said Dale, hearing a resignation in the officers' voices on the other end of the telephone line. "I think we just confirmed their thoughts about what conditions would be like in the next twenty-four hours over the Channel."

Dale's weather readings were apparently confirmed by other reconnaissance aircrews up that afternoon and by Royal Navy vessels strategically positioned at points around the British Isles. Strong southwesterly winds were now blowing over the Channel. Cloud and rain were lying low along the coast of western Europe. Furthermore, Group Captain Stagg's more detailed charts, showing a wider view, seemed to predict an apparently endless succession of low-pressure systems pushing in from the Atlantic and across the Channel. All the data seemed persuasive. General Eisenhower officially confirmed that the invasion would not happen as planned. A coded message, "Ripcord plus 24," was issued.

Later on Flight Lieutenant Dale realized that his weather information had helped determine that D-Day for June 5 was off for at least twenty-four hours.

The implications were serious. If the continuous weather depression maintained its influence over the Channel, as Gp./Capt. Stagg hypothesized, then the manoeuvres originally planned for Monday, June 5, might have to be postponed beyond twenty-four hours, perhaps until June 8. Those ships already at sea would have to turn back and refuel. New orders would have to be drawn up and issued. And if in turn, Thursday, June 8, was missed because of bad weather, SHAEF might have to wait another two weeks before conditions improved enough to suit its plans.

General Eisenhower, describing the situation, wrote, "The mighty host was tense as a coiled spring." Perhaps no one was more tense than he was.

If the gravity he heard over the telephone during his stop at Ford fighter station had not confirmed for Bob Dale that, as AVM Don Bennett had said, big things were about to happen, what Dale saw when he got back to Wyton later that afternoon certainly did. As he and Bicknell taxied their Mosquito to a stop on the flight line, they discovered that the station was a hive of activity. Ground crews seemed to surround every aircraft on the tarmac. And they were conducting other than their regular rigger and fitter duties.

"They were starting to paint black-and-white stripes on the wings and fuselages of all the aircraft," Dale said. "This was it."

The rest of Sunday, June 4, proved very tense indeed at Southwick House as the SHAEF meteorological staff watched the series of low-pressure disturbances settle over the invasion target. Furthermore, reports during the day revealed an intensity of weather that resembled mid-winter more than springtime conditions. To complicate things, at a time when every possible reading from the Atlantic west of the British Isles was needed most, observations from one of the key ships in the area went awry. Loss of that information left huge gaps in accurate predictions. However, just when the situation seemed darkest, forecasters could see the potential for conditions to ease.

Another SHAEF meeting was convened late that Sunday evening. Wind and heavy rains greeted the commanders outside Southwick House, while staff meteorologists inside forecast "a short spell of fairly clear sky, diminished wind and good visibility from the early hours of the morning of [June 6] until possibly the evening of [June 7]." Their promising forecast continued up to 4:15 the next morning, Monday, when a guardedly optimistic Gp./Capt. Stagg stated, "There will be considerable fair to fine periods on Tuesday [June 6] and Wednesday [June 7]."

The heavens had presented, quite literally, a window of opportunity.

Shortly after that, the Supreme Commander issued his final order that the Allies would launch the invasion on June 6.

Nearly two years earlier, a frustrated and adamant Joseph Stalin, premier of the Soviet Union and ally of the United States and Britain against Hitler, wrote to Britain's Prime Minister Winston Churchill: "The question of creating a second front in Europe: I am afraid it is not being treated with the seriousness it deserves." In the spring that followed, in 1942, both Churchill and American President Franklin D. Roosevelt acknowledged that "the Russians are today killing more Germans and destroying more equipment than you and I put together," and the two felt compelled to establish "a front to draw off pressure on the Russians."

By March, the Russians had successfully launched a counteroffensive to clear the Caucasus of German and Italian forces; the British and Canadian navies had turned the tide against German U-boats in the Battle of the Atlantic; Allied offensives had broken the stalemate in Tunisia in North Africa; and the

(British) Combined Chiefs of Staff had appointed Lieutenant-General Frederick Morgan to begin planning for "a full-scale assault against the Continent in 1944, as early as possible." In the interim between Stalin's demand for action and Morgan's orders, Canadians involved in the Dieppe raid had discovered first-hand how difficult such a task would be. Nevertheless, Allied intelligence devised a strategy for a return to the Continent and a breaching of Hitler's Atlantic Wall.

The directive was as broad as possible: an invasion anywhere from Belgium to Spain and anytime between the spring and fall of 1944.

Prerequisites soon narrowed the location and the date. The invasion point, or "lodgement area," had to lie within range of Allied fighter aircraft based in Britain. At least one major port had to lie near the landing site so that it could be taken from the land side and then be made operational to support an Allied invasion. In spite of the Americans' wish for an all-out attack across the Channel, Dieppe had demonstrated that a frontal assault on a fortified French port with towering cliffs could not succeed. Consequently, low-lying beaches that could receive hundreds of landing craft and thousands of storm troops made the most sense.

Where to land? The French Mediterranean coast or Brittany, while vulnerable, were situated too far from the Allies' ultimate objective, Germany's Rhine-Ruhr region. Belgium and Holland offered serviceable ports, but within easy striking distance of Luftwaffe bases. Le Havre at the mouth of the Seine or Cherbourg on the Cotentin Peninsula seemed best suited for the invasion, but the former posed geographical problems and the latter regularly faced severe Atlantic storms. The Pas-de-Calais coast in northernmost France appeared to be ideal, but too obvious an objective from the British south coast. Also, Calais had received the greatest attention from German

engineers building their impregnable wall of defensive fortifications. Indeed, to enhance German expectations of an invasion attempt at Calais, Allied planners created Operation
Fortitude, an elaborate deception of false radio transmissions,
sophisticated security measures, dummy armies, fake weaponry,
and a phony build-up near Dover, directly across the Channel
from the Pas-de-Calais.

Ultimately, the Calvados coast of Normandy became the
target of choice.

Geographically it made sense. Its shoreline lay a mere ninety
miles from the British ports of Portsmouth and Southampton.
Between the western Cotentin Peninsula, which offered protection from the worst of Atlantic weather, and the River Orne
on the east lay twenty miles of sprawling sand beaches connected by roads and offering a gradual incline leading inland.

Strategically it made sense, too. First, the port of Caen,
while small, might be captured on D-Day. A nearby airport at
Carpiquet could be used to service the aircraft of Allied Bomber
and Fighter Command if taken quickly. And the capture of
central Normandy would encompass the main highway and
railway communications across northern France, cutting off
the Cotentin Peninsula and putting Allied invaders on the road
to Paris almost immediately.

In military terms it also made sense. The River Orne had become the natural boundary between the Wehrmacht's Fifteenth
Army in the northeast and the Seventh Army in the northwest.
An attack near the river's mouth would penetrate the Seventh
Army sector, with its single panzer division, rather than the Fifteenth Army sector, with its five panzer divisions. A Normandy
landing along the Calvados coast would enable the Allies to take
advantage of the natural terrain, look like just another diversion
to German Intelligence, and ultimately allow the Allied forces
to land and fortify a beachhead before the German defenders

could react in strength. Surprise meant everything, yet no one knew for certain whether months of planning and practice would work. The entire enterprise had come precariously close to derailing on April 27.

That day German *Schnellbootes* (euphemistically named E-boats or "enemy boats" by the Allies) intercepted an American D-Day rehearsal, code-named Tiger, offshore at Slapton Sands in South Devon. The German gunboats sank two landing craft. More than 700 troops had been lost in the aborted exercise. Worse, German Intelligence had recognized the similarity between the practice beaches in Britain and the shoreline of the Cotentin Peninsula where the U.S. 4th Infantry Division intended to land at the beach code-named Utah. Hitler promptly called for reinforcement of the German defences in lower Normandy. Allied Intelligence watched the troop movements, and the strategists planning the return to the Continent suddenly grew concerned. Had the Germans unmasked Overlord? Did they now know where and when the most crucial military operation of the war in Europe would take place? Was the all-out attempt to open a definitive second front in Europe doomed before it began? Only by actually commencing D-Day operations could the Allies answer those questions.

Plans for Operation Neptune called for the landing of five British and Canadian infantry brigades and three American regimental combat teams—a five-division front spread over about 50 miles of Norman beach—as well as two airborne divisions on the right flank and one on the left. While he may have known the composition of a potential Allied offensive, the officer in charge of German defences in France could not confirm where or when the inevitable invasion would occur. In April, Field-Marshal Erwin Rommel thought the Allied assault would come the first or third week in May. When May passed without incident, he consulted moon and tide tables and deduced an

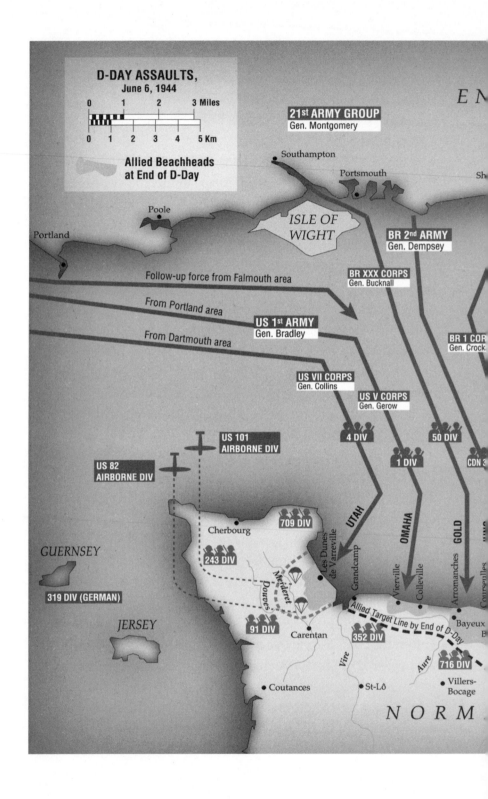

D-DAY ASSAULTS,
June 6, 1944

0   1   2   3 Miles

0   1   2   3   4   5 Km

Allied Beachheads
at End of D-Day

21st ARMY GROUP
Gen. Montgomery

E N

Southampton

Portsmouth

Sh

Poole

ISLE OF
WIGHT

BR 2nd ARMY
Gen. Dempsey

Portland

Follow-up force from Falmouth area

BR XXX CORPS
Gen. Bucknall

From Portland area

US 1st ARMY
Gen. Bradley

BR 1 COR
Gen. Crock.

From Dartmouth area

US VII CORPS
Gen. Collins

US V CORPS
Gen. Gerow

4 DIV

50 DIV

**US 101
AIRBORNE DIV**

1 DIV

CDN 3

**US 82
AIRBORNE DIV**

709 DIV

UTAH

Cherbourg

243 DIV

GUERNSEY

Les Dunes
de Varreville

OMAHA

GOLD

Grandcamp

Vierville

Colleville

Arromanches

Courseilles

Merderet

Douves

319 DIV (GERMAN)

JERSEY

91 DIV

Carentan

352 DIV

Allied Target Line by End of D-Day

Bayeux

B

716 DIV

Coutances

Vire

St-Lô

Aure

Villers-
Bocage

N O R M

ND

Dover

Strait of Dover

Hastings

Calais

47 DIV

49 DIV

Boulogne

Follow-up force from east coast

Le Touquet

BR 6 AIRBORNE DIV

Authie

344 DIV

85 DIV

Abbeville

348 DIV

Somme

le Tréport

Bresle

245 DIV

Dieppe

Béthune

84 DIV

Fécamp

15th ARMY
Gen. von Salmuth

346 DIV

17 DIV

Le Havre

Rouen

116 PANZER DIV

Cabourg

Deauville

ARMY GROUP B
FM Rommel

711 DIV

Risle

CinC WEST
FM von Rundstedt

Dives

Touques

12 SS PANZER DIV

Eure

Seine

Lisieux

Y

E N G L I S H   C H A N N E L

invasion wouldn't happen until after June 20. On June 2, he wrote his wife and told her, "There is still no sign that the invasion is imminent."

While he left calculations of the date of the coming Allied invasion to Nazi Intelligence and moon charts, Rommel left little to chance in his defence of Hitler's Atlantic Wall. As far back as August 25, 1942, German commanders in western Europe had ordered the construction of 15,000 permanent, fortress-like installations along the entire Atlantic coastline of Holland, Belgium and France, so "that no attack from the air, the sea or land shall appear to have any prospect of success." A year later, when Rommel became Inspector General of Defences in the West, only about 8,000 such installations had been completed. Effectively in charge of operational control of anti-invasion forces in the most threatened sector of France, Rommel recognized that coastal defences would not stand up to a concerted Allied naval or air bombardment, or both. He planned to augment the concrete and steel installations with obstacles and mines—a mined zone five miles deep along the entire coast, an estimated 200 million mines. In fact, some four million were laid amid a wide array of obstacles by the spring of 1944. In addition, inland from the coastal defences, he had poles, dubbed "Rommel's asparagus," erected in fields to discourage aircraft from landing.

During its defeats in the Soviet Union, North Africa and Sicily, the German Army had suffered serious losses of men and materiel. It remained, however, the strongest fighting force in Europe. France and the Low Countries, it turned out, had become a kind of rear echelon, where depleted divisions were refitted and returned to strength while new ones were trained. Consequently, by the end of 1943 the Wehrmacht in France had a strength of about 856,000 men, few of whom were battle-ready. To compensate for this inexperience, the German ranks contained younger leaders, some the notorious Hitler Youth who knew how to motivate green troops.

Along the coastline, Rommel inherited static units that had no means of rapid transport. Their best men were regularly transferred to the Eastern Front and the rest tended to be veterans from the Russian front or members of *Ostbataillone*, units made up of Soviet POWs or Polish conscripts. It was the firepower and mobility of the 10 panzer or panzer-grenadier (armoured infantry) divisions that arrived in late 1943, however, that suddenly made a deadly difference. Overnight an otherwise mediocre defence became a potentially lethal counterattack force, particularly on day two or three of an invasion.

Where the Allies planned to come ashore on D-Day, the German command had installed (from west to east across the Normandy region) the 243rd, the 709th, the 352nd and the 716th Infantry Divisions of the German Seventh Army as well as the 711th Infantry Division of the German Fifteenth Army. At the sector code-named Juno Beach, Force J and the Canadians would strike their D-Day blow at the 716th, a fighting force of nearly 8,000 men all dug in among resistance nests and fortified concrete. At their disposal were twenty-five mounted guns, including two 88-mm guns and eleven heavy mortars and scores of anti-personnel machine guns trained on the exposed beaches in front of Courseulles-sur-Mer, Bernières-sur-Mer and St. Aubin-sur-Mer. Augmented by Rommel's 21st Panzer Division, as well as the 12th S. S. Panzer Division of *Hitlerjugend* (Hitler youth) fifty miles inland, German defence of the Atlantic Wall across the Canadian sector would be formidable.

Last call, June 4, 1944—Ripon, England

Early June happened to be very eventful for the Turnbull family of Govan, Saskatchewan. In spite of tough times through the

Depression, during which her husband had died, and the toll the war years had taken on her grain and livestock farm north of Regina, Lillian Turnbull remained upbeat about the war. All three of her sons had enlisted and were members of the Royal Canadian Air Force serving overseas in Britain. All boasted exemplary wartime records. Eldest son Robert had completed two full tours in Bomber Command; he had been awarded a Distinguished Flying Medal and at age twenty-five had become the youngest wing commander in the RCAF. Second son Walter had successfully completed a tour as navigator on Lancaster bombers. And John was well on his way to completing a tour as a pilot officer on Halifax bombers with No. 6 (RCAF) Group.

The brothers had also defied the odds of wartime military-aviation survival. At the midpoint of the Second World War, during the average 1,000-bomber night operations over targets in Europe, as many as 10 percent or 12 percent of bomber crews did not return. The Commonwealth air forces, with aircrews from Britain, Canada, New Zealand, and Australia, were sustaining the highest casualties per capita of any Allied forces. Despite that grim fact, the Turnbulls' flight logs showed that on at least five different occasions, the three brothers flew bombing raids to the same target on the same night and that all made it home safely.

"That was sort of tweaking the nose of the dear Lord, just a little bit," John Turnbull admitted.

Excitement peaked for the family that spring when, on June 4, the air force informed twenty-year-old John Turnbull, stationed in north Yorkshire, that he would be awarded a DFC. That day, when he thought about it, several bombing missions stood out in his mind. There was the night he had flown "second Dickey" (observing from the co-pilot's seat) over Berlin. He recalled the first night he had led his own crew on a "gardening" (mine-laying) operation off the Frisian Islands. On his twentieth birthday, as he and his crew flew to a target at Mannheim, Germany, he recalled seeing "an awful lot of birthday candles" (anti-aircraft fire). There was also the trip he had made into the Alps; after bombing both ends of a mountain tunnel he had had to fight off a rapid descent because ice had formed on the engines and wings of his aircraft.

Yet the close calls—dealing with bad weather, being coned by searchlights over German targets, coping with flak-damaged engines while limping home on the remaining good ones, and escaping attacks by enemy night-fighters—all faded in the glow of the DFC announcement. Turnbull celebrated by taking his longtime crew members to a pub in Ripon for beer and fish and chips. Despite the significance of the party, one of Turnbull's crewmen quickly brought his pilot back to earth with one comment: "What the hell are you getting a DFC for?" his rear-gunner Joe Malec chided. "We earned it. You're getting it."

The remark and the way Turnbull took it in stride were typical of the close camaraderie that existed among his seven-man crew. Nobody's ego, not even that of the chief officer with a DFC, would ever be inflated if Malec, the six-foot tail-gunner from Biggar, Saskatchewan, had anything to say. Whenever his skipper made a less-than-perfect three-point landing, the intercom usually crackled to life.

"We're up. We're down," Malec would quip from the rear of the aircraft. "We're down. We're up."

Chemistry meant a lot on board John Turnbull's Halifax bomber, right from the moment they were crewed up in September 1943. Most of them were RCAF airmen from Ontario and the West. He enjoyed the good nature of his mid-upper gunner, Claude "Dusty" Hutt, and the reliability of his bomb-aimer Harold "Mac" McBain and his diminutive navigator Earl T. Albert, whom everyone just knew as "E.T.A." There was Frank "Mike" Michael who'd been a ground engineer and wanted so badly to be a flight engineer; he finally got his wish aboard Turnbull's bomber. And there was his wireless (radio operator) air gunner, Ron Gillett, from Stratford-upon-Avon in England.

Gillett described John Turnbull as quiet and determined. Even under pressure, Gillett said his pilot retained a resilient sense of humour. If a member of the crew left his intercom mike on, Turnbull would draw attention to it by saying subtly, "I can hear someone breathing. Switch it off or pack it in." It became a standing joke with the crew.

Turnbull's calm demeanour seemed to rub off on the rest. He was proud of his crew's discipline and control. If anything went wrong, if their plane was hit, if they had to take evasive action, nobody panicked. On a mission to Berlin late in 1943, as the crew closed the bomb doors, the Halifax took a heavy shell burst beneath its tail. The concussion yanked the controls from Turnbull's hands and the bomber lurched into a steep dive for several thousand feet. Everything that was loose inside the aircraft's fuselage crashed forward into the navigator's quarters, nearly destroying E.T.A.'s workspace.

"What's going on up there?" he complained. "Can't you keep this place any cleaner than that?"

While the crew found time and reason for fun, it also jelled as a fighting team in the air. The mission to Mannheim, the day Turnbull turned twenty, Ron Gillett remembers as a watershed trip. The flight required eight hours and ten minutes of flying to the heavily industrial and fiercely guarded Rhine Valley and back. On the way, the crew manoeuvred its Halifax bomber through tracer fire, searchlights, flares, markers, and flak. Yet in the final moments of the bombing run, Gillett recalled hearing none of the explosions of the erupting target below them, only the calm instructions of bomb-aimer McBain inhaling and exhaling steadily on the intercom as he counted down to the target. The crew seemed awestruck, he said, "but we returned jubilant because we had taken on the Third Reich."

That spring of 1944, things took a decidedly serious turn at No. 6 (RCAF) Group. At their Skipton-on-Swale station in Yorkshire, Halifax crews such as Turnbull's began more specialized activity. At night, Turnbull flew operational flights, and during the day he was also put through Officers Advanced Training School at the RAF College at Cranwell in Lincolnshire. Meanwhile, wireless air-gunner Gillett completed a course on "Fishpond," an electronic aid that enabled an airborne radar operator to spot fighters in a bomber's blind spots. By early June, Gillett had become a signals leader and the Turnbull crew began flying daytime operations.

During this period, operations consisted of a multitude of small- or medium-sized bombing raids. In some cases, aircrews flew two sorties within twenty-four hours. To those carrying out the operations, the planners and ground staffs seemed to be working harder now than at any other time during the war. This was true. In the late spring of 1944, Bomber Command was flying more than five thousand sorties per week, the same number of sorties flown in the first nine months of the war.

By the evening that Turnbull's crew celebrated the announcement of his DFC, the weather had deteriorated. The thermometer reading had dropped. The rain seemed more menacing. Turnbull thought the temperature was cold enough that they might have to deal with icing conditions if they did fly an operation. Nevertheless, orders the next day, June 5, called for an evening briefing. Each crew member attended a different session according to his trade—Earl Albert to the navigators' briefing, Harold McBain to the bomb-aimers' briefing, and so on.

"We were to fly south through England," John Turnbull said, and then head across the English Channel to the coast of

Normandy. "Our target was the gun emplacements at Houl-gate, near Cabourg." Turnbull remembered the last words from the officers leading the briefings as particularly emphatic.

"Your timing and accuracy are absolutely vital this time," they told the crews.

As John Turnbull's Halifax III crew took off with their sights set on the guns at Houlgate, that same night another 411 Hali-faxes, 551 Lancasters, and 49 Mosquitoes—more than a thou-sand aircraft—were flying toward coastal batteries at Fontenay, La Pernelle, Longues, Maisy, Merville, Mont Fleury, Pointe-du-Hoc, Ouistreham, and St-Martin-de-Varreville. More than five thousand tons of bombs were dropped that night, the greatest volume in one night thus far in the war.

Midnight, June 5, 1944, Bernières-sur-Mer, France

At least one of those bombs landed on or near the house of Paul Martin. He and his family lived in a modest cottage just two blocks from the beach in the Normandy resort town of Bernières-sur-Mer. Fortunately, his knowledge of explosives or perhaps his unpleasant recollections of time served in the French artillery during the First World War spared him, his wife Ida, and their two children from harm. As soon as that night's aerial bombardment began, Martin instinctively moved his family into the underground bunker he and his son Jacques had constructed some time before.

"It is better to be in a trench in the yard than in the base-ment of the house," Martin had told his son, "because if the house collapses into the basement we could be buried alive."

Paul Martin, at sixty, had been affected by the war in a num-ber of ways. A gun-shop owner in Paris in the late 1930s, he had been forced out of business when the Germans invaded. They had confiscated all his inventory, which forced him to lay off his staff. And because he lived close to the main station, which served trains from Germany, Martin was evicted from his home. His eldest son, an anti-aircraft soldier in the French army, had been captured early in the war and was a POW in Austria. In addition, Paul Martin knew that one day the Allies would invade and that Paris might become a battleground. So he had decided to move his family to the relative tranquility of the resort area in Normandy.

For four years the Martins had lived near the beach on Rue de la Mer across from l'Hôtel Belle Plage, where officers of the German occupation force stopped for food and drink most nights. While Martin's family was allowed to fish, the Germans prohibited civilians' use of boats; so each low tide, father Paul and son Jacques would dash across the exposed beaches and collect the shrimp and shellfish that washed up for the family to eat.

As Jacques remembered, his father had originally dismissed the possibility of the Allies' coming ashore in Normandy in any large-scale invasion. "There are too many islands uncovered at low tide. There is almost no water. How would the Allies conduct a successful landing?"

But Paul Martin had also witnessed Field-Marshal Erwin Rommel's troops coming to Bernières in February 1944. He had watched the Germans build a network of underground trenches and tunnels, machine-gun pillboxes, reinforced gun emplacements, camouflaged observation posts and anti-aircraft gun positions. At low tide, he had also watched the enemy fill the beaches with obstacles, each one made more lethal with contact mines. Martin was witnessing the construction of Hitler's Atlantic Wall, a system of 15,000 defence works, armed with more than 3,000 pieces of artillery, that stretched along 3,000 miles of French coastline. Paul Martin began to change his mind.

"Maybe we will have a landing here," he had speculated to his son Jacques in the spring of 1944. "The Germans are paying too much attention to these beaches."

Martin also told his son that an invasion would come when the moon was full, because the light would give the Allies greater visibility. Again he was right. June 5 was the night of a full moon, which, through broken cloud, illuminated many of the targets that Bomber Command would visit in those dark hours.

Around midnight on June 5, the first bombs fell on Bernières-sur-Mer. Jacques Martin, who would be twenty in nine days, remembered his father's telling the family to dress and rush out to the shelter. When the shelling continued intermittently through the night, the Martins decided to stay inside the shelter.

"Before long my mother and sister started to get demoralized," Jacques Martin recalled. "They thought we wouldn't survive. They thought we would be killed. So I got them to sing Boy Scout songs and it lifted their spirits for a while."

That's the way Jacques Martin remembered the beginning of the invasion. As for thousands of troops racing across the Channel toward this small town, his D-Day would be a long one. The aerial bombardment at midnight was only the beginning.

Midnight, June 5, 1944, Norfolk, England

There were more military weapons in the air over the Channel on the eve of D-Day than just explosives.

In its June 5 battle order, Bomber Command's 100 Group had despatched Lancasters with radar-jamming equipment, Stirlings with diversionary "Window" to drop, and Flying Fortress B-17s with "Tinsel" devices that transmitted engine noise onto the radio channels that German controllers used.

The aircrews aboard these specially outfitted bomber aircraft had been trained to interfere with and mislead the Germans along Hitler's Atlantic Wall defences about any military action from the Allied side of the Channel. One of the flyers involved in this airborne war of subterfuge was a young bomber pilot from Portage La Prairie, Manitoba, Murray Peden.

By the first week of January in 1944, Flying Officer Peden had completed thirteen operations as a member of 214 Squadron based at RAF Station Downham Market near the east coast of England. At nineteen, Peden had flown operations planting mines in German shipping lanes, dropping supplies to the French resistance, attacking V-1 rocket-launching sites, as well as main-force bombing runs against German targets, including some in the Ruhr area, a district known to aircrews as "Happy Valley." However, because squadrons using Stirling bombers (as 214 did) had suffered such heavy losses over those industrial targets, Bomber Command had decided to reassign Stirling crews to new duties and different aircraft. Peden and his colleagues in 214 Squadron accordingly joined Bomber Command's recently formed 100 Group, flying American B-17s. Their job on all operations, including those concerned with the interdiction campaign leading up to an anticipated invasion, was to mislead German defence operations.

"We went to war without bombs," Peden said, "but with Tinsel, ABC, Mandrel, Jostle, and all the other countermeasures invented by the Telecommunications Research Establishment."

As early as 1940, British Intelligence had opened ULTRA, a secret file on intercepted enemy radio signals, as it tried to decipher the German encoding device called Enigma. Among those experts involved, Dr. Robert Cockburn worked on the technical design of countermeasures at the Telecommunications Research Establishment (TRE), while British Scientific Intelligence specialist R. V. Jones and RAF Wing Commander

E. B. Addison endeavoured to anticipate German applications of science to warfare. To neutralize German radar, the countermeasures group invented "the theory of spoof," a means of "persuading (the enemy) that you are either (a) where you are not, or (b) not where you are." Among TRE's arsenal of electronic countermeasures were sophisticated jamming equipment and devices with "spurious reflectors" to fool German radar stations into believing there were more aircraft or ships facing them than there really were.

The crews of 214 Squadron, classed as 100 Group's heavy jamming squadron, assumed a leading role in spoofing the Germans.

Accordingly, Murray Peden and his crew had moved to Sculthorpe, 214 Squadron's new home in Norfolk. There they had adapted quickly to the strengths and idiosyncrasies of their new black-painted Flying Fortresses, while learning about the new weapons of warfare installed on board.

Among their new objectives was blocking the VHF communications between German night-fighter controllers and the fighter pilots themselves. Wireless operators aboard the B-17s used a three-stage jamming system, "black boxes" known as ABC (for "Airborne Cigar"). The Allied operator would tune his receiver to the radio bands the German controllers used, find a controller who was broadcasting instructions, and then set his ABC to the same frequency. This jammed the conversation so that nothing sent or received was intelligible. If the German controller flipped to a different frequency, the jammer followed and repeated the procedure. In some instances, special wireless operators fluent in the German language would flood German radio frequencies with credible erroneous commands and chatter.

Later, the B-17s were equipped with far more powerful jammers known as Jostle. Mandrel equipment too was used to lay a screen of interference in front of the long-range German radar, the Freyas system. Tinsel consisted of a small Marconi radio transmitter housed in a B-17's engine that simply transmitted engine noise when the wireless operator tuned his equipment to the same channel German radio controllers or fighters were using.

An equally vital spoof Bomber Command aircraft employed was a system called Window. This involved the release of tinfoil strips of a length corresponding to the wavelength of the German detectors—the long-range Freyas and the short-range Würzburgs—stationed in France. As the tinfoil fluttered down, it reflected echoes to the Germans' detectors that resembled the echoes of real aircraft where there were none; multiplied by hundreds of strands of tinfoil, the Window would flood the enemy's Würzburgs, confusing radar operators as well as the searchlight and anti-aircraft batteries depending on them for accurate defence. In a similar procedure, Operation Taxable, Allied aircraft flew at low altitude in elliptical courses over a small number of ships, giving German radar defences the impression of a large naval landing force approaching an objective far removed from the Normandy beaches.

At its June 5 operation briefing, just like John Turnbull's at Skipton-on-Swale in Yorkshire, Murray Peden's B-17 crew knew something big was in the wind. He recalled the palpable anticipation all felt "just before the curtains were parted to reveal the greatest secret of the war." At that point he learned that five Fortresses from 214 Squadron and sixteen Lancasters from 617 Squadron were to conduct the biggest jamming and windowing mission of the war to date.

That night the B-17s were to take off from the Oulton airfield in Norfolk and climb to an altitude of 27,000 feet over the English Channel. There they were to establish a strong patrol line about ninety miles northeast of the Normandy landing beaches and "seal off the flank of the invasion and, in effect, knock out [German] radio communications to the north and east of the landing site." They would continuously drop Window across the Channel at the same time to suggest that a main force of heavy bombers was headed inland, not toward coastal defences. At the same time, with their ABC and Mandrel equipment, the crews would throw a curtain of interference over every channel of communication the German night-fighters used.

"As we left England in F Fox [their B-17] to take our station," Murray Peden wrote, "we knew that beneath us in the darkness a tremendous drama was beginning to unfold. . . . We steered for our appointed patrol line, situated just north and east of Dieppe, and began our run inland almost perpendicular to the coastline.

"Our orders were to patrol our lengthy beat eight times [counting inbound and outbound legs separately]. So, for several hours we plied back and forth in the darkness, windowing and jamming for all we were worth."*

On this night, RAF 214 Squadron's cloak-and-dagger activity would really live up to its Latin motto *Ultor in umbris*— Avenging in the Shadows.

3 a.m. June 6, 1944—West Sussex, England

About the same time Murray Peden learned the secret behind the curtains in his briefing room, RCAF fighter pilot Charley Fox found out as well. There were plenty of signals that

---

* Shortly after the invasion operation, 214 Squadron received a congratulatory message from Bomber Command stating that its objectives that night had been successfully carried out. Murray Peden was eventually awarded the DFC, rose to the rank of Squadron Leader, and in 1979 wrote of his wartime experiences in the best-selling book *A Thousand Shall Fall*, quoted here.

the balloon might soon go up on the invasion. In late April, Fox's No. 412 (Falcon) Squadron had moved to Tangmere, the legendary Battle of Britain station in West Sussex that had witnessed nearly five years of briefings, scrambles, and fighter-aircraft sorties. As soon as they arrived, the pilots and ground crew of the squadron and all of 126 Wing went under canvas.

"We were living three guys in a tent," Fox recalled, "sleeping on cots, shaving with cold water, and this could only mean we were preparing for life on the Continent."

Not even these conditions or the boring taste of C food rations in the field bothered Flight Lieutenant Fox by this time. He was already a four-year veteran in the air force, and had been waiting patiently and with great anticipation for this moment. Charley Fox, originally from Guelph, Ontario, had taken a necessary detour to get here.

Unlike many of his squadron mates, after Fox received his air force wings and his commission at No. 6 Service Flying Training School in Dunnville, Ontario, in July 1941, he was not posted overseas immediately. The air force sent him to Central Flying School at Trenton, where he taught flying in the British Commonwealth Air Training Plan. For the next two years his home became the back seat of the yellow-painted Harvard trainer, instructing class after class of "sprog" pilots how not to kill themselves, how to take off and land safely, spin and recover, fly in formation and evade, fly on instruments day and night, and ultimately how to earn their wings in the RCAF and serve overseas on single-engine fighter aircraft, such as Hurricanes and Spitfires. As a senior instructor at Dunnville, Fox had trained, tested, and graduated scores of the rookies and sent them off to Fighter Command as his personal "calling cards for Hitler."

Finally in August 1943, it was his turn. Fox was posted on fighters overseas. At that point he had 1,500 hours of flying

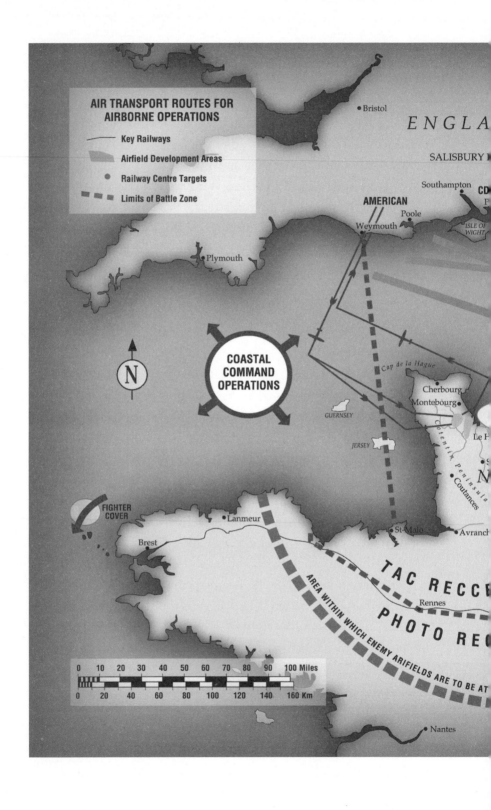

AIR TRANSPORT ROUTES FOR
AIRBORNE OPERATIONS

— Key Railways

Airfield Development Areas

● Railway Centre Targets

– – – Limits of Battle Zone

● Bristol

ENGLA

SALISBURY

Southampton   CD

AMERICAN   P

Poole

Weymouth

ISLE OF
WIGHT

● Plymouth

N

COASTAL
COMMAND
OPERATIONS

Cap de la Hague

Cherbourg

Montebourg ●

GUERNSEY

Le F

JERSEY

Cotentin Peninsula

N

Coutances

FIGHTER
COVER

● Lanmeur

● St-Malo

● Avranch

Brest

TAC RECC

AREA WITHIN WHICH ENEMY ARIFIELDS ARE TO BE AT

Rennes

PHOTO REC

| 0 | 10 | 20 | 30 | 40 | 50 | 60 | 70 | 80 | 90 | 100 Miles |
| 0 | 20 | 40 | 60 | 80 | 100 | 120 | 140 | 160 Km |

● Nantes

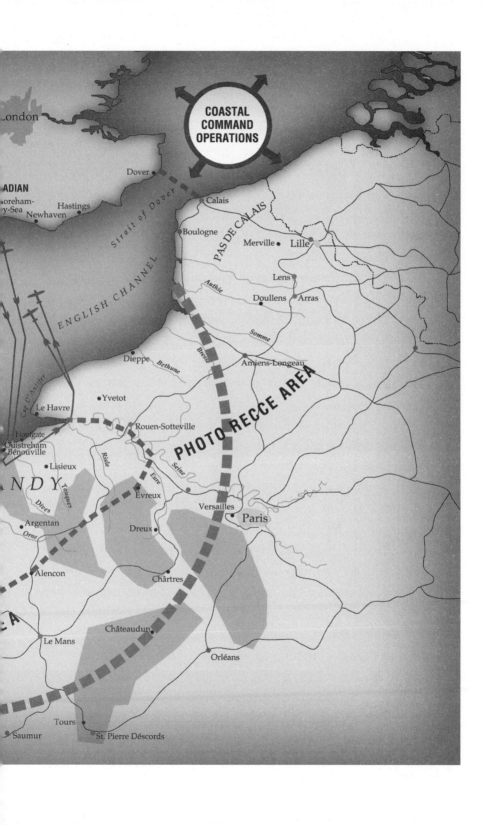

time under his belt, while some of his students who had completed a full tour on operations might have accumulated a total
of only 300 hours. Despite his superiority in hours flown and
perhaps even in rank, however, the ex-instructor–now fighter
pilot still had to prove himself. In fact, on his first sortie with
No. 412 in February 1944, Fox flew in fourth position, or tail-
end Charlie, to none other than Flight Lieutenant George
"Buzz" Beurling, who had already shot down thirty-two enemy
aircraft, tops in the RCAF.

"We took off four abreast," Fox said. "Of course, I really
wanted to do a nice takeoff, tucked right in behind the wing of
my number three [pilot]. But he was a little too nervous and
suddenly chopped back on the throttle, so I had to chop my
throttle too. When I throttled back up to catch up, my tail came
awfully high. It felt as if [my propeller] might have touched the
runway.

"Well, we did a sweep over to France. . . . The trip was
uneventful. Made it back. Greased it on the runway okay. I taxied into the gun bay, turned the engine off, and when the four
blades of the propeller stopped spinning I realized the tips of
each blade had been chopped off square. . . . Beurling really
bawled me out over that one. My introduction to operations."

Fox made a strong recovery from those first-flight jitters. In
his introductory months on Spitfires with the squadron, he had
plenty of opportunity to demonstrate his skill by escorting light
bombers, conducting ramrod sorties into France and Belgium,
and joining Fighter Command's preparations for D-Day. Among
other things, the air force experimented with the squadron's
Spitfire Mk Vs, using them to tow eight-man Hotspur gliders
carrying the service crew more quickly over the Channel in the
event of an invasion. They also transformed the Spitfire into
a dive-bomber by strapping a single 500-pound bomb under
the landing carriage and one 250-pounder beneath each wing.

Finally, they installed new gyroscopic gunsights so every Spit pilot could be as deadly in a dogfight as Buzz Beurling.

"The mechanism was controlled by twisting the grip on your throttle," Fox said. "It had a floating red dot in the centre all displayed on a screen at eye level in your windshield, with an adjustable ring of yellow diamonds. You put the dot on the enemy aircraft and brought the diamonds in until they framed the aircraft so the wing-tips were just inside the sight. Hold it steady. Press the gun button and you would hit your target."

By June 4, for security's sake, all personnel had been confined to the aerodrome and everybody with 126 Wing and 127 Wing was keen to know what the next day's operation might be. During the afternoon and evening of June 5, Fighter Command let the cat out of the bag. First, there was a mass briefing outdoors at Tangmere. Air Marshal Sir Arthur Coningham, the commander of the 2nd Tactical Air Force (TAF), which would take the lead in the air war over France, addressed aircrew from both wings, nine squadrons of eager pilots, and their just-as-eager ground crew. Charley Fox remembered that rigger Monty Montgomery and fitter Danny Daniels—his full-time ground crew when 2nd TAF moved to France—were both Canadians who had been overseas for almost three years and were champing at the bit as much as the pilots and COs.

"We've been preparing. We've been building up for this," Fox remembered Coningham telling them. "We don't know what you're going to meet up there. But we want to protect those beaches."

The briefings continued, wing by wing, squadron by squadron, all evening long. F/L Fox and the rest of 412 Squadron received specialized briefings about their role in providing cover for the naval and assault vessels the next morning. Fox would fly a thirteenth Spitfire, a spare, with a section of twelve other Spits. Preparations continued into the night, and by the time he'd found his cot inside his tent, with fellow Spitfire pilots Lloyd Berryman and Jamie Jamieson, it was well after midnight. Nobody got much sleep, maybe two or three hours' rest before everybody was wakened by activity on the flight line. Shortly after three o'clock, ground crew were up and already had the engines of 412's Spitfires running. Fox remembered being called and eating a quick breakfast of bacon and eggs; he was even served up a glass of real milk. Then he dashed to the flight line before four o'clock and strapped himself into Spitfire KLB, the personal aircraft of 126 Wing Commander Keith Hodson. It would not be long before Fox had his own airplane.

"The Spitfire never did have a lot of room in the cockpit," Fox said. "There's a half door on your left side, so when you get in with your seat pack [parachute] that you sit on, then your coup top [canopy], it's a pretty restricted area. But everything's right at hand."

As he closed the canopy over his head and rolled the Spitfire into position on the runway, Charley Fox made sure his wing lights were off. It was still dark, not yet dawn. As he throttled up along the runway and into the air, leaving Tangmere below in the darkness, he remembered what had kept him awake through the night. It was more than the excitement of the day's mission. It had been the steady drone of bombers and transports passing overhead. The sound had continued all night long. And along with the unending moan of the engines, he remembered noticing the black shadows passing steadily overhead.

3 a.m. June 6, 1944—Reading, England

Laurette Parsons heard the noise that night too. And she had a strong personal interest in that parade of outbound aircraft.

Just eighteen years old, the outgoing and self-confident Briton travelled every day from her home in Reading, west of London, into the city to the London Royal Free Hospital School of Medicine for Women. She had plans to become a doctor, but one of the conditions her mother had made requisite for Laurette's attending medical school was that she must commute. Clarissa Parsons had already lost her only son— killed in a Fleet Air Arm combat operation over Norway in 1941—and her husband, Norman Parsons, seemingly worked around the clock at the Miles Aircraft plant in Reading. So being protective of her daughter was natural.

On Monday nights, Laurette came home from her studies early enough to put in some volunteer hours at the Navy, Army, and Air Force Institutes (NAAFI) canteen at Reading railway station. That night, June 5, she put in a particularly long shift. She had arrived at the canteen at nine o'clock and worked through the night, preparing and serving confections to servicemen and -women passing through the busy London-area station.

"In the middle of the night we heard these planes going over," she said. "So we ran outside. It was so exciting because they all had their [navigation] lights on. . . . It was like a starlit night all of a sudden. . . . After all the years of complete blackout, to see all these planes going over with lights . . .

"Of course, I also thought, 'I bet I know who's in one of those planes.'"

A year earlier, Laurette's parents had permitted her to attend a cricket match in Aldershot, Hampshire, where the Canadian troops had been residing, training, and preparing for an eventual invasion of Europe. Her escort for the day was a family friend, Capt. Bill Rushton. During the game, Rushton introduced her to Richard Hilborn, a young Canadian military officer with the Canadian Scottish regiment. The two chatted, stopped by the officers' mess, and had tea.

A few days later, the Parsons household received a telephone call from the same officer. "Would you like a game of tennis?" he asked Laurette.

"Fine," she said.

"I could come over," he said.

Again she agreed, gave him directions, and at the appointed time the Canadian arrived on the doorstep . . . with a suitcase. He had just brought along a change of clothes. One thing led to another and Laurette's parents invited him to stay.

"He left the next day," Laurette said, "and that was the beginning. . . . I found out afterwards that Bill Rushton had played matchmaker. . . . Sometimes he'd come to dinner with Mum and Dad and he'd say, 'You want to go out?' . . . It was all planned."

Not that Laurette minded. Even when Hilborn was transferred to an airborne regiment, the 1st Canadian Parachute Battalion, the couple carried on the relationship with her parents' blessing. As the spring of 1944 arrived, the courtship became a long-distance one. Laurette became more preoccupied by her studies when the London campus was bombed and she had to move to another hospital. She always hoped that this Canadian paratrooper would play a role in her future.

Then June 5 came and the nighttime flypast of what was clearly an airborne assault force. Laurette knew that Hilborn, with whom she had fallen in love, was somewhere in that armada of tug planes and gliders passing overhead.

"I was scared," she admitted. "I remember when my brother was killed. The three of us were at a movie theatre in Reading and they announced, 'Would Mr. Norman Parsons please go to the office?' and Mum said immediately, 'It's your brother.'

I remember thinking, 'Oh, for heaven's sake, Mum.' But she was right. He'd been killed in action."

As she anxiously hurried into the street outside Reading station to watch the stream of aircraft navigation lights passing overhead, Laurette Parsons expressed the concern and prayers of many that night. Not just one bond hung in the balance. More than civilians were worried. Both the generals and the general public would pass a sleepless night. That night a BBC news broadcast would be interrupted by a report that contained the words "Eileen is married to Jo. . . . It is hot in Suez. . . . The compass points north. . . . The dice are on the table." In France, 5,000 resistance members would know this was the signal to attack specific railway lines, roads, and telephone exchanges. The greatest plan in the history of warfare was about to be tested. The D-Day invasion had begun.

A LEAP OF FAITH

WITHIN MINUTES of issuing his "Okay. We'll go" order to launch Operation Overlord, on June 6, the Supreme Allied Commander faced an equally tough second decision. At Southwick House in Portsmouth on the south coast of England, General Dwight Eisenhower sat across from Air Chief Marshal Sir Trafford Leigh-Mallory, the commander-in-chief of the Allied air forces.

Their discussion focused on Operation Neptune, the assault phase of Overlord, and in particular the role of the parachute and glider-borne forces, whose task it would be to secure the flanks of the main invading army. The aim of the scheme was relatively straightforward. D-Day planners had chosen a section of the coast of Normandy, stretching from St-Martin-de-Varreville on the Cherbourg peninsula east to Ouistreham at the mouth of the River Orne, as the target for the main assault.

"To assist them on the right flank," Eisenhower stated in his despatch, "it's believed that two airborne divisions be employed ... still leaving one airborne division to hold vital bridges in the Orne/Dives rivers area to the northeast of Caen."

Leigh-Mallory doubted that the two airborne divisions, the U.S. 82nd and 101st Airborne Divisions, dropped into the south Cotentin Peninsula on the far west of the Allied invasion force, would be able to muster even half that number when the ground battle began. He was equally apprehensive about the British 6th Airborne Division's accomplishing the same on the far east of the Allied landing.

The operation was scheduled to begin in less than twenty-four hours.

In the end, Eisenhower relieved Leigh-Mallory of "the heavy responsibility of deciding the airborne operation" and again gave the "We'll go" order personally. Over the next twelve hours, Leigh-Mallory leapfrogged across southern Britain from one airfield to another to speak with airborne troops and glider crews.

"There's no doubt in my mind of their determination to do the job," he reported, "[but] I would describe their demeanour as grim and not frightfully gay."

10:30 p.m. June 4, 1944—Salisbury Plain, England

Jan de Vries did his part to lift spirits among his buddies in the Airborne that night. They were definitely deflated, especially when the entire division had to stand down because of the bad weather on June 4, the eve of the original D-Day.

Since the end of May, the 600 members of 1st Canadian Parachute Battalion had been caged inside a security transit camp in the south of England. Once within the barbed-wire compound, nobody came in and nobody left. The four companies of the battalion could only try to keep fit with exercise, stay dry under the canvas tents, and deflect any feelings of boredom. So the paras did calisthenics. They played draw poker. They hung out at the Navy, Army, and Air Force Institutes (NAAFI) canteen. They gathered for singsongs while Jan de Vries accompanied them on his Marine Band C harmonica.

The men sang "Mademoiselle from Armentières," "It's a Long Way to Tipperary" and "There's a Long, Long Trail a-

Winding." As a change of pace, de Vries played the mournful "La Paloma." In fact, he could play almost any tune if he heard it often enough and locked the melody in his head. Most of all, though, the men of the battalion liked to sing a paratroopers' song they called "He Ain't Gonna Jump No More." To the tune of "The Battle Hymn of the Republic," the song began:

> He was just a rookie trooper and he surely shook with fright.
> He checked all his equipment and made sure his pack was tight.
> He had to sit and listen to those awful engines roar.
> He ain't gonna jump no more.
>> Gory, gory. What a helluva way to die.
>> Gory, gory. What a helluva way to die.
>> Gory, gory. What a helluva way to die.
>> He ain't gonna jump no more.

And it finished with a verse designed to scare most new recruits out of their wits:

> They placed him in a blanket. Then they laid his soul to rest.
> They notified his next of kin. His funeral was the best.
> And on his monument of stone they scribed this little verse:
> He ain't gonna jump no more. . . .

Sometimes they sang it as a drinking song, other times when they marched.

"We always sang on a march," de Vries said. "Maybe not when we started, but after two or three miles, somebody would start a cadence count and before long everybody was singing. It was always a good sharp beat. It helped you pick up your step especially when you were tired. Singing was a great lift. . . .

"When returning to barracks after a gruelling twenty-mile forced march, we always passed the word along to keep singing and straighten up just to show those in camp it was just 'a walk in the park' for our company."

Volunteers in the 1st Canadian Parachute Battalion had been marching and singing for almost two years. The battalion had been created on July 1, 1942, when Minister of Defence J. L. Ralston and the War Cabinet Committee approved its structure. The battalion would be trained in keeping with the American system and organized according to the British model—a battalion headquarters, a headquarters company and three rifle companies, twenty-six officers and 590 other ranks in all. Its initial purpose was for home defence against any enemy attack on remote areas of Canada. Not surprisingly, the idea of such a force was really hatched in 1940, when the Allies witnessed 30,000 German airborne troops, *Fallschirmjager*, parachute into Holland in force to capture strategic locations.

A German invasion was something Jan de Vries' family, originally from the Friesland area of northern Holland, understood only too well. His father, a tradesman in the Dutch city of Leeuwarden, had lived through tough times in the First World War and decided he disliked Dutch politics and the volatility of the country's economy. So in 1930 he had moved the family to Canada, settled in Toronto's east end, and taken work maintaining a fleet of trucks. When the Depression hit, Jan's father became a freelance mechanic while his mother cleaned homes to help the family survive. Toward the end of the decade, the family bought a gas station and garage, where Jan and his brother worked after school until war broke out again in 1939. Jan's brother enlisted in 1940 and Jan signed up in 1943.

"I tried to get into the air force because the thought of flying kind of appealed to me," de Vries said. "They decided I was partially colour-blind and that was no good for aircrew.... I left the air force recruiting office and was thinking of the navy. Then I saw some paratroops walking down Bay Street.... It was the look, the way they carried themselves, the high brown boots and berets. . . . I went into the closest army recruiting office and said, 'I want the paratroops.'"

Many 1st Canadian Parachute Battalion volunteers received their American-style training at the U.S. School of Infantry in Fort Benning, Georgia. De Vries was shipped to western Canada instead, to the Canadian Parachute Training Centre in Manitoba's brand new Camp Shilo. Following a battery of physical and psychological tests, de Vries and his fellow recruits were handed over to instructors who "put the boots to our fannies." In a matter of weeks the new paras learned how to handle weapons and explosives, how to attack and demolish bridges, pillboxes, barbed-wire entanglements, and casemates, as well as how to pack a parachute and leap from a moving aircraft. By June 1943, de Vries had first-hand experience in all the paratroop essential skills except one, when one morning he and the latest recruits were assembled in the Camp Shilo parade square.

"You've got an option," an officer told them. "You can take your first jumps next week or you can take five days' leave, because you're going overseas."

De Vries chose the leave, but within a week he was in Halifax, shoehorned aboard the ocean liner *Queen Elizabeth* with 20,000 other troops and steaming his way to the 1st Canadian Parachute Battalion's headquarters in the south of England. At Bulford train station near Salisbury, perhaps to keep up appearances, if not to remind reinforcements such as de Vries just how serious this posting really was, the new paras detrained and immediately trekked through a valley, across a creek, and into the Carter Barracks on the Salisbury Plain. The march punctuated an important moment in the career of Jan de Vries and the rest of his C Company. For the next eleven months, the new paratroops would sweat out a rigid training regimen for the D-Day they knew was coming.

Private de Vries made his first jump soon after arriving. An instructor took him and four other first-timers about 600 feet aloft in a basket hanging beneath a tethered balloon. Each novice approached the hole in the centre of the basket and listened to the specifics of parachute-jumping.

"Arch your back," the instructor said, "so your chute clears the edge of the hole, or else the chute tips you forward and you hit your head on the far side."

"Lots of broken noses," de Vries thought.

"Okay, number one. Go!"

De Vries remembered slipping through the hole and then dropping and dropping. He felt as stiff as a board: "When the hell is that thing going to open?"

Finally after nearly 200 of the 600 feet, the chute opened. He heard a nice rustling sound as it slowed his descent. Then, he relaxed and enjoyed the ride, looking around at the countryside until an instructor on the ground "gave me hell for not paying attention." It was all over in eighteen seconds.

Next, he did a jump at night. Then a jump from a converted Whitley bomber, which the instructors called a flying coffin. By September, de Vries had completed the required eight jumps. He got his paratrooper's high brown boots and beret. Best of all he received a set of graduation "jump wings" pinned to his chest by the commanding officer, Lieut.-Col. George Bradbrooke, in front of the battalion on the parade square.

"It felt great," de Vries said. "We were qualified. All set. The cocks of the walk."

Next morning, the troops were back to work with a five-mile run before breakfast. On the routine went, through that fall and winter and into the spring of 1944. De Vries also got more armament training on semi-automatic guns and .303 rifles. His superiors decided that he was no standout as a marksman, so they assigned him the job of section bombardier; he became a walking dispensary of guns, shells, mortar bombs, and grenades. This responsibility he carried in addition to his regular full-combat pack.

Then the marching and running intensified. A 10-mile run once a week became 15 miles and then 20 miles. Once, their battalion commander ordered a 50-mile forced march in full equipment and weapons. The troops had to finish the route within eighteen hours or do it a second time. They only had to do it once.

The cadence counting and the singing helped boost the men's spirits as they marched. It helped them endure their aches and pains, forget the rain and mud, while covering the miles to get home in time. On the night of June 4, when all four companies of the battalion transported their gear to the airfields prepared to launch their D-Day jump, and then had to stand down because of bad weather, the singsongs and even de Vries' harmonica-playing helped ease their agitation and get them through one more night of waiting inside the security transit camp.

The tension was palpable. For those who remembered the failure at Dieppe, the postponement of D-Day meant twenty-four more hours during which German counter-intelligence could get wind of the Allied plans, twenty-four more hours for a breach of security to undermine the element of surprise.

Nevertheless, the one-day delay gave everybody, from untested privates to seasoned commanders, one last chance to review his role in the invasion. Specifically, in joining the 6th British Airborne Division phase of Operation Neptune, the 1st Canadian Parachute Battalion had been assigned the job of securing a firm base on the left flank of the beach bridgehead that would allow a future Allied breakout to the east of the River Orne. The battalion was ordered to capture intact the bridges over the river and its canal, and to destroy the enemy coastal battery at Merville and five bridges over the River Dives as well as deny the enemy access to the high ground between the two rivers. The schedule called for some members of the Canadian battalion to land one hour ahead of the rest of the brigade to secure the Drop Zone.

That meant that the Canadians would be the first Allied troops to set foot in occupied France on D-Day if things went according to plan.

One final piece of advice resonated in the thoughts of C Company's bombardier, Pte. Jan de Vries. He remembered something British Brigadier James Hill had told the battalion in those final hours: "No matter how well you've been trained, no matter how good you feel about yourself, when you land, don't expect anything to be what you thought it would be. It will most likely be total chaos."

De Vries did not realize then how right Brigadier Hill would be.

6 a.m. June 5, 1944—Salisbury Plain, England

D-Day minus one. When reveille wakened those who had been able to sleep inside the Canadian compound, June 5 was dawning with little promise. The wind was still driving a heavy rain. Nevertheless, at nine o'clock platoon commanders began rallying their men as if the operation had been given the full go-ahead. Men and vehicles began to repeat the ritual of the previous day. Equipment was checked, weapons made ready, and everything reloaded onto the trucks that arrived outside the barbed wire. A, B, and Headquarters companies embarked for the RAF station at Down Ampney, while C Company, the main advance group, was driven to Harwell airport in Oxfordshire to board eleven Albemarles, the transport planes that would ferry them to Drop Zone V in Normandy.

De Vries arrived with his stick—a group of ten paratroops—at Harwell, where the Albemarles were ready and waiting. Only then did they get word the jump was a go. Through the evening, de Vries' stick loaded its gear aboard its allotted aircraft. As well as a jump bag strapped to his knee and running down his shin to the top of his foot, de Vries wore a veritable arsenal around his torso: a Sten gun and a bandolier with seven Sten magazines across his chest, four additional Bren-gun magazines, six 2-inch mortar bombs tucked under the chute harness on his back, and smoke grenades sewn into his jump smock and filling every available pocket—more than seventy pounds of added weight. Eventually he took his spot in the aircraft. He would jump eighth in his stick.

As he sat down, he made mental note of the faces of the men with whom he would jump into France. There were Roy Rushton, a Bren gunner, and Art Shank. There were Peter Braidwood, who spoke with a strong Scottish burr, and Joe Villeneuve from Quebec. And there was his platoon sergeant, George Kroesing, whom de Vries always remembered getting ready to jump with a Bangalore torpedo draped around his neck.

There was very little conversation as the men loaded themselves and their gear into the belly of the Albemarle. They painted their faces and any exposed skin with charcoal. They ate the extra sandwiches they had been issued at lunchtime. Some smoked final cigarettes and had a last nervous piss. The picture was repeated across the entire airfield. C-47 Dakota transports also loaded paratroops, while Halifaxes and Stirlings prepared to tug gliders full of paratroops and their equipment to the drop zones in France. Meanwhile, Mosquito fighter-bombers and Lancaster bombers winched explosives into their bomb bays to fulfill their roles in Operation Neptune.

At the edge of the tarmac, war reporter Richard Dimbleby and a technician from the BBC program "Radio Newsreel" had set up to record the sounds of the airborne departure on a vinyl disc. The British public was just as starved for information about the long-awaited invasion as the Canadian soldiers were eager to get aloft. For nearly five years, they had heard nothing but bad news on their radios. Tonight that would change, beginning just after 10:30 p.m., June 5.

"There she goes now, the first aircraft leading the attack on Europe," Richard Dimbleby announced into the microphone. He paused to let the sound of the Albemarle's twin-engines register with his listeners. "No sooner has she gone down the runway, level and straight, now I can see her . . . over the brow of the hill, lifting into the sky."

Just forty-five seconds later, the second Albemarle is in position and rolling away. And the next. Dimbleby is nearly shouting over the engines' roar.

"Even as the very first machine to go climbs into the sky, her white tail light can be seen lifting and lifting against the clouds, and the second one disappears below the hill to follow. . . . So the third begins revving up her engines and bit by bit pulling towards the tarmac. . . ."

As the eleven Albemarles carrying C Company climbed and moved into formation for the run over the Channel, the paratroops said and did little as they sat along the inside length of the plane. De Vries was struck by the men's silence and stillness. No one smoked. Nobody moved, except those men near the fuselage portholes. In the moonlight and broken cloud they strained to see the cliffs of southern England slipping away and then the coastline of France approaching fast.

The first signs of trouble were the flashes ahead of them, then the noise of anti-aircraft flak and tracers rushing up to meet them. None of the Albemarles sustained significant damage, but the pilots were forced to take evasive action. They had been instructed to fly in loose formation and to follow their leaders in the release of the paratroops; however, when a leader made an error, so did those who followed. Some aircraft were now off course and had lost altitude, flying below 600 feet.

When the red ready light came on near the pilot's cabin, the closest paratrooper called out, "Red light!" This meant two minutes to the drop. Everybody moved to his ready position, checking to make sure his static line was securely hooked to the cable running along the left wall of the fuselage. De Vries' thoughts turned inward as he wondered what would happen next and whether everything would go the way it should. The red light switched to green. Somebody yelled "Go!" and the men in front of de Vries began to disappear one by one through the bathtub-like hole in the plane's belly.

"It seemed to be forever," de Vries said. "I thought, 'Jesus, I'm not going to be anywhere near where the other guys are because it's taking so long for the others to get out.' . . . Then jump. It's black, just total black. You couldn't see a blessed thing. Just black. . . . The chute opened with a jerk. I had my hands up to control, but I didn't know whether to go forward, backward, or anything. So I just hung there ready if anything happened. It was just seconds and, bang, I'm on the ground."

It was twelve minutes after midnight. D-Day.

De Vries had landed in a grassy farmer's field. Nothing he saw there looked like anything he had seen on the maps or the miniature models on the briefing-room sand tables. He was fairly certain he had been dropped too far inland, so he started to creep through the darkness toward what he thought would be the Drop Zone. He figured he was 300 to 400 feet from his nearest platoon mate. But nobody he heard sounded like another trooper. When he did hear voices, he realized they were speaking German and figured they were a patrol out looking for whatever had come down from the passing aircraft.

"All I kept thinking was what they'd told us: 'If you get captured by the German army, you'll become a POW. If you get captured by the SS, you'll be shot.'"

Like many in his company, de Vries was alone and would have to make his own way to the company objective. More than the coastal flak had thrown the delivery aircraft off track; Allied bombing of coastal targets was affecting the airborne assault negatively too. Even though accompanying British airborne troops had by now set up a series of Eureka beacons (green lights) on the ground to guide the main paratroop force into the Drop Zone, smoke and heavy dust kept drifting in from the coast and obscuring the beacons. Of a possible 110 paratroops involved in the advance party drop, only thirty had landed inside the Drop Zone. The rest were scattered as far as nine miles from the intended target.

12:12 a.m. June 6, 1944—
River Orne and Caen Canal, France

At almost precisely the same moment that de Vries landed, 12:12 a.m., six Horsa gliders towed across the Channel by six Halifax bombers were released and descended slightly to the west of the Canadian Drop Zone. On board was a special force of 180 men from the 2nd Oxford and Buckinghamshire Light Infantry and thirty Royal Engineers, all part of the 6th Airborne Division. Their coup de main mission this night was to attack two vital bridges, one spanning the River Orne and the second the Caen Canal, together code-named Ham and Jam.

Under the command of Major John Howard, these special British troops had trained during the same months as the

Canadian paras to drop with precision and to seize intact the two bridges in the dark. If they succeeded, the Allied assault forces landing on the Normandy beaches later on D-Day could just as quickly break out into the French countryside to meet an anticipated German counterattack.

By 12:19 a.m., just seven minutes later, five of the six gliders had made controlled crash-landings within a stone's throw of the two targets. Major Howard and his unit had overrun pill-boxes guarding both bridges, and with very few shots fired—two British troops dead and 14 wounded—had seized the Caen Canal bridge and the River Orne bridge, the next day renamed Pegasus bridge and Horsa bridge, respectively, in the soldiers' honour.

"Ham and Jam!" shouted the radio operator into his wireless. "Ham and bloody Jam!"

11:53 p.m. June 5, 1944—Varaville, France

One paratrooper from C Company of the 1st Canadian Parachute Battalion who managed to land within a few hundred yards of his designated Drop Zone was Corporal Dan Hartigan. He admitted reciting the Lord's Prayer during his short descent, which did nothing to improve the location of his landing. After extricating himself from an apple tree and cautiously making his way to a road, he suddenly heard voices and the sound of feet clomping along the pavement. With nowhere to hide, he dove into the dirt on the shoulder of the road and contemplated tossing a Gammon bomb toward the people coming his way. Then he realized they were French farmers in wooden shoes trying to escape the Allied bombing. The group passed so close to him that he could have reached out and tripped some of them, but he let them pass. They never spotted him.

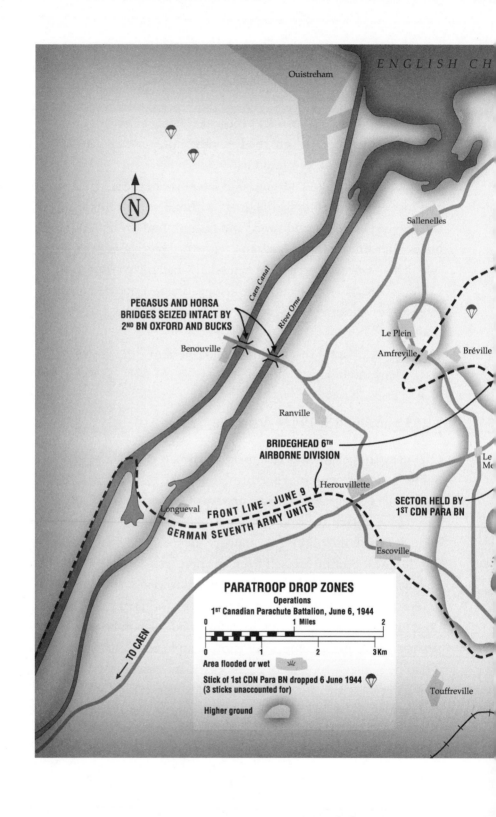

ENGLISH CH

Ouistreham

Sallenelles

N

Caen Canal

River Orne

**PEGASUS AND HORSA
BRIDGES SEIZED INTACT BY
2ND BN OXFORD AND BUCKS**

Le Plein

Amfreville

Bréville

Benouville

Ranville

**BRIDEGHEAD 6TH
AIRBORNE DIVISION**

Le
Me

Herouvillette

FRONT LINE - JUNE 9

Longueval

GERMAN SEVENTH ARMY UNITS

**SECTOR HELD BY
1ST CDN PARA BN**

Escoville

TO CAEN

PARATROOP DROP ZONES
Operations
1ST Canadian Parachute Battalion, June 6, 1944

0   1 Miles   2

0   1   2   3 Km

Area flooded or wet

Stick of 1st CDN Para BN dropped 6 June 1944
(3 sticks unaccounted for)

Higher ground

Touffreville

Cabourg

Dives-sur-Mer

Le Petit Homme

Divette River

ONE STICK
DROPPED NEAR
HEULAND
4 MILES EAST

Le Marais

ARMY UNITS

P ZONE
PARA BDE LESS
BATTALION

Varaville

**GERMAN
STRONG
POINT**

River Dives

Dives Canal

Robehomme

**BRIDGE
DESTROYED**

Plain Lugan

Goustranville

VENT

**BRIDGE
DESTROYED**

Bures

St. Richer

**BRIDGE
DESTROYED**

St.
Samson

Troarn

Hartigan began making his way toward his rendezvous point, about halfway between the village of Varaville and the Merville Battery. He could hear the sound of explosions just ahead. From his pre–D-Day battle briefings, he figured that Allied bombers were now striking their targets, including the German guns at Merville. In fact, he was closer to the bombing run than he would have preferred, as he could hear the sound of one Lancaster's engines coming straight at him, accompanied by the whine of its single bomb. Again, he went to ground behind some dirt at the base of a hedgerow. The ensuing blast covered him in "the soft chunks of Normandy earth . . . seeming to bury me alive" and nearly deafened him. He managed to dig himself out from beneath several inches of soil, shook it off, and continued carefully toward his rendezvous, avoiding the roads. At one point, as he pulled himself over a gate, he was stopped by a sharp jab in his backside from a bayonet.

"Punch!" came a firm whisper in the darkness.

It was the battalion's password sequence this night. "Judy!" Hartigan blurted out and he looked up the rifle into the face of Eddie Mallon, a private from his own stick of paratroops. Hartigan swore at him.

Mallon laughed, as glad to see Hartigan as to have scared him half to death.

11:30 p.m. June 5, 1944—Salisbury Plain, England

By the time members of C Company's advance party had begun orienting themselves and taking stock on the ground in France, the C-47 Dakota transport aircraft carrying A, B, and the Headquarters companies were just taking off from Down Ampney aerodrome in England. Of the twenty-six aircraft carrying the main 1st Canadian Parachute Battalion force to the Drop Zone, nine would drop their sticks in the flooded area around the River Dives, a couple of miles east of the target area; five would drop theirs near the village of Breville; and the remainder would disperse their cargo over a wide area around Battalion Drop Zone V.

Paratrooper Richard Hilborn and his Vickers machine-gun platoon with Headquarters Company would be delayed slightly more than the others. When Lieutenant Hilborn arrived at Down Ampney, he had found his transport pilot, Flying Officer Graeme Metcalf trying to locate a mechanical problem in one of his Dakota's engines; once he had deduced its magneto was malfunctioning, he quickly ordered the entire stick to transfer to a spare aircraft. That had delayed their takeoff about an hour. Then out over the Channel, Metcalf and his navigator discovered they had incorrect charts for the radio beacons guiding their aircraft into France. The pilot decided to use dead reckoning to find the Drop Zone.*

"As I approached the French coast," Metcalf said, "I came in low to try to pick up some mark. Just as I got there, there was quite a party going on ahead with a tremendous fireworks show, and a Stirling bomber went in. I saw the tail plane on the Stirling quite clearly as it blew up."

Metcalf had to steer clear of both the exploding bomber and the lethal wall of anti-aircraft fire ahead of him, by yanking the control column of the Dakota as hard as he could.

"It happened just as we were getting organized to jump," Hilborn said. "So about five of us ended up crashing into the lavatory at the back of the plane in a heap."

Somehow, Metcalf recovered and spotted the mouth of the River Orne. He figured that, at approximately 130 miles per

---

* "Dead reckoning" is navigation by use of predetermined vectors of wind and true airspeed and precalculated heading, ground speed, and estimated time of arrival—in other words, a calculated guess.

hour, if he flew along the coast for about two and a half minutes and then directly inland for another minute and a half, he would arrive at the Drop Zone.

"My orders were to land [the] men somewhere in France," the pilot said in jest some years later.

Hilborn was number four in his stick. He managed to jump from the Dakota cleanly, but when the chute jerked open, the strap holding his kit bag to his knee broke and he made the rest of the short descent with his gear down around his ankle. He had never come to earth so quickly in his life. Miraculously, he dropped into an orchard about a mile northwest of the Drop Zone, managed to cut himself free of his rigging, and set off across the countryside in the direction of gunfire he heard in the distance. Mounting the first fence in his path, Hilborn quickly learned that he was no longer in the relative sanctuary of the Salisbury Plain training grounds. He heard a clatter, looked up, and saw a metal sign that read *Achtung Minen*. Before long he had met a few other members of his stick, not far from a farmhouse with inhabitants.

"We saw a crack of light under the front door," Hilborn said. "We thought there might be Germans inside. I knocked and a man came out. We grabbed him and went inside. A French family was there, all loyal and friendly. I produced my map, and using my limited vocabulary of French [asked] where we were. He took us to the nearest road and he sent us off in the proper direction."

By five o'clock in the morning Richard Hilborn and company had reached their objective, Le Mesnil crossroads between Breville and the Bois de Bavent west of Varaville.

1 a.m. June 6, 1944—Robehomme, France

Lieutenant Hilborn was one of the few Canadian paratroopers to arrive at his rendezvous point with his full kit and weapons packs. Between the low altitude, the scattered nature of the drop, and the smoke-obscured conditions on the ground the battalion lost much of its fighting gear. One other hazard that the Allied airborne-assault planners had not anticipated to a large degree, but which the Germans wisely guessed might deter any invasion attempt, was the defensive use of water. The farmland adjacent to the River Dives provided a natural flood plain. So the German engineers responsible for defending the French coastal area dammed the flow of river water to the sea, which flooded acres of orchards and pasture along the River Dives and, as it turned out, a portion of the 1st Canadian Parachute Battalion's Drop Zone.

"I was never afraid of heights," paratrooper Mark Lockyer said. "I'm also a fatalist. What's going to happen is going to happen."

Born in 1924, on a 125-acre farm in Whitby Township north of Lake Ontario, Lockyer was the youngest of three sons. He generally got the hand-me-down jobs at home, such as moving hay bales to the highest point in the hip-roof barn, some fifty feet off the ground. Farm work had given Mark a strong upper body, and his spare time spent shooting rabbits (for the seventy-five cents his father could get for each pelt at the St. Lawrence Market in Toronto) had made him a crack shot and therefore an ideal prospect for the army.

Not having advanced beyond Grade 10, Mark chose to stay and help out on the farm when the war broke out. He considered staying there, too, in an essential service, until Lloyd Brush, his older sister Dorothy's husband, was taken prisoner in the ill-fated Dieppe raid. Then Mark knew he had to enlist, even if he was only seventeen. When the 1st Canadian Parachute Battalion accepted him, the recruiters refused to send him overseas with the rest of the battalion because he was underage. Instead they sent him to Wainwright, Alberta, for an additional training course.

When he finally turned eighteen and was allowed to join the battalion in England, Private Lockyer already had his jump wings, training as a sniper, and additional expertise in the use of explosives. He joined the fourth platoon of B Company during the final preparations for the jump into Normandy. The sticks with which he jumped would be responsible for reconnoitring, seizing, and destroying a small strategic bridge over the River Dives near the village of Robehomme. Under Captain Peter Griffin, the group including Lockyer would rendezvous at the objective in the middle of the night, and with the assistance of Royal Engineers, who were bringing explosives, would destroy the bridge. The objective was to stop or slow down any mechanized counterattack by German tanks on the Allies' left flank.

Though he knew he was just another citizen soldier, Pte. Lockyer treated every aspect of a jump professionally. Aboard the Dakota en route to France, he mentally walked through each move, securing his gear, checking his static line, and making a quick exit. Then, once he was actually through the door, he knew that, if he kicked the leg on which he had tied his .303 rifle in the same direction as the Dakota's flight path, his body would turn directly into the Dakota's prop wash to fully inflate his parachute. Each step went like clockwork.

"Once out, you got rid of the pack on your leg," he said. "It was tied in two places with a slip knot; that let the pack down to the end of a twenty-foot rope. That'll tell you where the ground is as you come down. . . . In my case, though, I hear a splash and think, 'Oh-oh, water.' So I had my hand on the harness release, because if the water below is going to be deep I want to get the hell out of that harness."

Despite his fears, he hit the water and his descent stopped with his jump boots hitting terra firma about four feet beneath the surface. Oddly, he felt at home. The ground was mucky, yet grassy—farm pasture. As far as he could see in the darkness, there was water. He quickly released his chute, retrieved the waterproof kapok container with his Lee Enfield rifle inside, and faced his next challenge. Where was Robehomme? Where was the River Dives? And the bridge they were supposed to destroy?

As many as five sticks of B Company paratroopers splashed down into the marshy flooded areas around Robehomme. The paras later nicknamed the area "Satan's Quadrangle" for very good reason. Lockyer learned that many of his comrades who never showed up at the rendezvous point had been so laden with the excess weight of their extra ammunition and heavy weapons that they were dragged down and drowned in the deeper irrigation ditches.

Members of the company, singly and in groups of two and three, collected what weapons and ammunition they could muster and set out for their objective, the Robehomme bridge over the River Dives. One group under Lt. Norm Toseland met a young French woman bicyclist, who led the men across a farm field to within sight of the bridge. By two o'clock, in the darkness, about a dozen paratroopers had gathered at the bridge, and they sat tight until the designated demolition crew of Royal Engineers arrived to complete the mission. By three o'clock the sappers had still not arrived.

"Anybody here worked with plastic high explosive?" Toseland asked.

"I have, sir," Lockyer said. Not only did he know about PHE, but he had trained others back in Canada how to use it. It would now be up to him to collect the right mount of explosive from his comrades, place it correctly along the two supporting girders of the bridge, and cripple or destroy the crossing. At that moment, Lockyer was more grateful to the D-Day drop organizers and one recce pilot than anybody else. First, the planners had ensured that every paratrooper jumping into France carried his own small quantity of plastic high explosive in the space between the shock-harness and the metal roof of his helmet. Second, Allied air force reconnaissance had supplied B Company's pre–D-Day briefings with a photograph of the bridge.

"This Mosquito pilot had taken a picture, probably doing three hundred miles an hour," Lockyer said. "And how big was the I-beam under the bridge? Fortunately, there was a Frenchman going across [the bridge] on a bicycle in the photograph. So based on that, we knew we were going to need a hell of a lot of PHE to blow up that ten-inch I-beam. But that guy did a damn good job of photographing that bridge."

As Private Lockyer gathered about thirty pounds of PHE and the explosive from some disarmed Gammon bombs and grenades, a Royal Engineer finally appeared. The two men set to work to prepare the bridge for demolition. In fact, at one point, the sapper held Lockyer by the feet so that he could dangle over the side of the bridge and tape the explosive along the bridge supports. Within twenty minutes, they had strung out the explosive wire and warned everybody to take cover.

"Okay, Canada," the Royal Engineer said. "It's yours."

At 3 a.m., Lockyer pushed the plunger. When the dust cleared, the I-beams had been broken and the centre of the bridge had collapsed on itself; otherwise the structure remained intact. The mission was only partly complete.

With more paratroops arriving seemingly every other minute, the bridge demolition group grew in number to include intelligence officers, field ambulance medics, and a British machine-gun crew. This enabled the men to set up defensive positions at the western entrance to the bridge until daybreak, when more Royal Engineers arrived with the explosives necessary to blow the bridge completely. Once the bridge was destroyed, B Company's paratroops began a methodical move west toward the battalion headquarters at Le Mesnil crossroads. For Pte. Mark Lockyer, it had been an adrenaline-filled D-Day. In less than forty-eight hours, however, the flow of adrenaline would mark the only difference between life and death.

1:30 a.m. June 6, 1944—Le Mesnil, France

The 1st Canadian Parachute Battalion had four medical officers, one assigned to each company. A group of paratroopers had been trained to provide assistance to the medical officers to act as medics. The assistants learned how to conduct triage, serve as stretcher-bearers, and establish dressing stations for the wounded in the field. Twenty-year-old Torontonian Ernie Jeans had been with the battalion since its formation. He took his first parachute jumps at Fort Benning in Georgia and learned about explosives and marksmanship at Camp Shilo. Not until late in his training regimen was he streamed away from weaponry and into first aid. The night of June 5, Cpl. Ernie Jeans came across the Channel in one of the Headquarters Company aircraft with about twenty other paratroopers.

Like the other aircraft in the main force on the way to the Drop Zone, the Dakota carrying Corporal Jeans' stick ran into flak, taking a direct hit to its left engine. Perhaps the anti-aircraft fire or the inadequacies of the navigational aids rattled the crew, because the drop operation seemed disorganized and slow. After the green jump light flashed on, only two-thirds of the paratroopers jumped. At that point the aircraft dispatcher at the doorway suddenly told the remaining few paras to stop and sit down again. Ernie Jeans and his fellow medic, Sgt. Dan

Wright, were eighteenth and nineteenth in the jump line.

"Here we've come all this way," Jeans said to himself, "and we're turning back to England."

The pilot had actually banked the Dakota for a second run over the Drop Zone. Then a quick red light flashed, then a green light and a second signal to go. Jeans and Wright and the few remaining members of the stick jumped into the night. Nearly all of those who had jumped on the Dakota's first pass over the Drop Zone failed to make their way to battalion head-quarters; they were killed, wounded, or taken prisoner. The two medical paratroopers landed safely and made their way toward the objective, where they helped the 224th Field Ambu-lance set up a field hospital at a château near Le Mesnil cross-roads.

About the time Ernie Jeans saw his first dead paratrooper, one of the officers at battalion headquarters told him and Wright that the HQ doctor, Capt. Colin Brebner, had been taken prisoner; it was therefore up to the two of them to set up a first-aid station. Jeans remembered the confusion and the severity of the first wounds to arms, legs, and bodies that he saw. All the two medics could do was stabilize the wounded who were brought in to them; later, the brigade evacuated a farmhouse and converted it into a field hospital.

"We worked from dawn till dusk," Jeans said. "It was never easy. I guess my training came through. But those first days were the worst . . . being a twenty-year-old thrust into the busi-ness of looking after the wounded and trying to comfort the dying."

3 a.m. June 6, 1944—Varaville, France

As the disparate sticks of four Canadian airborne companies began making their way toward the makeshift battalion headquarters within the intended defence position, individual soldiers or small groups continued to blaze their own D-Day paths forward. Cpl. Dan Hartigan and Pte. Eddie Mallon had found each other in the dark near the road between Varaville and the Merville Battery. Along the way, they ran into a group from the British 9th Parachute Battalion, and then a local civilian. Since Private Mallon spoke French, he explained to the Frenchman who the paratroops were. The man, realizing that the Allied invasion had begun, promptly threw his arms around Mallon and kissed him. The two Canadians laughed out loud; neither had ever seen one man kiss another in his life.

About daybreak, Mallon and Hartigan located a Canadian-held anti-tank ditch overlooking the grounds of Le Grand Château de Varaville. They were greeted by a burst of enemy machine-gun fire; the château was evidently not yet in Canadian hands. Worse, Hartigan discovered, the earlier engagement with German gunners had killed C Company's commander, Maj. Murray MacLeod, platoon officer Lt. Hugh Walker, and several other paratroopers.

Itching to break the stalemate, Corporal Hartigan approached his superiors. He warned them that daybreak might bring a German counterattack. More important in his view was the fact that the Canadian red berets had to gain the position before the British green berets—commandos who were trying to make their way up from the beaches—arrived to take it for them. The battalion officers in charge agreed to allow Hartigan to conduct a solo reconnaissance to see if the Canadians could direct a successful assault on the entrenched enemy troops. While passing through the château gatehouse where his commanding officer had been killed during the night, Hartigan first faced a truth about warfare that he had not expected.

"The room was a shambles, but more," he later wrote. "A pair of legs hanging . . . over part of a wrecked bunk bed. A torso . . . lying on a pile of brick and covered in brick mortar dust. Simply an insignificant little remnant clothed in a dirty tee-shirt. It was something which had been a young man a few minutes earlier."

The drama of the battle was not complete. As Hartigan poked his way toward the German trenches adjacent to the château, C Company officers began pressing the German defenders to surrender. During the exchange, there was an explosion in the distance. The Canadians knew it meant that members of their battalion had achieved yet another objective: they and Royal Engineers had successfully blown up one of the Varaville bridges over the Divette canal, cutting off one avenue of a potential German tank assault on the troops landing on the beaches.

This seemed to increase the likelihood of a surrender. The Germans let the Canadians know they wanted to send out their wounded; they had no medical personnel in their position. With Capt. John Hanson's permission they returned to their lines to bring out their casualties. Two German soldiers emerged pushing a cart tht carried their wounded, and several other men who were able to walk also stepped forward. To the Canadians' astonishment, a German machine-gun crew abruptly opened fire on their own surrendering men. This caused the Germans who were approaching on foot to start running, triggering another exchange of small arms and mortar fire between the two sides.

Having located the heart of the German defence, a 75-mm French field piece, which the Germans had adapted to serve both as a field gun and anti-tank gun, Corporal Hartigan pulled out some two-inch mortar bombs and his mortar. He worked his way on his belly through a series of ditches and depressions to within a distance from which he could fire his mortar in a relatively flat trajectory. Bracing the weapon almost horizontally against the base of a tree, he fired four bombs in succession into the gun position and then several smoke bombs to cover his own exit. One of his mortar bombs struck the artillery gunsight, knocking out the weapon. His action and the continued pressure of the rest of the company forced the issue. A few minutes later, a white flag appeared from the German bunker and the Canadian paras accepted the surrender of the forty-three remaining enemy troops. The radio signal incorporating the code word "blood" was transmitted. The Canadians had captured Varaville.

"Within an hour of the seizure of Varaville," Hartigan wrote later, "a count of the enemy was made . . . a total of roughly 80 prisoners and casualties, two enemy soldiers for every Canadian paratrooper who fought for Varaville. . . . They had the plentiful weapons . . . and the strength of numbers in their favour. We, the paratroopers, had the determination and the airborne mystique on our side."

10 a.m. June 6, 1944—Wiltshire, England

By the middle of D-Day morning, about the time the assault troops were establishing a beachhead behind them, survivors of the 1st Canadian Parachute Battalion had achieved all the objectives assigned them in Operation Overlord. They had captured the Merville Battery and destroyed its guns. They had overrun or isolated remaining pockets of German defenders. All the bridges lying between Troarn and Varaville had been demolished or made impassable. Meanwhile, through short, sharp battles of their own, the other battalions of the 6th British Airborne Division had taken intact the two important bridges over the River Orne and the Caen Canal to the west of Ranville. For the moment, the flanks of the assault area on the beaches were secure.

Altogether, thirty-seven paratroop sticks had dropped into Normandy on the eve of D-Day. The battalion's losses were

significant. Of the 27 officers and 516 other ranks who participated in the drop, 113 men were lost, killed, wounded, or taken
prisoner within the first twenty-four hours of the operation.
The Allied air force crews sustained losses during the mission
as well; of 264 aircraft and 98 glider combinations working to
deliver the entire 6th British Airborne Division to Normandy,
seven aircraft and 22 gliders and their crews had been lost.

In some ways, however, anecdotal evidence reveals more
about the losses than the statistics do.

Though he flew no sorties on D-Day, RCAF pilot Ralph
Campbell was itching to participate. On June 5, he had been
with No. 196 (RAF) Squadron at Keevil in Wiltshire, England, for only six days. He and his Stirling crew were still considered too green for operations. Consequently, they did not
fly on the night of June 5 or during the day of June 6. As word
filtered back and aircraft returned from those operations,
Campbell's commanding officer consoled them.

"You'll have lots of ops," he told them. "This war is a long
way from over. Anyway, we can't send everyone, and so we have
picked only the crews with experience."

To illustrate his point, the squadron crews were taken to the
tarmac. They were shown one of the Stirlings that had dropped
paratroops during the night of June 5/6. Wrapped around the
base of one of its propellers was a mangled parachute.

"The planes in front of us flew too high over the dropping
zone," read the pilot's report, "and . . . we hit this poor chap's
chute. He's dead, of course, and all because of some bloody
poor flying. . . ."

The incident, Campbell explained, illustrated the human
tendency to make what seemed to be minor corrections in the
interest of one's own safety without fully appreciating how
costly those minor slips could be. If the orders called for an officer to drop troops from a plane at 500 feet, those carrying out

those orders faced a temptation to go up to 525 feet, and for the next wave after that to creep up to 550 feet, and so on. The higher the release point, the greater the likelihood that the troops would drift off target or be shot on their way down. Ultimately, those who were following orders precisely were placed in dilemmas not of their own making. This particular Stirling pilot had maintained the proper altitude and had killed a paratrooper as a result.

Even as the greatest military invasion plan in history was unfolding in the air, on the sea, and on land in Normandy, the Allies were learning many lessons at very high cost.

BEYOND

PICCADILLY CIRCUS

Dawn, June 4, 1944—Portland Harbour, England

B AD WEATHER on Sunday, June 4, had the Allied invasion plans by the throat.

If need be, most aircraft involved in Operation Neptune could climb above the cloud cover. Infantry could temporarily hunker down under canvas until the downpours and the wind blew themselves out. Storms moving across the British Isles that weekend, however, threatened to paralyze Allied military shipping completely. Vessels out on the English Channel reported sea swells of five and six feet, as wind velocities were peaking at force four. Force-five winds would have chased most medium-sized and small vessels off the North Sea and the Channel indefinitely.

However tempestuous the situation was on the water, what concerned Ray Mecoy aboard the Canadian minesweeper HMCS *Fort William* far more were the pre–D-Day warnings from his skipper. At the June 4 church service on board, Mecoy remembered Lt. Hugh Campbell and a navy chaplain laying out generally what was going to happen on D-Day, whenever it took place.

"[We] figure two-thirds of all the ships in the invasion are going to be hit [and] won't make it back," they said. "There's a good chance you're going to end up in the water and nobody is going to pick you up right away. You'll be on your own."

In spite of his superior officers' dire forecast, at twenty-two, Leading Stoker Mecoy felt extremely confident about himself. His civilian and wartime records showed he had plenty of skills to offer. In school he had taken electrical courses. To help his family make ends meet during the Depression, he had worked as a labourer at a bread factory, making twenty-three cents an hour. When he was eighteen he had worked in a machinist's job at the Toronto plant of Sangamo Electric, where they built the recording devices that the navy used in anti-submarine "ASDIC" (Anti-Submarine Detection Investigation Committee) devices. His wife-to-be, Margaret Neal, worked in the same plant making components for aircraft instrument panels. They met on a double date.

Mecoy had joined the 48th Highlanders in Toronto in 1939, but after participating in manoeuvres on a cadet weekend at Niagara-on-the-Lake, where the food was cold and greasy and the shooting practice hot and boring, he decided to scratch army off his list. Instead, in August 1942, he was accepted as a stoker (engineer) trainee in the Royal Canadian Navy. He paid his navy dues by learning auto mechanics, welding, and sheet-metal work; he built future landing craft, then cleaned soot and corrosion out of the boilers aboard RCN destroyers and corvettes docked in Halifax. Finally, in April 1943, he was drafted as a stoker, one of a crew of eighty-three, aboard the newly repaired minesweeper HMCS *Fort William*.

The world of an RCN stoker aboard a Bangor-class mine-sweeper had a rhythm and responsibility that Mecoy enjoyed.

Four hours on and eight hours off around the clock, he worked in one of two boiler rooms below decks. As one of twelve stokers, Mecoy kept the main steam-engine bearings oiled and cool; he ran the evaporator, which distilled water for the boilers; and he maintained the reciprocating steam engine that powered the ship's tiller. During some of his hours out of the engine room, he assisted launching depth charges or manning the guns on deck.

In February 1944, the *Fort William* set sail from Canada and joined a Canadian flotilla of sixteen minesweepers in the waters around Britain. In U.K. ports, shipyard workers upgraded the Bangor sweepers with new deck armament, including twin, electrically powered, 20-mm Oerlikon guns and all the winches and tackle they would need for the coming invasion.

Next, *Fort William* and the rest of the Canadian sweepers began their workups, or training. The Canadian minesweeper crews faced one of the most dangerous and most technically exacting missions of any of the ships involved in the invasion. They were expected to sweep and mark a series of approach channels through known German minefields in the English Channel, right to the shallow water along the French coast. Their navigation would have to be precise and their sweeping thorough. The training exercises through April and May were assigned a most unlikely title, "Pious Dream."

Despite Lt. Campbell's gloomy predictions of low survival rates on D-Day, Mecoy took some comfort in the new equipment he had been issued for the coming operation. To replace the flimsy balloon-type life jackets the crew had had to inflate themselves and strap around their waists, each man received a brand new life-vest. This improved model offered protection and some warmth from the neck to the crotch. Its bonnet and collar, with small batteries and a light attached, would hold a sailor's head up in the water. And the hooks on the vest would easily connect him in the water to a Carley float, the life raft. Each navy crewman also received a steel helmet.

"It was a really queer feeling," Mecoy said, "because here you are, going out there, and you have no control over where you are going to go, or what you can do in an emergency."

So, with a sense of the heightened responsibility and with his captain's grim premonition of more than 60 percent losses in mind, Leading Stoker Mecoy went to his battle station below decks on a Canadian minesweeper that Sunday morning, June 4. *Fort William* sailed from Portland Harbour and joined a massive flotilla of more than 7,000 vessels all making their way beyond the Isle of Wight and heading toward the assembly area, which officials had code-named "Piccadilly Circus."

Once beyond any protection that southern England's harbours and the Solent (the strait between England and the Isle of Wight) provided, even the most substantial of the vessels found the winds and swells nearly overwhelming. Cloud cover hovered barely above the surface of the sea. Driving rain reduced visibility even further. Deteriorating conditions on the Channel appeared to endanger the entire operation. At that point, word filtered down from SHAEF's inner circle that the invasion scheduled for the next day, June 5, would be postponed at least twenty-four hours. The decision seemed only sensible but, for everybody, standing down only dragged out the tense waiting game.

Dawn, June 4, 1944—Isle of Wight, England

To a sailor, soldier, or airman, postponement of the mission was truly excruciating.

For Reg Weeks, the delay was almost disaster. Since January 1944, Lieutenant Weeks had worked as an intelligence officer at 3rd Canadian Infantry Division headquarters on the Isle of Wight, the island across the Solent from Southampton. In addition to compiling written and photographic data on German troop activity in occupied Europe, Weeks and his corps of eleven other intelligence officers drew up and kept secret all the maps the naval and assault infantry landing forces would use on D-Day.

"Up until that point, people could only speculate about D-Day," Weeks said. "Everybody was guessing where it was going to happen and when it was going to happen. They could speculate. But we knew."

During the previous four years, Reg Weeks had come to know a great deal more than the average soldier about the information of war. That knowledge had happened quite by accident. Born and raised in Britain, Weeks had earned a scholarship to attend school in the United States in 1940. When he graduated from Tabor Academy in Massachusetts the following year, he was nearly broke. He figured the quickest way home was to join the Canadian Army and be posted back to Britain. He therefore hitchhiked to Buffalo, New York, boarded a transport aircraft to Toronto, convinced officials at the airport that he was a landed immigrant, and enlisted in the army. He expected that when his outfit, the Lorne Scots (Peel, Dufferin and Halton Regiment), was shipped to Debert, Nova Scotia, he would soon be on his way home. Unfortunately, one day while cleaning windows inside an officer's quarters at Debert, Weeks began humming a piece of classical music.

The officer entered, stopped abruptly, and asked, "Where did you learn that?"

"I've always known it, sir," Weeks said. "I like real music."

"Private soldiers don't hum things like that."

"Well, I have been."

"Well then, you ought to be an officer." And with that, his superior arranged to send Weeks to officers training school—at the opposite end of the country, at Gordon Head on Vancouver Island.

In August 1943, Weeks finally received his commission. Someone noticed in his transcripts that he could speak French and German, so the army sent him to Kingston, Ontario, where he studied war intelligence. Through three months of intensive training, Weeks examined every intelligence textbook the library had to offer. He learned how to interrogate. He learned what constituted intelligence, how to separate fact from fiction, how data are gathered for intelligence reports, and the difference between "being concerned with blades of grass at the unit level, and at divisional level where you're concerned with the fields and forests."

In the fall of 1943, Weeks was finally sent overseas to Cambridge. In his homeland at last, he took more sophisticated British Intelligence training and at the beginning of 1944 was posted to Canadian army headquarters on the Isle of Wight. It was there, inside a compound of a few buildings and tents for living quarters and surrounded by barbed wire, that he joined a select circle of the few who knew the invasion would happen soon.

"Within ten minutes of my arriving, I was taken down to the map rooms," Weeks said. "My first question was, 'Where do I land and when?' They said, 'We can tell you the hour but not the day . . . about 0700 hours on D-Day.' They showed me on a map [where I would land], but no place names were shown. The map was complete with shoreline, topographical features, but no names. They would be added later."

Weeks and his team began creating and copying the detailed set of maps with the place names inserted and an exact duplicate set of maps without those labels. Each map, approximately three feet square, showed key buildings, wooded areas, defensive gun locations, streets, seawalls, and beach topography, including areas where the Germans had installed obstacles and mines. Each map was designed to offer the troops the information they would need about the coastal village and the roads that would lead them up from the beach and on to their expected objectives at day's end. Each map sheet would be relevant to about a brigade's worth of men: one map for the Canadian Army's 7th Brigade, 8th Brigade, and the 9th Brigade in reserve. Each intelligence officer gathered as much information as he could about what the invading troops would encounter in their sector—troops, armament, and defensive positions.

In the first days of June 1944, Weeks' IO team left the Isle of Wight. They took with them a transport truck full of their precious cargo. Each set of maps, with the exact D-Day locations clearly marked, was wrapped in paper and bound with string. Each was clearly designated for a particular command ship, such as an infantry landing ship (LSI), a tank landing craft (LCT), an infantry landing craft (LCI), and so on. Each was to be handed directly to the commanding officer of each vessel. It was then to be locked away in the safest possible place on board and guarded until the vessel was under way and sailing for France.

Weeks remembers the false alarm on Sunday, June 4, when many ships of the invasion armada had already been launched to their assembly points near and beyond "Piccadilly Circus" out in the Channel. Then everything was postponed at least twenty-four hours. All the maps carefully stored aboard ship now had to be unloaded until the actual "go" signal was issued. Even though he knew the inclement weather had forced the stand-down, Weeks wondered fleetingly if the false alarm was just another practice run, another test of the intelligence corps' ability to keep the D-Day secret secure. The stress, he admitted, taxed everyone.

"There was always the element of doubt," Weeks said, "that you were giving someone some bad intelligence and that the bad intelligence you gave them might cause problems, even death.... We were a small staff but all people in whom I learned to have an enormous amount of confidence."

Midday, June 4, 1944—Ramsgate, England

One of the same packages of top-secret maps and charts for Operation Neptune was delivered at Ramsgate in Kent to the coastal forces naval base of the Allied Dover Command. Until a week or so before D-Day, this had been the home base for the 29th Canadian Motor Torpedo Boat Flotilla. The eight original MTBs were slightly longer than seventy-one feet and powered by three U.S.-built Packard engines. They nearly hydroplaned over the Channel waters at their maximum speed of forty-one knots. Bristling with armament, torpedoes, depth charges, a 2-pounder pom-pom gun, twin 20-mm Oerlikon guns, and two Vickers .303 machine guns, the MTBs were produced to meet the cross-Channel threat of German gunboats. Therefore, even without knowing the specific D-Day orders, the crews of the 29th Flotilla realized they would be responsible for protecting the eastern flank of the invasion forces. A second group of MTBs, the 65th Canadian Motor Torpedo Boat Flotilla, would defend the extreme western flank.

One sub-lieutenant aboard MTB *459*, Jack Foote, remembered the Confidential Books (CBs) arriving in a canvas sack just before the 29th Flotilla moved to Portsmouth.

"We got the charts for the whole flotilla when we left Ramsgate. And we had to store them in a place that could be locked," he said. Fulfilling the security requirements presented a real problem. "We ended up putting them in the heads in the officers' wardroom."

The heads, or washrooms, aboard an MTB were cramped at the best of times and it took all three officers—Lt. Tony Law,

1st Lt. John Shand, and Sub-Lieutenant Foote—to cram the flotilla's bags of CBs into the toilet area. Space was at a premium throughout MTB 459. With private quarters on board for only the skipper and his second, Foote usually set down a mattress in the radio voice-transmission room or on the open deck to sleep when his watch was over. The sleeping arrangement did not bother him in the least. Foote had made his way onto an MTB for more than the privilege of occupying a bunk.

He joined the navy partly because a mariner's life was in his blood. His father was a merchant sea captain, first a skipper on a Great Lakes oil tanker, then aboard one of the Park merchant ships (each named after a Canadian park) hauling crude oil from Aruba to refinery ports along the east coast of the United States during the war. After numerous attempts, Jack got himself into the Royal Canadian Navy as a probationary sub-lieutenant in 1943 and took officers training, which taught him to read navigational charts, send and receive signal communication, and, of course, study King's Rules and Admiralty Instruction (KRAI). Eventually he served aboard a Fairmile motor launch operating out of St. John's, Newfoundland. When the call came for MTB volunteers, though, he jumped at the chance.

"I wanted to be closer to the action," he said, "and I wanted to be on Motor Torpedo Boats. . . . The speed was wonderful and the power. . . . If we were sailing at night and it was a bright night, there would be this unusual fluorescence from the wake of the ship. It was great to see, but as we learned in time it was dangerous, too. It made us visible."

While not necessarily dangerous, the weather was uncooperative for despatching a naval armada to France during those early June days and nights. The Channel waters were nearly impassable, particularly for smaller craft. Anybody on the open MTB bridge in rough seas, Foote observed, was soaked to the bone and found refuge to warm his extremities and dry his gear only below decks in the relative shelter of the MTB's engine room. Despite the poor weather and sailing conditions early that month, the 29th Canadian Motor Torpedo Boat Flotilla moved from Ramsgate to Portsmouth. That relocation, too, turned out to be difficult. When the flotilla navigated its way past the gate vessel toward the harbour, Lt. Law began searching for his docking area, HMS *Vernon*, and could barely draw near it because "craft buzzed around it thick as flies in a jam pot." In fact, when he did find space and moored the MTB flotilla, Law had to walk over hundreds of craft to get to a shore phone to check in with "Aunty," the Confidential Books officer.

"For God's sake!" she shouted into the phone at Law. "Get them over here and into the vault! The ones you have are wrong and have been recalled."

Back at MTB *459*, Jack Foote and some of the crew extricated the bags from the officers' washroom, loaded them onto a launch, and quickly delivered them to the CB office, which, like the boat heads, was stacked to the ceiling with bags of secret documents. As Law described it, the office was in utter confusion with ships' officers returning old CBs and picking up new ones. And in the midst of it all was Aunty on a telephone.

"My dear, I think I'm going crazy!" she exclaimed. "I've had hundreds of ships return their CBs. What a day!"

Such was the difference a day made in the run-up to launching Operation Neptune on June 6.

5:35 p.m. June 5, 1944—The Solent, England

The Canadians, in particular, grew anxious with every moment of delay. The ghosts of Dieppe haunted them. Postponement heightened the possibility that the best-kept secret might not stay that way. The return and exchange of Confidential Books and maps invited leaks of the plan. The so-far-successful deflection of German attention from the Allies' true intentions might be undone. Preservation of the vital psychological weapon missing at Dieppe—the element of surprise—was threatened with every additional hour that the assault forces had to stand down.

Still, the invasion planners looked to another legacy of Dieppe to ensure success this time. To reverse the tactical failure of the earlier raid, the Chief of Staff to the Supreme Allied Commander (COSSAC), Lieutenant-General Frederick Morgan was directed in the summer of 1943, among other things, to plan "a full-scale assault against the Continent in 1944." By February 1944, the COSSAC plan emerged as the "Initial Joint Plan." This introduced a combined authority of naval forces, commanded by Admiral Sir Bertram Ramsay; army forces, under Field-Marshal Sir Bernard Law Montgomery; and air forces, led by Air Chief Marshal Sir Trafford Leigh-Mallory. In other words, under the Supreme Commander, Gen. Dwight D. Eisenhower, all three expeditionary forces would work in tandem, in close communication and co-operation, from the earliest planning of the invasion to its ultimate implementation.

The prototype was already in existence, a permanent force devoted to amphibious operations born during Operation Jubilee at Dieppe, and that organization became known as Force J. Thus, Operation Neptune on D-Day would direct the principally Canadian attack of Force J, including the 3rd Canadian Infantry Division, on the stretch of Normandy beach now code-named Juno.* Similarly, the combined British task force, known as Force S, would direct its assault, by the 3rd British

---

* One amusing story about the coding origins for the Normandy landing sites suggests that SHAEF contemplated naming the British and Canadian beaches after fish; that is, Gold Beach as in goldfish, Sword Beach as in swordfish, and Jelly as in jellyfish. A Canadian, the story continues, informed the British that jelly had a much different and less attractive connotation in North America. Consequently they chose Juno instead.

Infantry Division, at the beach code-named Sword. At the same time, Force G, a combined British task force with the 50th British Infantry Division, would assault the beach code-named Gold. The British and Canadian groups comprised the Eastern Task Force. Meanwhile, in the Western Task Force, Force O with the U.S. 1st Infantry Division would attack Omaha Beach, and Force U with the U.S. 4th Infantry Division would come ashore at Utah Beach.

Early on Monday morning, June 5, 7,016 Allied vessels—110 of them Canadian—lay at anchor, as Winston Churchill put it, "like a vulture poised in the sky over the thoughts of the most sanguine." The order to go finally arrived just after 4:15 a.m. Somewhere between the Allied naval force moored on the south coast of Britain and its objective on the Normandy coast, *Kriegsmarine*, the German navy, still had 230 surface ships in active service, as Allied intelligence knew. The German seaborne force comprised about 16 destroyers, 50 E-boats (*Schnellbootes*), 60 R-boats (*Raumbootes*), as many as 130 U-boats and assorted armed trawlers, minesweepers, and other smaller support craft. Equally dangerous and nearly invisible, a belt of German water mines roughly ten miles wide lay directly in the path of the invasion ships. These explosives were mines moored by long wires and weighted to the bottom of the Channel.

It was up to the 31st Canadian (Minesweeper) Flotilla to clear the way through one of ten approach channels to the Normandy beaches.

HMCS *Fort William* set sail for a second time late in the afternoon of June 5. As it moved through Piccadilly Circus, the flotilla began to spread out into formation for sweeping its allotted section of water—approach channel number three—roughly 1,200 yards in breadth. Each sweeper plied the channel 800 yards astern and 200 yards to port of the ship ahead. At seven o'clock that evening, the 31st Flotilla entered the mine belt.

"First we'd swing the [torpedo-shaped Oropesa] float [tethered to the stern of the sweeper] with underwater fins out several hundred yards from the ship," Leading Stoker Mecoy explained. "A sweep wire dragging under the surface of the water was razor sharp and it would saw through the cables anchoring the mines. And the mines would come up to the surface. . . . Normally, once we had done the sweep, we'd come back to blow the mines up with fire from the Oerlikon [guns] or we'd put enough holes in them that they'd sink. But not on D-Day . . ."

The planners had decided that detonating the mines that day would draw too much attention to the sweeping activity. So orders stated that the crews were to allow all mines that floated to the surface to drift out of the approach channels, with the help of the strong Channel current, unless the Germans became aware of the sweepers' presence. To ensure the safe passage of the thousands of assault ships through the lanes a few hours later, British trawlers followed the sweepers and dropped lighted Dan buoys at half-mile intervals to mark the borders of each channel.

The entire operation depended upon absolute precision. Correct navigation through every mile of each channel put tremendous pressure on the sweeper crews. Also, the Dan buoys had to go overboard at the correct moment, each with two 175-pound weights tethered to about 600 feet of wire. The entire operation went on in complete darkness and across an easterly moving tide that inconveniently reversed itself at ten o'clock that night, right in the middle of the procedure. In addition, Neptune orders prescribed that the sweep was to continue without deviation no matter what opposition confronted the sweepers, even German warships or U-boats. There was no room for error; by the time the sweepers and the Dan-layers had completed their fifth mile, the first invasion landing craft would be entering the channels they had created.

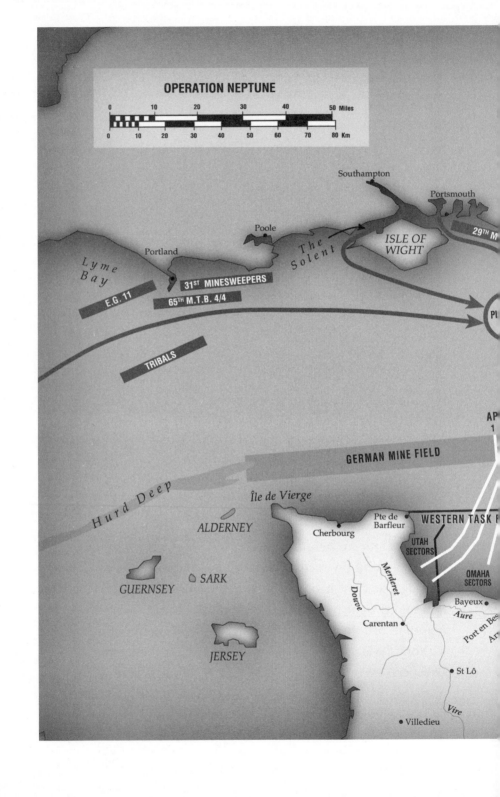

OPERATION NEPTUNE

0 10 20 30 40 50 Miles
0 10 20 30 40 50 60 70 80 Km

Southampton

Portsmouth

29TH M

Poole

Portland

ISLE OF WIGHT

*L y m e
B a y*

*The
Solent*

E.G. 11

31ST MINESWEEPERS

65TH M.T.B. 4/4

TRIBALS

Pl

AP
1

GERMAN MINE FIELD

Hurd Deep

Île de Vierge

ALDERNEY

Cherbourg

Pte de
Barfleur

WESTERN TASK F

GUERNSEY

SARK

UTAH
SECTORS

OMAHA
SECTORS

Merderet

Douve

Bayeux

Aure

Port en Bes

Ar

JERSEY

Carentan

St Lô

Vire

Villedieu

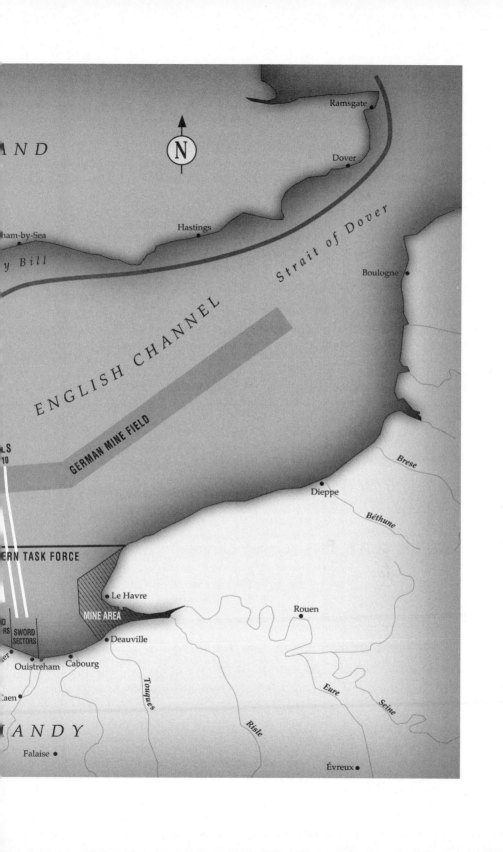

Fort William and the rest of the 31st Flotilla completed their southward sweep of approach-channel number three just after ten o'clock. They methodically swept another eighteen miles toward the beaches, and just past midnight they began clearing an area where the transports and warships coming through their channel would assemble for bombardment of the coast and debarkation of troops. The weary crews swept even closer to the shore, finishing at 3 a.m. just as the full moon poked through the clouds and, for several minutes, advertised the entire flotilla's presence a mere one and one-half miles offshore. The same operation was conducted in ten separate approach channels by ten different sweeper flotillas off the Normandy beaches. By 5 a.m. the work of the sweeping-and-Dan-laying tandems was finally done, and all ships in those vanguard flotillas were returning to their anchorage stations. Despite the dire predictions of two-thirds losses, not one sweeper had been lost.

"When I came off my watch, we were anchored," Mecoy said. "I came on deck to see what was going on and all I could see were all these ships going the opposite way we were facing. Of course, they were on their way in."

5 a.m. June 6, 1944—English Channel

In fact, the ships of the 31st Flotilla were not the first Allied naval vessels to ply the waters off the German-occupied beaches of Normandy that morning.

The Canadian minesweepers and the British Dan-layers that had just cleared a swath of safe water across the English Channel owed some of their accurate navigation through the mine belt to two midget submarines, which had been lying quietly on the sea floor just offshore for three nights and two days. Code-named Gambit, the operation had despatched the mini-subs, called X-Craft, to act as lightships and guide the first landing craft and/or their escorts in toward their appointed beaches. The American naval command feared the Germans might spot the mini-subs and arouse suspicion, and so rejected their use at Utah and Omaha beaches. British and Canadian naval commanders calculated that weather conditions and smoke from shelling might obscure the shoreline and decided in favour of them.

Each X-Craft carried no armament, only its diesel engines, navigational equipment, and a radio beacon, which was a flashing light at the end of an eighteen-foot telescopic mast. There was virtually no room inside the sub for its crew of five. The men shared two bunks, situated on top of the batteries, and at best enjoyed five feet of headroom when at their control positions. The limited amount of oxygen smelled of diesel fuel and left the sub's occupants dizzy and claustrophobic. The only way a crewman could find relief was to enter a watertight compartment atop the sub, shut the door behind him, and open the hatch above his head. If the compartment flooded, the water had to be pumped out before the next man used it.

Crossing the Channel in the dark, Lt. George Honour and his Royal Navy crew aboard X-23 had reached shallow water less than a mile off the British and Canadian landing sectors by 4 a.m., Sunday, June 4. At eight o'clock they had moved to periscope depth to verify their position, careful not to break the surface because, as Honour noted, they would have been spotted.

"Through the periscope looking to shore," Honour said, "we saw there were lorry-loads of Germans coming on to a certain bit of the beach, probably cleared of mines, so they could have their Sunday afternoon swim. They unloaded and played on the beach and some were swimming in the water. And as we watched, we thought 'Little do they know what's coming.'"

The mini-sub crewmen had dealt with a setback of their own when later that night they received the radio signal informing them that D-Day was postponed for at least one more day. It meant another twenty hours of imprisonment in the sub, hiding on the bottom of the Channel, saying little, moving even less, and worrying whether they could retreat to England before their oxygen failed. Several times during the day they had heard the sound of propellers in the vicinity and they had waited until the last possible moment to surface for air. Honour and each of the crew had taken his turn in the hatch during the night. Finally the mini-sub received the welcome signal that the invasion was actually under way.

Just before 5 a.m. on June 6, *X-23* surfaced, initiated its radio beacon, raised the mast, and flashed its light north toward the oncoming armada. What the crew witnessed then was ample reward for their sixty-four hours of stuffy submersion off the Normandy coast.

"As dawn broke on the 6th," Honour said, "looking seaward, there was just a solid line of ships, starting with the small landing craft, destroyers, cruisers, battleships, and all types of craft as far as the eye could see. They were steadily coming towards us. And although we knew they were on our side, it was a very frightening sight. One can only imagine in the observation posts all along the coast the Germans seeing this. They must have been very surprised and I should think very frightened."

11 p.m. June 5, 1944—English Channel

Nine war correspondents also crossed the Channel with the Canadians in Force J on the eve of D-Day.

William Stewart and Ross Munro would report home to the Canadian Press news agency. Ralph Allen of the *Globe and Mail* had been chosen by lot to represent a consortium of Canadian daily newspapers. Charles Lynch would report for the Reuters news agency. Joseph Willicombe would feed material to the

International News Service, and Ronald Clark to the British United Press. Lionel Shapiro represented the North American Newspaper Alliance. Finally, CBC Radio would broadcast reports from its English and French correspondents, Matthew Halton and Marcel Ouimet, respectively. Ouimet and Allen spent the night of June 5/6 aboard a Royal Navy frigate. At about the same hour that troops who were aboard the landing craft plying south across the Channel were first allowed to see the maps complete with place names, the correspondents were examining them too.

Marcel Ouimet was a French CBC Radio reporter who had described the progress of the Canadian troops as they invaded Sicily in 1943. Then, he had travelled close to the front as they fought the bloody Italian campaign to Ortona. Back in London with Matthew Halton, he had paced around the CBC Overseas Unit office waiting for word of the invasion of France. Among his first broadcasts back to Canada on June 6 was his account of the eve of D-Day aboard a British frigate in the Channel:

"The wardroom is being used as a headquarters for one of the Canadian formations. [Ralph Allen] and I listened to the Major give us the details of the great operation of the day ahead. The map is in front of us on a table covered with a navy-blue cloth . . . [the map] is similar to the one the officers have been studying for several weeks, but the difference is that it doesn't have fictitious names. We have known for two days where the landing will happen; the only thing left was to give us the plan of the attack. Within an hour, we know the big picture."

Mindful that Canadians at home would want very specific news of each regiment involved in the landing, Ouimet carefully matched the regiments with their beach objectives. In the first wave, he said, the Queen's Own Rifles of Canada and Régiment de la Chaudière were to take Bernières-sur-Mer, while to the west, at Courseulles-sur-Mer and Graye-sur-Mer, the Royal Winnipeg Rifles, the 1st Battalion of the Canadian Scottish, and the Regina Rifles would take the lead. To the east, the North Shore (New Brunswick) Regiment would land at St-Aubin-sur-Mer. Then, in the second wave would be the North Nova Scotia Highlanders, the Highland Light Infantry of Canada, the Cameron Highlanders of Ottawa, and the Stormont, Dundas and Glengarry Highlanders. He itemized the armoured support, the 1st Hussars, the Fort Garry Horse, and the Sherbrooke Fusiliers as well as the artillery of the 12th, 13th, and 14th Field Regiments.

It was 11 p.m. as Ouimet and Allen queried the major for specifics.

"What are the German defences like?" Ouimet asked.

"There are casemates, pillboxes, concrete bunkers, and underground fortifications that even the heaviest anti-tank shells cannot pierce," the officer said. "Bombers have been attacking them for six weeks and some of them are neutralized. But there are still some that we'll have to take by force. . . ."

"What about mines?"

"There are some. But not as many as we had thought. We know the beaches because we even had some of our soldiers strolling on these beaches a few days ago without being discovered. The attack will take place in full daylight. . . . Ultimately, for this operation, it will take 100,000 sailors to get 130,000 soldiers ashore. . . ."

At roughly the same hour, Ouimet's CBC colleague, Matthew Halton, pored over the maps aboard another Force J assault ship on its way to Juno Beach. Halton had covered the war almost from its beginning. First, as European correspondent for the *Toronto Daily Star*, he had reported on the rise of Nazism, covered the Battle of Britain and the Blitz in London, and then spent nearly two years with the British Eighth Army in North Africa, before becoming the CBC's senior war correspondent in 1943. He reported on the Allied landing in Sicily and the jump into Italy. Halton was now covering his third Allied amphibious landing.

"In the lounge of our ship," Halton recalled in one of his D-Day reports, "we played bridge or gathered 'round the piano and sang. We were going where our fathers and brothers had gone twenty-five years before. And we sang the same songs they sang . . . one more than others—'There's a Long, Long Trail a-Winding.' And I began to wonder if it wasn't a dream . . . playing bridge and singing as we approached the beaches of Hitler's Europe."

The officers aboard his headquarters ship notified the war correspondent that the assault on the beaches would begin at the first light of dawn. Halton referred to it as "the start of the mighty enterprise." The assault troops would go ashore on a rising tide so that the surf would carry the landing craft over underwater obstacles, or "hedgehogs." These were four-foot-high tripods of steel or wood anchored to the beach, each implanted with a mine or shell designed to explode on contact. D-Day planners also hoped enough of the hedgehogs might be exposed to enable marine engineers to clear some of the mines before most of the landing craft hit the beaches.

"It was absolutely astonishing to stand on deck in the early morning before H-Hour, the moment when the battle was to start," Halton's report continued. "It was bewildering. There was this enormous armada anchoring right off the coast of France in broad daylight and nothing was happening. Not a thing. Not a gun. Not a bomb. It was fantastic. . . . We stared at the villages and the tall church spires of Normandy and there was not a sound. . . ."

This same morning, Peter Stursberg, Halton's CBC colleague in Italy, finished filing one of the biggest stories of the war. Just hours earlier, the American troops had reached the outskirts of Rome. The CBC audio feeds back to Canada about the imminent victory contained a live broadcast by Pope Pius XII. Yet both the broadcast and the liberation of Rome were about to take a back seat to events unfolding before the eyes of correspondent Halton at Juno Beach.

6:50 a.m. June 6, 1944—off Juno Beach

At dawn, the bulk of the navy assault force had emerged from the approach lanes and lay at anchor or was patrolling off the Normandy beaches. There were warships, troop carriers, head-quarter ships, assault landing craft, tank landing craft, and assorted other vessels. Rough water off the coast delayed the launch of landing craft momentarily. Now the heavily armed battleships, cruisers, destroyers, and corvettes of Britain, the United States, Canada, Australia, France, Norway, Greece, Poland, and the Netherlands were lined up along nearly sixty miles of coastline, ready to engage the enemy.

Forty-five minutes remained before H-Hour, 7:35 a.m., the appointed time for the actual landing to begin.

Eleven Fleet-class destroyers were now homing in on the coastal targets of the Juno Beach sector, among them two Royal Canadian Navy destroyers, HMCS *Algonquin* and HMCS *Sioux*. Each carried four single 4.7-inch guns as its main arma-ment, along with eight torpedo tubes, twin 40-mm Bofors guns, and several batteries of 20-mm Oerlikon guns. Among *Sioux*'s targets were the large seaside buildings sheltering 75-mm German guns east of St-Aubin-sur-Mer; *Algonquin*'s first target was a 75-mm gun battery immediately west of the village. As the early-morning cloud and fog were lifting, some of the dust and smoke left over from the overnight air-force bombings obscured some of the target area. Those conditions prompted the ship's war diarist to note: "God damn air force is messing up our target again."

Lieutenant Commander Desmond Piers was skipper aboard the *Algonquin*. He and his crew had filled the days and hours leading up to the "open fire" order with the intense study of maps and charts, preparing to escort the headquarters ship HMS *Hilary* through the approach channel, and ensuring that two members of the press corps on board were well informed of the operation's progress. One of the highlights of the day for the seasoned captain in the run-up to D-Day, however, was his crew's gathering around the ship's torpedo tubes for a pep talk.

"I could sense the high morale of the men," Piers recorded in his diary. "Confidence beamed from their smiling faces. Their good humour could not be subdued by the serious possibilities I presented to them, such as being mined, dive-bombed [or] shelled. I felt more like Bob Hope at a Navy concert without a script."

The Channel crossing presented none of those anticipated threats. *Algonquin* safely escorted the Force J command ship, HMS *Hilary*, to its vantage point off Juno Beach. But even for an experienced naval captain, the calm in the anchorage area was eerie and unsettling. While Operation Neptune so far had gone off without a hitch, Piers "began to wonder if we were in for a nasty surprise in the form of some new German secret weapon." Nevertheless, Piers and his officers focused their attention on the final stage of their invasion preparations, "softening up" German defences along the Atlantic Wall.

Precisely at the appointed time on June 6, *Algonquin* opened up on its targets. Piers said his gunners quickly silenced the 75-mm gun west of St. Aubin and then they surveyed the beach for other possible hiding places for snipers and machine-gun nests. When his chief engineer came up from the engine room, the captain picked out a target in his honour and the crew proceeded to dismantle it with gunfire. No doubt the air force bombers, which arrived shortly thereafter for another run at the enemy, could also complain about navy gunners obscuring their targets with smoke and dust.

As the bombardment began, two long low vessels emerged from approach channels six and seven. The two troopships, *Prince David* and *Prince Henry*, had operated in Canadian waters before the war under the flag of the Canadian National Steamships line. They were converted to armed merchant cruisers when the war began in 1939 and then to troop carriers, Landing Ships Infantry (LSIs), for Operation Neptune. During the night of June 5/6 each had led more than twenty merchant vessels down the mine-swept lanes to Juno Beach. For this mission, they had been officially camouflage-painted. Like many of the RCN and Canadian merchant ships, their crews had added their own unofficial markings as well; both *Henry* and *David* now proudly displayed a green maple leaf on each side of a funnel.

Few aboard *Prince David* were prouder of those Canadian insignia than Able Seaman John Henry Gorsline.

"I respected the Royal Navy ensign [flag]," he said, "but passing through the Panama Canal [en route to England], the Americans kept saying, 'Pip, pip, old chap.' They assumed we were British. But we were Canadians . . . and that maple leaf was very important to me."

Gorsline had been raised within sight of the shipbuilding yards of Collingwood, Ontario, and passed his senior matriculation there. In 1942 he found work as a pipefitter's assistant at the yards. During the war, the small Lake Huron town was alive with the construction of corvettes for the Canadian Navy, and Gorsline spent that summer at a furnace bending the steel beams for the framework of those corvettes. That autumn, he took a job as a chemical analyst at the Aluminum Canada plant in Toronto, later deciding to follow his older brother, Allan

Gorsline, into the navy. When he finished his training at Halifax in 1943, John Gorsline asked for a posting and was eventually sent to Esquimalt, B.C., as a radar operator aboard the newly refitted merchant cruiser HMCS *Prince David*.

He felt very patriotic during the workups for the invasion as well. In addition to putting ashore a group of Royal Marine engineers on D-Day, *Prince David* was also transporting several companies of Le Régiment de la Chaudière to the Normandy beaches. And since another of Gorsline's jobs aboard ship was helping to run the canteen, he used his high-school French when serving the young French-Canadians.

"They had a real commando look about them," Gorsline recalled. "They were very intense-looking guys. We kind of joked among ourselves when things were delayed twenty-four hours. We said, 'Hope to hell we get rid of them soon, because if we don't they're liable to turn on us.' They couldn't get off the ship fast enough! On the other hand, there's no way I would want to be crowded into one of those landing craft."

All the crewmen aboard *Prince David* had seen pictures of Stuka dive-bombers and of the massive guns the Germans had lined up along Hitler's Atlantic Wall. Gorsline remembered his skipper, Cdr. Thomas Kelly, sharing the same predictions that other commanders did, of 60 percent losses among the ship's 350-man crew; at the same time he expressed his utmost confidence and pride in "the boys of P.D." *Prince David*'s passage through the approach channel from England to France took eight long hours, most of which Gorsline spent at his action station, sharing duty with AB Al Francis in the radar cabin.

"We were radar operators on a [Type] 285 gunnery set," Gorsline said. "Our job was to line up any radar specks on the screen. These [data] would be sent to the gunners at our four-inch, high-angle guns. The screen duplicated the points for the gunners. Then they could line up with my fixing. A green light would come on, the guns would be loaded, fuses set, and I could then pull the trigger. . . . But we never had to fire the guns that night."

During the night, the ship's crew worked on two watches instead of three, four hours on and four hours off. Nobody slept through that night. By the time *Prince David* reached its assigned anchorage about six miles offshore, Gorsline said he had smoked his way through an entire pack of Players cigarettes. When he finished his watch in the radar cabin the following morning, he came up on deck to watch and listen to what was going on ashore.

"All during the night there was a constant roar from hundreds of bombers passing overhead," he said. "Then as we neared the coast and reached our anchorage, the heavy naval bombardment of the coastal defences began. You could hear the shells from the [British battleships'] fifteen-inch guns coming from behind us and going over, a 'whoomf' sound every few seconds."

Gorsline and the crew of *Prince David* had practised the run-up to the beach in numerous training exercises. The Marines would neutralize the mines on the beach and the Canadians would follow through with the running assault past them and up the beaches. To ferry these troops ashore, *Prince David* carried the six assault craft of the 529th Canadian Flotilla. Gorsline watched as the soldiers were loaded aboard the landing craft and then lowered away from his vessel into the water.

"Heavy seas, beach obstacles, and mines destroyed all of our landing craft except one," Gorsline said.

Prince David's assault landing craft (LCAs) were forty-one-foot wooden vessels designed to carry thirty to forty men ashore. Each craft was flat-bottomed and lightly armoured. The conditions in front of Bernières-sur-Mer complicated the efforts of the LCA crews to navigate their way ashore. They faced a quartering sea, winds blowing at a forty-five-degree angle to the beach. The mined hedgehogs embedded in the sand were just visible above the rising tide. If the Royal Marines were successful in clearing the water of those obstacles, the LCA crews figured they could manoeuvre their craft, unmolested, right up onto the shore.

Able Seaman Fred Turnbull was a crewman aboard LCA No. 1151: "We had been told of the minefields guarding the beaches, so we moved in at half speed ahead. As I looked over the bow and saw the dead bodies of the Marine commandos floating in the water, I realized what we were facing."

Turnbull's LCA, which the troops had nicknamed "Daisy Mae," soon faced a beach littered with mined hedgehogs and a strong and rising tide pushing the craft headlong into the minefield. As the crew struggled to pilot Daisy Mae into shore, the German mortar-bomb crews and snipers found the landing craft within their range. The LCA seemed to drift within inches of the hedgehog mines. Minutes later, most of the flotilla's LCAs had miraculously managed to get through three rows of hedgehogs; but the fourth proved to be deadly. Turnbull turned to see the LCA to his right blown in two. Others took hits through their hulls and began sinking rapidly.

"I couldn't believe we were still afloat," he said. "Our craft kept going, and when we could get no further our ramp went down and our troops rushed ashore. We had come safely through the minefield, the only one in our section."

Despite the destruction all around them, most of the crewmen with the 529th Flotilla had made it ashore alive. Most of the flotilla's 400 troops had also landed safely. Yet the travails of the Daisy Mae were not over. The single surviving LCA crew decided to try a return trip to *Prince David*. They might have reached the vessel, had the next wave of oncoming infantry landing craft (LCIs) not forced them out of the cleared waterway.

Daisy Mae ran over a steel-spike obstacle in the water and the crewmen again had to abandon ship. They jumped onto a passing tank landing craft (LCT), and it too struck an obstacle and began to sink. Yet another LCT managed to pick them up.

Turnbull turned to look back at what was left of his flotilla landing craft, "holes blown through their sides, sunk to the gunwale, but maple leafs still above the waterline."

7:35 a.m. June 6, 1944—English Channel

If Lt. George Honour, peering through his miniature submarine periscope, enjoyed a front-row seat for the invasion, Allied aircrew returning from overnight bombing, strafing, and spoofing missions delighted in a balcony view.

Between mid-May and the first week of June, bombers of No. 433 (Porcupine) Squadron with No. 6 (RCAF) Group flew hundreds of "softening up" sorties against targets in France. Recently promoted Flying Officer Phil Marchildon knew the invasion was coming. He had a good reason to want to see the war over and done with. In 1941, the Philadelphia Athletics had signed him to pitch professionally in the American Baseball League; he had won ten games in his rookie year and seventeen in 1942, before returning to Canada to join the air force. Overnight on June 5/6, 1944, he and his Halifax bomber crew had hit a railway marshalling yard. Coming home, seated in his tail-gunner's position in the rear turret, Marchildon looked down through the broken cloud.

"There were so many . . . ships that you almost couldn't see the water between them," Marchildon later wrote. "I called out through my head-set for the other guys to take a look at history in the making."

Marchildon would have to wait until 1946 to make his historic comeback in the major leagues; on his twenty-sixth bombing mission, later in the summer, his Halifax was shot down over Denmark and he spent the rest of the war as a prisoner of war at Stalag Luft III in Germany.

Another Canadian who had entertained audiences before the war had a bird's-eye view of D-Day proceedings as well. Like all the Allied troops in the south of England around the end of May, peacetime musician Sam Levine found himself cordoned off from the rest of the world. Formerly a bass player with such Toronto-based band leaders as Jimmy "Trump" Davidson and Cliff McKay, Levine had joined the air force as a radar mechanic; in 1943 he had been reclassified as an "Entertainer B" and recruited by the RCAF troupe known as The Blackouts. They performed for servicemen and -women in Nissen huts and under canvas all over Britain rather than in the West End theatres or the Piccadilly pubs.

"We wound up in a barracks on the south coast of England," Levine said. "Every night we would go to different [bases] and play for these guys getting ready for the invasion. . . . On June 6, we stood on the cliffs of Dover and watched the armadas going out and the planes flying above us. . . ."

Overcome by the magnitude of what they were witnessing, Levine and Murray Lauder, another bass player stuck within the restricted zone, paid the outbound troops the highest compliment they could think of. The two musicians pulled out a book of standard string exercises, set up their bass viols facing the Channel, and began playing duets to serenade the outbound invasion troops.

"That's the way we did our bit for democracy," Levine said.

On that first day of the Normandy invasion, the ships of the largest fleet ever assembled managed to put ashore the largest payload in military history: 9,989 vehicles, including 900 tanks and 600 guns, and 6,070 tons of food and ammunition. In all,

110 Royal Canadian Navy ships and 10,000 Canadian sailors had helped launch the Second Front against Germany. On D-Day the Americans had landed about 57,500 troops from the sea, and British Commonwealth forces had set ashore more than 75,000 in their landing craft. Of those, nearly 15,000 were Canadians. Of those 15,000, 47 were captured, 574 were wounded, and 340 did not live to see the end of D-Day.

"NOBODY'S COMING HOME"

7:49 a.m. June 6, 1944—Mike Red Beach, France

A WEEK BEFORE the ramp on his landing craft dropped open in front of Courseulles-sur-Mer on D-Day, Cpl. George Meakin had written a letter to his mother and sister from behind barbed wire at a security-transit camp in southern England. He was daydreaming about being back home in Birnie, Manitoba, where the summer heat would have enticed most kids in town to jump into the nearest pond.

"If there was only some way for us to get to a big swimming hole," Meakin wrote, "but no such luck."

On D-Day morning most of his regiment, the Royal Winnipeg Rifles, had more than enough water around them as they stormed ashore just west of where the River Seulles emptied into the English Channel. Many of the first to leave the landing craft leaped into rising tidewater up to their waists or higher.

"All of us are scared. It would only be lying to say we aren't," Meakin admitted in his May 24 letter home. His was a close-knit prairie family. Several years before, when George had finished his embarkation leave at home in Birnie, his mother,

Jennie, and his sister, Ellen, walked him to the highway to meet the bus. Then, within two years, George's younger brother Frank had enlisted and also joined the Winnipeg Rifles overseas training for the invasion.

To add to the Rifles' rude awakening at Normandy on the morning of June 6, the tank and advance assault vehicles that divisional planners anticipated would precede the assault troops just before 8 a.m. had not yet arrived on Juno Beach. Worse still, the men faced intense machine-gun fire, mortar bombs, and artillery shelling because, according to the battalion diary, "the [Allied naval and aerial] bombardment . . . failed to kill a single German or silence one weapon." The regiment, known as the Little Black Devils since 1885, had to storm an entrenched enemy cold.

For the Meakin brothers and their platoon mates in A and B companies, as many as 700 yards of water-covered or open beach lay between the lowered ramps of their landing craft infantry (LCI) and any sort of protection. Running seemed impossible. Twenty-four hours of seasickness during the Channel crossing had weakened many of them. Others were weighed down with extra weapons, communication gear, or ammunition bandoliers, and sank like stones in the rough water, never to resurface. Several men carrying grenades, Bren gun magazines, and Bangalore torpedoes full of explosives died when German gunfire hit their packs and ignited them.

Frank Godon, an anti-tank gunner, came ashore in B Company with the Winnipegs. He jumped from his LCI into water up to his neck and waded as fast as his arms and legs could propel him forward. Maybe it was his youth—he was seventeen and underage in the military—or his long hours of farm labour as a teenager in southwestern Manitoba, or possibly the times he had had to defend himself with his fists from taunts about his Métis background that helped him survive those first steps onto the French shore. He had been told not to expect much.

"None of you guys are coming home," an officer had announced to Godon's platoon during training in England.

Given his first few minutes ashore, Godon began to believe it. Members of his company, men he had trained with for two years or more, crumpled all around him. Orders were to keep going, not to stop. When he managed to slog out of the water, he dashed across the beach, zigzagging with every step.

"The Germans had been waiting for us for years," he said.

Godon was right. If fatigue or misfortune didn't cut into the ranks of the assaulting Winnipeg Rifles that morning, the maze of lethal obstacles the Germans had laid in their path surely did. The first barrier was rows of wooden or concrete stakes, about six feet high and pointing seaward. Next were rows of pyramid-shaped obstacles made of three wooden, steel, or concrete bars bolted together, or hedgehogs shaped like tripods, all armed with anti-tank mines or artillery shells with pressure igniters set to explode on contact. In some areas, particularly in front of Bernières and Courseulles, the Germans had added steel anti-tank obstacles, which Allied Intelligence dubbed Element C. They were also known as "Belgian Gates," since they resembled the obstacles the Belgians had erected on their border with Germany before the war.

When those who survived the dash through the obstacles reached the limited cover of the few sand dunes along the shoreline, they faced nearly impregnable *Widerstandsnester*, or resistance nests, overlooking and commanding the beaches. The Germans had placed these defensive fortifications about 2,000 yards apart so that no enemy landing anywhere on the beach could do so without coming under some kind of fire. Each nest had as its focal point a massive concrete pillbox or casemate, some camouflaged to look like innocuous cottages or seaside patisseries, constructed of as much as seven feet of reinforced concrete on its roof and its seaward side. Each nest protected a 50-, 75-, or 88-mm gun that was nearly always installed to fire at the beach in enfilade from the side, and usually in one direction only. Positioned in at least six locations and further shielded by concrete, 50-mm anti-tank guns could fire down and along the beaches in both directions. Then, surrounding these concrete casemates, a virtual warren of trenches ran to and from mortar-bomb and machine-gun positions, each lined with more concrete that was flush with the surface of the ground.

As a final deterrent to any invasion from the sea, the designers had protected each configuration of nests, gun positions, and trenches with a vast minefield and band after band of barbed wire. Between the villages of Courseulles and Bernières alone, the Germans had buried 14,000 mines. Such were the features of Hitler's Atlantic Wall that the Royal Winnipeg Rifles faced at both Mike Red and Mike Green sectors of Juno Beach tht morning.

The cost was heavy. Of 136 men in B Company of the Winnipegs, for example, fewer than thirty made their way safely off the beach.

The persistence and heroic actions of individual soldiers stand out in the survivors' memories. Among the indelible images recalled by the company's Sgt.-Maj. Charles Belton was that of one corporal named W. J. Klos. Nicknamed "Bull" because he was broad-shouldered and weighed well over 200 pounds, Corporal Klos had earned a reputation for using his fists to assist any RWR buddies in need. On D-Day Klos's landing had been a rough one. He had been shot in both the stomach and legs before he even left the landing craft. Despite severe bleeding and loss of his rifle, according to Belton, Klos pressed on to reach a resistance nest whose persistent gunfire had felled most of his platoon. When gunfire from the pillbox ceased and the next wave of Winnipegs entered the casemate, they found that the unarmed Klos had overpowered all three Germans inside by sheer brute physical force.

"I looked through one of the gun slits," Belton said, "and saw Corporal Klos dead, but with his hands still gripped around the throat of [the third] dead German, whom he had strangled."

9:30 a.m. June 6, 1944—Mike Red Beach, France

William Stewart found similar scenes when he came ashore a short time later in the Mike Red sector. The Canadian Press war correspondent had come through the approach channels aboard the British frigate HMS *Lawford* overnight. Like Marcel Ouimet and Matthew Halton of the CBC and Ralph Allen of the *Globe and Mail*, on the way over Stewart had received a full description of the intended targets and the assault plans from a brigade major in the ship's wardroom. He had then written his first D-Day story, packed the copy into a canvas bag marked with red stripes and stamped with the word "Press" to be returned to England on the first available ship, and slept just a few hours. By 6 a.m., June 6, he was up, had eaten breakfast, and was climbing aboard a landing craft with two British forward observation officers (FOOs). By nine-thirty Stewart had stepped from his LCI onto the Mike Red beachhead and toward a concrete pillbox seized ninety minutes earlier by the assault troops.

"Seven dead Canadian infantrymen were in a line in front of one of these strongpoints," he said. "One or two had been killed before they reached the barbed wire. One was caught in it. The others fell as they silenced the position. The last man sprawled almost at the top of the pillbox and his helmet had rolled a bit farther on."

After he had absorbed that scene, Stewart looked to the east toward the Mike Green and the mouth of the River Seulles, where he saw more Canadian troops lying dead in the sand as well as other "wounded men shaking from the effects of shock." He watched a while longer as more wounded Canadians made their way slowly back down the sand dunes to the beach. Close to the mouth of the river he spotted a group of disarmed German soldiers; they were unguarded and apparently needed no surveillance. By this time, the Royal Winnipeg Rifles and 1st Battalion troops of the Canadian Scottish Regiment were fighting their way through the village above the beach. Stewart now needed to find a place to write his second D-Day story.

Even though the beachhead around him seemed secure, Stewart had learned to be cautious while covering the 1st Canadian Infantry Division in Sicily and Italy in 1943. During that campaign he had frequently dug a makeshift bunker in case mortar or sniper fire came his way. On Juno Beach the dunes were eight feet high, so, with a trenching tool, he cut a slit trench into the seaside slope, preparing one shelf to sit on and another to serve as an impromptu desk. He had brought his typewriter wrapped in waterproof tape and a Mae West life preserver as well as a briefcase of paper, a twenty-four-hour ration pack, a bandage pack, and a second red-striped press bag. Stewart then sat down to write about the scenes on the beach, the defences the Canadians had overcome, and the courage of these citizen soldiers.

"Imagine. They are assault infantry, just young guys, all volunteers," he said. "They learn where they're going when they get out on the Channel. They're told they're going to attack the Germans' Atlantic Wall. They're twenty years old. They're put in landing craft and landed on the beach. . . .

"Ralph Allen wrote about the bearing of Canadian soldiers, from the way they marched, not rigid, but very military, heads upright, a reflection of pride. They had a job to do and they were going to do it as well as they could. . . . I have undying admiration for those Canadian soldiers."

7:05 a.m. June 6, 1944—aboard HMS Hilary

As hungry as the SHAEF commanders—General Dwight Eisenhower, Admiral Sir Bertram Ramsay, General Sir Bernard Law Montgomery, and Air Chief Marshal Sir Trafford Leigh-Mallory—were for progress reports on the amphibious run into the beaches this day, one Canadian officer had nearly paced through the deck of HMS *Hilary* with his concern and second-guessing. Brigadeer Stanley Todd, the Commander Royal Artillery (CRA) and officer in charge of the Fire Plan to support the landings, had spent perhaps the most anxious night of his life aboard the headquarters ship off Normandy.

"I wondered if I had done everything . . . if I had forgotten anything," Todd wrote years later. "I was alone on deck . . . and I had the living daylights scared out of me. . . . I would be personally responsible for those who were going to die in the next few hours. If we did not succeed in getting ashore or were unable to stay, like Dieppe, the war would be set back four or five years."

Raised in Ottawa, commissioned into the Royal Field Artillery in 1916, Todd had served in the 1st Field Brigade of the Canadian Artillery since 1921. As a militia officer in the 1930s, he had devoted himself to the science of artillery, studied gunnery, and experimented on a miniature artillery range.

He was posted overseas to the 5th Field Regiment during the war and dissected the strategy of artillery warfare in the aftermath of Dieppe. First, he knew the Allies had learned they could not attack a defended port such as Dieppe, nor could they succeed in any landing without synchronized artillery support. Second, since they could not now invade France at its closest

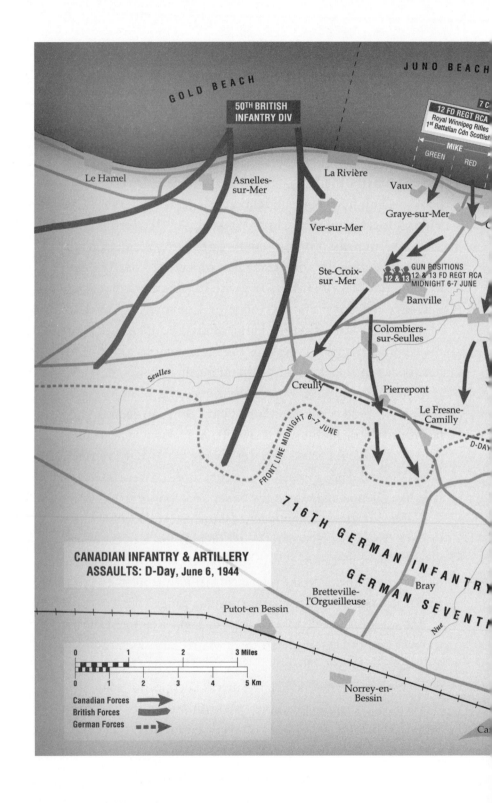

GOLD BEACH

JUNO BEACH

50TH BRITISH INFANTRY DIV

7 C

12 FD REGT RCA
Royal Winnipeg Rifles
1st Battalian Cdn Scottish

MIKE

GREEN · RED

Le Hamel

Asnelles-sur-Mer

La Rivière

Vaux

Ver-sur-Mer

Graye-sur-Mer

Ste-Croix-sur -Mer

12 & 13 GUN POSITIONS
12 & 13 FD REGT RCA
MIDNIGHT 6-7 JUNE

Banville

Colombiers-sur-Seulles

Seulles

Creully

Pierrepont

FRONT LINE MIDNIGHT 6-7 JUNE

Le Fresne-Camilly

D-DAY

716TH GERMAN INFANTRY

GERMAN SEVENT

CANADIAN INFANTRY & ARTILLERY ASSAULTS: D-Day, June 6, 1944

Bretteville-l'Orgueilleuse

Bray

Putot-en Bessin

Nue

| 0 | 1 | 2 | 3 Miles |

| 0 | 1 | 2 | 3 | 4 | 5 Km |

Canadian Forces ➡
British Forces ➡
German Forces ┅➡

Norrey-en-Bessin

Ca

N INFANTRY DIV
N INFANTRY BDE
-ght Infantry
-Glengarry Highlanders
-tia Highlanders

8 CDN INF BDE

14 FD REGT RCA
-égiment de la Chaudière
-Queen's Own Rifles

19A FD REGT RCA
North Shore
(New Brunswick)

NAN
WHITE
RED

N

S W O R D   B E A C H

3RD BRITISH
INFANTRY DIV

-nières-
-r-Mer

St-Aubin-
sur-Mer

Luc-sur-
Mer

Lion-sur-
Mer

Ouistreham

Tailleville

Douvres-la-
Délivrande

-asly

21st PANZER DIV

-by-
-aon

Anguerny

Anisy

-ons-les-
-ussons

Les
Buissons

Biéville

FRONT LINE

6TH AIRBORNE DIV

MIDNIGHT 6–7 JUNE

River Orne

Canal de Caen à la Mer

N AREA

-ron

Caen

point, the port of Calais, and had chosen instead the open beaches of Normandy, the operation would require a whole new set of gunnery guidelines. Deployment would have to be altered, as would the actual equipment and the training, not to mention the means of transporting the guns across ninety miles of Channel, not twenty.

What had been a private subject of interest for Brig. Stanley Todd became his life's focus in April 1943, when he joined Maj.-Gen. Rod Keller at the War Office in London. There Todd learned that the 3rd Canadian Infantry Division would join the assault on Normandy and that he would spearhead the preparations for artillery support. His job would be "to encounter and learn to overcome problems the ordinary soldier never thought about," such as loading equipment on and off landing craft, firing artillery while moving toward the beaches and ultimately adapting to artillery that was self-propelled rather than towed into battle.

Brigadeer Todd took his artillery troops to Scotland for training. The crews worked with six Landing Craft Tanks (LCTs), learning to load last-off vehicles first and first-off last, all of them facing the exit ramp at the front of the LCT. Each LCT would carry four six-man gun crews and their guns to the beach, with each crew trained to fire no fewer than 100 shells on the run-in to the landing. The gun crews aboard the LCT would therefore begin firing about 10,000 yards from shore. By continuous practice, at the end of the mobile-firing phase, crews were able to empty an entire LCT in one minute and forty-five seconds. The LCT crew would then practise the reverse, winching the craft off the beach and escaping out to sea.

On the surface, loading, shooting on the move, and then putting the guns ashore seemed straightforward. The entire process became much more complicated when each artillery piece changed from a truck pulling a 25-pounder gun to a 105-

mm gun mounted on a self-propelled tank-like vehicle, or SP. Suddenly, the gun-crew driver, who was used to towing the gun with a truck, had to become a tank driver who could handle a tracked vehicle using a system of brakes and no steering wheel. In addition, until that point Canadian artillery had calculated gun sightings by degrees and minutes; however, the SPs (also known as "Priests") that Canadian gunners would now use during the landing employed a metric system in millimetres. As well, the range-setters in the SP guns were in metres, not yards. That meant changing all the drill manuals, converting calculation tables for wind velocity and temperatures from standard Imperial measures to metric.

"It meant retraining nearly 3,000 artillerymen," Todd wrote in disbelief. "Good God, we'd had these men over in England for three years and we were pretty darned near as perfect as regular soldiers. Then everything we ever owned was taken away from us, our guns, our range tables and all our equipment. So we said, 'OK, boys, let's start all over again.'"

Redrafting the Fire Plan required eighteen hours per day, seven days a week of intensive work through the winter of 1943 and the spring of 1944. Even then, there would be last-minute changes. When General Montgomery returned from the Middle East to take charge of the infantry component of D-Day, he decided that the invasion would require three divisions, not two, and since there weren't enough landing craft to move three divisions, each existing division would have to give up one-third of its craft to make two-thirds of an additional division. Todd then grappled with the dilemma of finding places for one-third of his guns on only two-thirds the original number of landing craft. He decided to leave behind many of his support vehicles—with food, water and administrative supplies—to make room for the full complement of SPs. He also had to alter the loading tables to allow for the loss of one-third of his boats while adjusting the Fire Plan aboard each LCT, which now carried more SPs.

All this when there were just six weeks to D-Day.

All alterations were complete by April 23, 1944, when intelligence discovered that the architects of Field-Marshal Rommel's Atlantic Wall had expanded the beach defences along the French coast beyond the beaches and underwater just offshore. Allied planners accordingly decided to launch the invasion at low tide, to allow the engineers to remove many of the obstacles before any troops landed. That meant that Brigadeer Todd had to alter 100 pages of landing tables yet again. What had taken three months to adjust before April 23 would now have to be done in four weeks.

One other enemy action caused the Royal Canadian Artillery great frustration in the final days before the invasion. On May 29, a single German aircraft attacking from the sea scored a direct hit on one of the 13th Field Regiment's self-propelled guns. Since the SPs were parked so close together in preparation for loading aboard the landing craft, the resulting fire also engulfed four other SPs, two Sherman tanks, a jeep, and three motorcycles.

By June 4, the waiting game had begun, with ships and landing craft all berthed at the Southampton docks or at anchor in the Solent. With the actual launch of the armada delayed from June 4 to June 5, the invasion gun crews, like the rest of the troops, spent Sunday crowded into the harbours along the southern English coast and bobbing on the Channel waters like corks. Then, even with the break in the weather, the nighttime crossing added to the crews' discomfort. Men crowded into the holds were seasick and drenched by the salt spray thrown over the pitching bows of their landing craft. No wonder that Brigadeer Stanley Todd seemed at his wits' end, endlessly pacing the decks of HMS *Hilary* on the eve of D-Day.

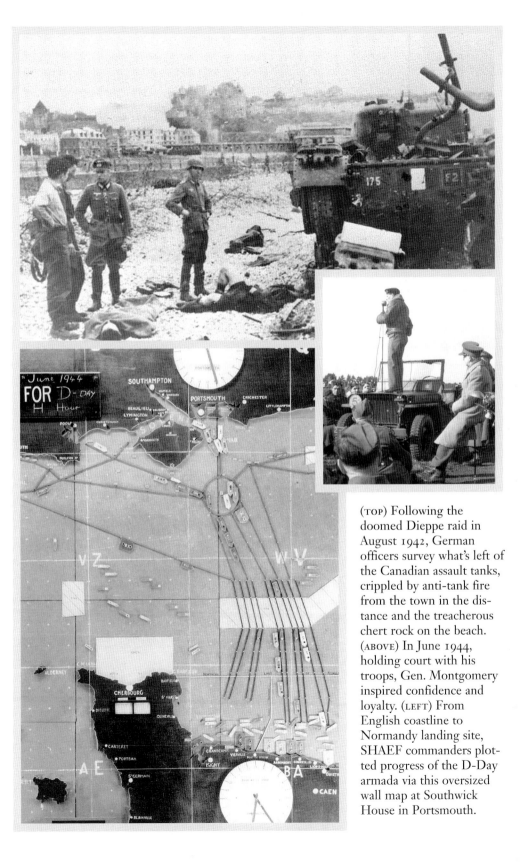

(TOP) Following the doomed Dieppe raid in August 1942, German officers survey what's left of the Canadian assault tanks, crippled by anti-tank fire from the town in the distance and the treacherous chert rock on the beach. (ABOVE) In June 1944, holding court with his troops, Gen. Montgomery inspired confidence and loyalty. (LEFT) From English coastline to Normandy landing site, SHAEF commanders plotted progress of the D-Day armada via this oversized wall map at Southwick House in Portsmouth.

(TOP RIGHT) Sir Arthur Coningham fought with the New Zealand infantry during the First World War, but on June 5, 1944, as an air marshal, he briefed Allied pilots at Tangmere on the invasion plan. (TOP LEFT) Among those he briefed was fighter pilot Charley Fox, shown here with his Spitfire fully armed to cover Canadian troops landing at Juno Beach. (RIGHT) Navigator Bob Dale's Mosquito battled time and the elements to help SHAEF decide the timing of D-Day. (BELOW) Overnight, ground and aircrew painted zebra stripes on wings and fuselages of every Allied aircraft, like this Spitfire. The hope: to prevent incidents of friendly fire.

(TOP) John C. Turnbull (middle) piloted this Halifax II bomber to targets at Houlgate, France, on the eve of D-Day with his regular crew: (l to r) wireless operator Ron Gillett, gunner Claude Hutt, navigator Earl Albert, bomb-aimer Harold McBain, and rear gunner Joe Malec (Don Board subs for regular engineer Frank Michael). (LEFT) F/L John C. Turnbull proudly wearing his wedgie cap in July 1944. (ABOVE) Nearly tripping on the red carpet caught by a gust of wind, Turnbull narrowly averted falling into the arms of King George VI when receiving his DFC, Aug. 11, 1944.

Richard Hilborn (upper right) has his gear checked; 1st Canadian Parachute Battalion troops preferred these British chutes partly because of their "hard slap, half turn" quick release. Paratrooper Jan de Vries (upper left) was hard pressed in 1944 to say if he was proudest of his new beret or wings crest. Mark Lockyer (lower left) at practice attention was proudest of his para jump boots.

Most Canadian paras jumped with a leg kit-bag strapped to the right leg, resting on top of the foot and nearly doubling pack weight to 175 pounds. Of 20 men in his stick of paratroopers, Ernie Jeans (above) was one of only two not to become D-Day casualties. Dan Hartigan (inset) said the paras succeeded that day because "we had airborne mystique on our side."

Had German aircraft penetrated the skies over Southampton, no camouflaging could have hidden all 7,016 Allied vessels preparing for the invasion. As an intelligence officer, Reg Weeks (bottom left) had to keep secret the true Normandy destination until his top secret maps were unwrapped and viewed by the troops (bottom right) as the armada set sail on June 6.

(LEFT) Leading Stoker Ray Mecoy (bottom left) smiled in this D-Day snap with his buddies (clockwise from top: Walter Borako, Ted Clarke, and Herb Crowe) aboard minesweeper HMCS *Fort William* (top), but also for the 1944 state-of-the-art life preserving gear they'd just been issued.

(RIGHT) Able Seaman John Gorsline and his ship HMCS *Prince David* (below) made it safely across the Channel and back in 24 hours; what stuck in his memory was the "noise" of D-Day.

(LEFT) Watching from the aft gun position aboard a motor torpedo boat, crewmen of the 29th Canadian MTB Flotilla marvel at the ships (with tethered anti-aircraft balloons) stretching from Britain to Normandy.

(RIGHT) Assault troops, such as these Royal Winnipeg Rifles, covered the final stretch of the Channel crossing in matchbox-like landing craft. The war diary of the Canadian Scottish (who landed with the Winnipegs) said the last seven miles to the beach seemed like seventy.

(LEFT) While assault troops had to brace themselves for the rough ride in, the unsung Royal Canadian Navy crews had to ensure the rendezvous was on target and on time.

June 3rd 44 Binie
Man
My Dearest George.
Hello Son and hows
well I supose you are

say chinis for now". I
always your most
dont Mr. George.

Like ships passing in the night.
Just a week before D-Day, brothers
George (left) and Frank Meakin
(with the Royal Winnipeg Rifles)
wrote their mother and sister from
southern England. They didn't
know the letters would be their
last. When their mother, Jennie,
wrote letters to her sons from
Manitoba on June 3, 1944, she
didn't know she would never see
them again. D-Day and events
immediately after intervened in
their lives.

Your Ever
loving son.
Frank
x x x x x x

"Betsy," CBC's first on-location van, carried both state-of-the-art broadcast equipment and shrapnel from many a close call. Covering the Canadians' 1943 Italian liberation campaign, the CBC broadcast team gathered for a portrait (below): (l to r) Matthew Halton, Capt. John Howard (conducting officer in the field), Marcel Ouimet, engineers A. J. McDonald and Paul Johnson, and Peter Stursberg.

(ABOVE) Paul Martin (right) emerged from his bombed-out house in Bernières June 6 only to be mistakenly arrested. Chaudière Sgt. Rosaire Gagnon (left) freed Martin and his son Jacques (behind Gagnon) all in the same morning. A Fort Garry Horse tank is in the background. (LEFT) Never far from the frontlines, CBC war correspondent Marcel Ouimet described Canadian troops "with rage in their hearts and knowing what it was to measure themselves against the enemy."

(RIGHT) Once Bernières was secured, Sgt. Gagnon gladly told the residents of his Quebec regiment's commitment to train and fight to liberate France. A week later he was killed in action.

(LEFT) The DD (Duplex Drive) Sherman tank was a D-Day secret weapon. Its waterproof canvas skirt was made rigid by inflatable hoops and compressed air and its two built-in rear propellers enabled the tank to "swim" from landing craft to shore and land firing shells.

(RIGHT) Born and raised on the prairies, Lt. Bill Little knew about horses, hunting, and auto mechanics, but for D-Day he prepared not only to lead an armoured troop onto Juno Beach, but also to "swim" his tank ashore. Wounded on D-Day he returned to his unit and at the war's end was awarded the Military Cross.

(LEFT) This Flail tank pounded the earth in front, exploding land mines before they disabled a tank or its crew. The flail and the DD tank were inventions of Maj. Gen. Percy Hobart, and were known respectfully as "Hobart's Funnies."

"At 6 a.m. we were committing 20,000 men to battle, all Canadians, none of whom had ever been to war before," he wrote. "We were going to land on a coast against trained enemy soldiers that had already been through war for four years. They were entrenched in cement emplacements and knew exactly what they had to do. I wondered why in God's name I had been chosen to be the guy responsible for designing and implementing the Fire Plan."

The pre-dawn silence was agonizing for Brigadeer Todd. As the naval bombardment finally began and the assault landing craft were launched, he went below to what had formerly been a lounge aboard HMS *Hilary*, the passenger ship converted to the headquarters ship for Force J in front of Juno Beach. The lounge now contained a mass of wireless communications radios so that every unit could be reached for reports. Todd listened for word that each stage of the Fire Plan was proceeding according to the schemes the crews had rehearsed for months.

Just after seven o'clock, the SP crews aboard the LCTs carrying the 12th and 13th Field Regiments spotted a blue flag on the masthead of the motor launch that controlled fire in their sector. That meant that the guns were within 9,000 yards,

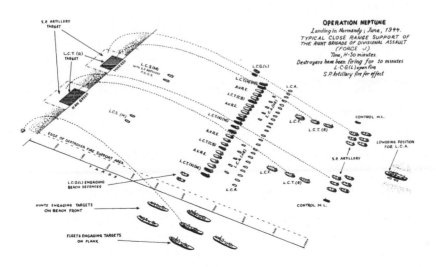

the opening range for the 105-mm SPs. They fired their opening salvos against the 7th Canadian Infantry Brigade's target beaches, Mike Green, Mike Red, and Nan Green. Within thirty minutes, the 14th and 19th Field Regiments were within range of the 8th Canadian Infantry Brigade's target beaches, Nan White and Nan Red. Shellfire from all ninety-six Priests persisted for half an hour, each gun firing 100 to 150 rounds. Holding position 2,000 yards offshore, the LCTs in turn gave way to the landing craft infantry and awaited orders to land the guns.

A gunner with the Royal Canadian Artillery, 14th Field Regiment, recorded his thoughts on the run-in to his appointed beach in the Nan White sector. Sgt. Wes Alkenbrack, with the "Dog 4" SP gun crew, remembered a quick breakfast from self-heating cans of cocoa and oxtail soup that took the chill off the cold morning air. By seven o'clock on D-Day morning, orders being shouted across the short length of the LCT were nearly drowned out by the roar of the naval shells passing over the crews and slamming into the coastline ahead.

"There was no difficulty in carrying out this operation," Alkenbrack wrote. "With our guns fixed facing forward as they were on the craft and at zero traverse on their mountings, we were aimed directly toward the shore."

As the distance to the beach shrank, Alkenbrack's crew merely corrected the gun's elevation in descending hundreds of yards to keep the SP's 105-mm weaponry on target. He recalled that most of the Priest crews began firing at about seven-twenty and continued to pump out round after round as their LCTs advanced toward the beach.

"In those last tense moments, as we loaded and fired and loaded and fired like automatons," he wrote, "the shore of France was fully visible, rent and torn with violent explosions and with a dense pall of smoke. . . . And then the beach itself became visible with a few figures scattered across it, some running, some standing and some lying motionless on the sand."

The SP crews suffered their share of losses landing on the beaches too. German mortar fire met the SPs of the 12th Field Regiment as they came ashore to back up the Royal Winnipeg Rifles; the shrapnel killed a signaller and wounded three officers. Shelling and sniper fire killed two officers with the 14th Field Regiment on its way in to the Nan White beach sector and a gunner with the 19th Field Regiment at Nan Red. In the Regina Rifles assault area, the 13th Field Regiment suffered heavier casualties. An exploding mine wiped out an entire landing party in one craft. Shells killed two officers in another, and a forward observation officer (FOO) drowned when his landing craft overturned. When shelling intensified on Nan Green beach, another forward observation group suffered numerous casualties, leaving one surviving signaller. Gunner Jack Holtzman carried on. He managed to radio gunners from his 13th Field as well as a Royal Marine battery, who returned fire on a pillbox that had pinned down a group of Regina Rifles troops. The action silenced the German strongpoint and earned Holtzman a Military Medal, probably the first decoration won by a Canadian on D-Day.

8:15 a.m. June 6, 1944—Nan Green Beach, France

The Regina Rifles were scheduled to land just as the artillery's Fire Plan ended.

Sister regiment to the Royal Winnipeg Rifles, the Reginas' objective on D-Day morning was Courseulles-sur-Mer. A Company was to land at the centre of the village, B Company slightly to the east of it, and C Company was to back up both. Given the high winds, the rapidly rising tide, the mass of shipping on its way to a multitude of objectives, and the not surprising fog of war that morning, at least one of the LCIs ferrying

Regina Rifles troops ashore brushed disaster even before reaching the German defences.

Three miles offshore, Maj. Stuart Tubb and members of C
Company realized their landing craft was headed for the church
spires of Bernières, not Courseulles. While the Royal Navy
crew corrected the heading, Tubb reported his LCI then crossed
the path of another vessel with a 4.7-inch gun about to fire a
shell on a low trajectory at its coastline target, whether an LCI
full of Reginas was in its path or not. Again Tubb's LCI quickly
altered course. Then, on the carrier's final run-in, Tubb witnessed the application of one of the Allies' secret weapons re-
served especially for D-Day. Broadside to the coast, looking
more like a church organ with its sounding chimes aimed at the
beaches, were LCT barges loaded with hundreds of 5-inch
rocket launchers. The sight and sound of this new weapon
clearly stunned the Canadian infantrymen.*

"As we watched, these soared away in successive volleys
with a great and satisfying swooshing roar, clouds of smoke and
showers of sparks," Tubb wrote. "We had not seen this particular weapon before and were duly impressed and encouraged."

7:30 a.m. June 6, 1944—Courseulles-sur-Mer, France

As uplifting as the Allied firepower was to the inbound troops,
the night of air bombings, naval shelling, and then the early-
morning artillery barrage meant something completely different to those living in Courseulles-sur-Mer. To the east of the

---

* The Landing Craft Tank (Rocket) carried 792 5-inch rocket projectors
from which to "drench" beach defences about five minutes before touchdown. Operation Overlord marked the first deployment of the Landing
Craft Assault (Hedgerow), which could deliver over a short distance a salvo
of twenty-four 60-pound bombs designed to create gaps in enemy minefields
and barbed wire for the passage of troops and vehicles.

River Seulles and several hundred yards up from the beach in the village sat the house of Casamir Martin, a French citizen who worked as one of the mechanical staff in a local sugar factory. During the night, the Bomber Command air attacks had chased Martin, his wife, and three children, including his seventeen-year-old son Bernard, into their basement. As the first bombs fell and exploded nearby, the Martins found they had visitors.

"Two young German soldiers came down the stairs of our cellar," Bernard Martin said. "They wanted something to eat. My father had been in the First World War and he didn't like Germans. But we gave them some cider and they went away."

The Germans did not look much like soldiers. Bernard remembered that they had no gas masks nor bayonets. They did not even have full uniforms, looking "more civilian in their pants and civilian shoes" than like the soldiers of the 716th German Infantry Division that were garrisoned in Courseulles. Despite four years of German occupation in his village, Bernard Martin felt some empathy for these young, ill-clad, and hungry soldiers. The last time he saw them, they were seeking cover from the shelling in a crater behind the house, where the German infantry had set up an artillery battery.

Convinced that something unusual was happening, Bernard spent much of the night between bombardments climbing to the upper floor of the house. Just after seven o'clock that morning, he looked from the top-floor bathroom window to see a black line on the horizon. As the dawn illuminated the view to the north, Bernard realized that the line was warships. His father could not believe how close the ships were coming to the shore and worried that he and his family might be about to witness another Dieppe. When he realized the ships would soon be firing in their direction, Casamir Martin again herded his family down into the basement. Within minutes, one of the first naval-bombardment shells landed on the second floor of the Martin house and shattered it.

"Because of the concussion from the explosion," Bernard Martin remembered, "we all had sore ears, bloody noses, and our eyes were full of dust."

As the morning went on, the family could hear shells flying both ways, from the German artillery behind the house and from the landing craft pulling onto the beach. When Casamir and his son finally managed to push the debris away from the basement door, Bernard climbed through the rubble up to a hole that had been a first-floor window. He saw soldiers he later discovered were the Regina Rifles, first crawling toward the coastal road, then marking a path through the minefield next to their house. Fearless, Bernard dashed from his home to get a better look. One of the first sights he saw has stayed with him: the two young Germans who had come into the cellar looking for food during the night lay dead beneath a nearby tree. Sickened but not deterred, Bernard raced on to the village water tower. He still craved a better view of the battlefield on the beach and quickly climbed the twenty-five yards to the top of the tower.

"I saw ships shuttling back and forth on the water," he said. "I was truly captivated by what I saw. The beach was alive with hardware, tanks, bulldozers swarming everywhere."

That's when he heard the first ping of a bullet ricocheting near him off the water tower. Another ping and he saw a British soldier crouched in the nearby cemetery with his rifle resting on a tombstone, and aimed at him. The man shouted and signalled at him to come down. No sooner was the young French boy off the tower than the soldier had him pinned face down to the ground. The soldier yelled at him first in German and then poked his bayonet at him to raise his arms. Moments later he was in front of other troops getting a full interrogation in

English. Bernard might well have been imprisoned immediately had the village mayor not recognized him and explained who he was to the British interrogators.

A Regina Rifles officer addressed him in French: "Do you want to see?"

Bernard lit up at this unexpected chance to go to the beach.

"Come," the lieutenant said. "I'll show you." Then he put a first-aid dressing on Bernard's arm where the soldier in the cemetery had roughed him up, put the boy in a jeep, and drove him through rows and rows of vehicles back to the Nan Green beachhead.

"What I saw out on the beach was atrocious," Bernard said. "A shoe with a foot in it. . . . Devastation everywhere. It's not like a movie. The sea was giving back all these bodies. It immediately gave me the conviction that war was never pretty. . . . That was the day I stopped being a boy."

By day's end, what was left of the Martin home had a new, if familiar, next-door neighbour. Where until that morning a German artillery battery had been firing, Canadian anti-aircraft guns had now been installed. This battery had four guns, a searchlight, and troops who offered Bernard Martin's family cigarettes, chocolate, and fresh tea, all luxuries the French civilians had not known for many months.

A greater culinary treat awaited the Canadian Press correspondent, William Stewart. Once he had written up his first impressions of the Royal Winnipeg Rifles' assault on Mike beach, Stewart put away his typewriter and was quite content to lunch on the contents of his twenty-four-hour ration pack, a small tin of canned meat, compo tea (powdered tea, sugar, and milk), and cereal cakes. He then abandoned his "office" in the sand dunes and followed a soldier leading him and other correspondents up from the beach.

"The dirt track led to the village of Graye-sur-Mer," Stewart wrote, "where an old couple invited the little group of correspondents and their conducting officers into their small stone house, where they served strawberries and cream at a glass-topped table in their parlour. . . .

"The conducting officers delivered our stories to the beach to be given to naval craft going back to England. We chatted with the French couple who invited us to stay overnight in their house. Our first sleep in France was in soft beds between white sheets, another remarkable D-Day surprise."

In a letter sent from England to his mother a few days before D-Day, George Meakin had told Jennie Meakin and George's sister, Ellen, how much he missed them and life back home in Birnie, Manitoba. He had even enclosed a couple of snapshots of himself and his brother Frank. Both men in the Royal Winnipeg Rifles were preparing themselves for the invasion.

"This may be the last chance I get to write before the big day, so if you don't hear from me for a while, please try and not worry," he wrote. "We will be OK. And no matter what happens, I can always say I have the greatest mother and sister. . . . We are all coming back and all in one piece. . . . I am as always your most loving son and brother—George."

On September 14, 1944, more than three months after D-Day, a letter written by Jennie Meakin on June 3, 1944, and addressed to Cpl. George E. Meakin, Royal Winnipeg Rifles, Canadian Army Overseas, was returned to Birnie. In the letter, Mrs. Meakin updated her son on the 100 chicks she and daughter Ellen were raising on the farm. She told him the weather had been damp, but helpful to their new garden. She finished by saying, "The train will soon be here, so I must get this posted . . . so I will say 'Cheerio. Good luck and God bless you till we meet again.' . . . from your loving mother." Jennie Meakin's June 3 letter also contained a stick of chewing gum.

George Meakin never received the letter. Nor did Frank, George's brother, receive the letter his mother had written and sent to him on June 3.

Mid-afternoon on June 8, D-Day plus two, the Meakin brothers and the rest of A Company of the Royal Winnipeg Rifles tried to hold their ground in Putot-en-Bessin, about nine miles from where they had come ashore. Counterattacks by the 26th S.S. Panzer Grenadier Regiment cut off several platoons of the Winnipegs. The Germans then captured about forty-five Canadians, and by the end of the day the S.S. had executed all of them, including the Meakin brothers, at the Château d'Audrieu.

On June 26, 1944, Jennie Meakin received two separate telegrams from the Director of Records in Ottawa. They informed her that both her sons, George and Frank, reported missing in action three days earlier, were now confirmed as killed in action. When the undelivered letters she had sent her sons on June 3 came back in September, both still contained the chewing gum.

The two Meakin brothers were buried on high ground near the village of Bény-sur-Mer, inland from the coast. By the end of the Normandy campaign, more than 2,000 Canadian war dead lay there, including nine pairs of brothers, as well as the three Westlake brothers, Thomas, Albert, and George, who were killed in Normandy within a week of D-Day.

THE SWIM TO FRANCE

7:30 a.m. June 6, 1944—Nan Red Beach, France

BILL LITTLE arrived at his designated piece of the Normandy beachhead shortly after seven-thirty on D-Day morning. Lieutenant Little led the 5th Troop in C Squadron of the Fort Garry Horse ashore. His tanks were to provide fire support for the North Shore (New Brunswick) Regiment at Nan Red sector in front of St-Aubin-sur-Mer on the extreme east flank of Juno Beach.

As a tank commander, Little's regular vantage point would have been in the turret atop his Sherman tank. From there he would communicate steering directions to one of his two drivers or firing instructions to his gunner and loader below and inside the tank. Instead, during this first stage of the D-Day landing, he was positioned on the rear outer surface of the tank with his hands wrapped firmly around a tiller bar.

"My tank went into the water about a thousand metres [yards] from the beach," Little said, "and our DD tank swam to shore."

The DD stood for Duplex Drive. The two propellers affixed to the tail-end of the tank, in combination with the tiller bar that Little pushed back and forth, transformed his 35-ton Sherman into an amphibious armoured vehicle. This manoeuvre alone represented one of the most unconventional forms of tank warfare any military organization had ever attempted. On this historic morning, Bill Little was commanding one of forty tanks with the 10th Armoured Regiment (the Fort Garry Horse), which joined forty more in the 6th Armoured Regiment (the 1st Hussars) that would leave their tank landing craft (LCTs) well out at sea and literally navigate their own way onto Juno Beach.

He had only just learned about the outrageous scheme six months earlier. In December 1943, all members of both B and C squadrons, comprising about 200 men, were rounded up and transported in great secrecy to a small lake near Great Yarmouth in Norfolk on Britain's east coast. There, on an otherwise deserted lakeshore, the Canadians were introduced to a British officer. As the man briefed the assembled crews, Little said he noticed a small boat circling out on the lake.

"You're going to see something here you've never seen before," the officer announced.

Little remembered all his men standing there very conscious of the security and the hush-hush nature of the trip, and with no idea why they had been summoned to this remote location. Meanwhile, he noticed that this boat on the lake was drawing a little closer. He tried to ignore it.

"We are about to show you," the officer said, "the reason for coming here."

As he spoke, he pointed to the boat that moments before had been gently plying the surface of the lake. Now it was suddenly powering non-stop toward the men on shore. It motored through the last few yards of shallow water just as a screen that had looked like the hull of the small boat suddenly dropped flat down to reveal a Valentine tank with its tracks now churning up the sand and its gun apparently ready to fire. It was a regular tank, similar to those in which Lieutenant Little and his squadron crews had trained through the winter of 1943–44. As of that moment, however, the tank had become amphibious. This development would change the complexion of the D-Day landing.

The Duplex Drive tank, as Bill Little learned in those months leading up to D-Day, was yet another innovative weapon the Allies would hurl at Hitler's Atlantic Wall. And just like the counter-intelligence activity of ULTRA, the radio-jamming of Mandrel and Jostle, and the window-spoofing of Operation Taxable, the development of the DD tank was designed to catch the Germans off guard. What could be more dramatic and effective as part of the largest amphibious invasion in history than four squadrons of tanks launched hundreds of yards from shore, landing under their own power, with their guns blazing.

Little later found out that the inventor of the DD, or swimming tank, was a tank commander like himself, Maj.-Gen. Sir Percy Hobart, commander of the British 79th Armoured Division. When the Second World War broke out, Hobart was actually retired and had become a corporal in the British Home Guard. Winston Churchill re-activated him. Like so many other painful lessons learned on August 19, 1942, Dieppe had persuaded the prime minister and his military planners that army engineers would never be able to destroy obstacles, build roads, clear minefields, overcome anti-tank ditches, or neutralize fortifications if they themselves were under heavy fire. Churchill trusted Hobart to come up with some practical solutions.

The resulting fleet of armoured vehicles, known affectionately as "Hobart's Funnies," played key roles in the D-Day landings. Hobart developed the Crab, or flail, tank, a Sherman with a revolving drum and hanging chains built into it. The chains flew around ahead of the tank, exploding mines before its treads ran over them. He also invented Roly-Polys and

Bobbins, lengths of steel mesh and matting that enabled vehicles to cross unstable sand or patches of gooey clay. Hobart's Fascines carried huge bundles of logs that could be dumped into anti-tank ditches to allow vehicles to pass over them. Petards were tanks adapted to throw bombs from a short-muzzled mortar, and Crocodiles threw flame farther than the flamethrowers the infantry carried. Finally, the Duplex Drive Sherman employed twin propellers affixed to the rear of the tank and a canvas skirt supported by a steel frame with thirty-six inflatable tubes so that the tank, completely waterproofed, could navigate short stretches of water. As soon as the tank's tracks made contact with the beach, the skirt dropped and the tank would roll ashore into action.

"It operates on the Archimedes principle," Bill Little's British instructor had explained. "A basket full of stones will float until you put too many stones in it. . . . You have so much freeboard. If you increase your freeboard, you increase your ability to float."

Astounded at first, the DD-tank crews of the 1st Hussars and Fort Garry Horse adjusted quickly to the new training regimen, and it was organized so secretly that not even members of the other non–DD-tank squadrons knew what was going on. As with all such preparation, Bill Little depended on the chemistry among the men in his crews to meet the rigours of their tight training schedule. They had six months to work on waterproofing their new Shermans, learning how the Duplex Drive gear worked, and mastering the pros and cons of actual amphibious landings. Little had one other factor working in his favour: the men in the young lieutenant's own tank and many of those in his squadron were virtually neighbours—they all come from his part of Manitoba.

"I don't think there was another part of Canada that produced more people who served in the Second World War,"

Little said. No fewer than thirty of his neighbours from a single block of Dufferin Street in Selkirk, Manitoba, were in the services. "We all felt a strong sense of duty, I guess."

Bill Little's radio operator and loader, Blair Gunter, came from Selkirk. So did half a dozen other members of the squadron. His gunner, Earl Kitching, was from Stony Mountain, Manitoba. His two drivers, Barney Stamm and Tom Mitchell, hailed from around Winnipeg. And Bill Little's own brother, Harold, served in one of three DD tanks in the 2nd Troop of C Squadron.

The consequence, of course, was that the loss of any and all squadron men felt like losing members of the family. The Channel crossing had taken a physical toll. Little remembered that seas were so rough that when the "matchbox" landing craft climbed each wave, all the men inside could see toward the bow was sky. Of the twenty-five tank crewmen on board, twenty-three were seasick coast to coast. In some cases, when the launching of the DD tanks began, Little was actually lifting some of his crewmen into their vehicles.

With the DD tank's canvas skirt fully inflated, Little directed his Sherman down the open ramp and out into choppy seas about 1,000 yards from shore. Right away, he spotted holes in the canvas from incoming small-arms fire, but to that point no bullets had penetrated either the inflated uprights supporting the skirt or the metal containers supplying the air. By the time the tracks on Little's tank finally touched down on the beach and he had dropped the skirt, ready to attack, his troop of four tanks had already lost men and equipment.

"A tank commander always had to have his head up [above the protective armour]," Little said, "and that's how Sergeant P. Parkes, my troop sergeant, and his operator, Lance Corporal [Bob] Stevenson, were killed. Both shot by sniper fire. . . . And

Sergeant Spud Murphy, a shell hit his tank and down it went."

The wreckage of Fort Garry tanks and North Shore Regiment assault landing craft seemed to fill the water. Bodies of the infantry were already rolling up in the rising surf fifty yards in front of the seawall at St-Aubin-sur-Mer. Among the living, making their way to shore, were a North Shore soldier and a man wearing a Red Cross armband and a priest's collar. Rifleman Joel Murray and Reverend R. M. Hickey were pushing their way through the flotsam and seawater when Hickey grabbed a fellow New Brunswicker who had taken gunfire and fallen beside him. He dragged the young soldier all the way to cover next to the seawall, only to find that he was already dead.

"I knelt for a second that seemed an eternity," Reverend Hickey wrote, "and anointed him—the first of the long, long list I anointed in action."

Without regard for himself, Reverend Hickey joined a regimental doctor, Captain J. A. Patterson, and some stretcher-bearers as they dashed back and forth across those fifty yards several times, retrieving more wounded soldiers. The enfilade of machine-gun fire and mortars rained down all around them. Hickey heard bullets and shrapnel cutting into the sand and each shell concussion produced another shower of stones and debris. Making matters worse, as some of the Fort Garry tanks arrived and powered their way up the beach, he watched them run over some of the wounded. During one of his attempts to retrieve those out in the open, Hickey reached three badly wounded infantrymen just as a shell smashed into them. He was the only one to survive the explosion.

In spite of the carnage on the beach, the remaining tanks and infantry were making some headway. In time, an Assault Vehicle, Royal Engineers (AVRE), arrived with pioneers (advance engineers) who used one of Hobart's modified Petard tanks to blast a hole in the seawall. Immediately afterward, the Canadian troops and vehicles swarmed over the strongpoint on the beach and began clearing pockets of German snipers and machine-gun nests through the town. Reverend Hickey and the doctor ran into the open to catch up with the troops, the former wondering why no sniper had picked him off. He marvelled at the bravery of the stretcher-bearers who retrieved wounded from exposed ground. On his way toward the advancing troops, Hickey came upon two such men carrying a third out of harm's way, when one of the stretcher-bearers stepped on a mine and all three were killed.

In St-Aubin, Alexandre Constant, a civilian, approached Hickey and Patterson seeking their help. He led them to a house where his wife lay on the floor, wounded. As the doctor administered first aid, Reverend Hickey looked around to see three terrified little girls watching the doctor work. He spoke to them to try to ease their fears, without success.

"Then I remembered I had three chocolate bars in my pocket, part of my day's rations," Hickey wrote. "I gave them to the little girls. Oh, the power of a chocolate bar! The terror vanished from six brown eyes."

The two Canadians left the house confident the woman would survive her wounds, though they would never know for sure. They continued southward out of St-Aubin, again following the North Shore infantry and the Fort Garry tanks, this time to the village of Tailleville, which the D-Day planners had calculated was an enemy headquarters. As was often the case in occupied Normandy, German troops had converted a local château into a strongpoint protected by bunkers and a network of trenches, mines, and apparently endless walls of barbed wire. The North Shores advanced as far as they could and then awaited backup from the Fort Garry tanks.

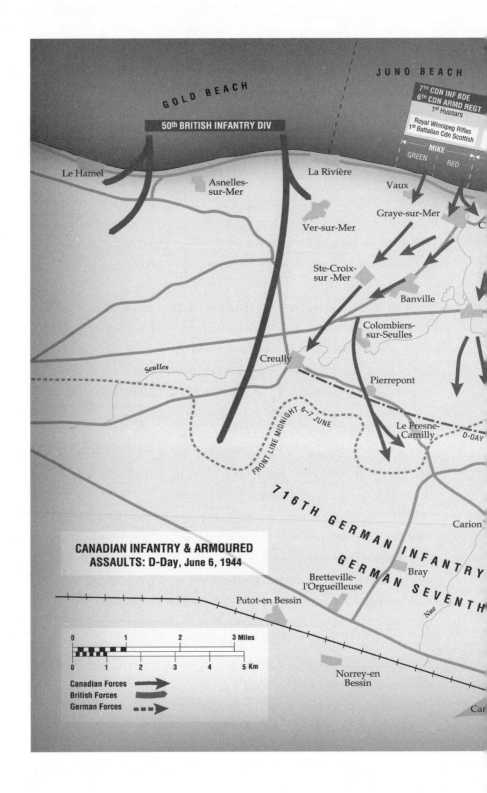

JUNO BEACH

GOLD BEACH

50th BRITISH INFANTRY DIV

7TH CDN INF BDE
6TH CDN ARMD REGT
1st Hussars
Royal Winnipeg Rifles
1st Battalion Cdn Scottish

MIKE

GREEN | RED

Le Hamel

Asnelles-
sur-Mer

La Rivière

Vaux

Graye-sur-Mer

C

Ver-sur-Mer

Ste-Croix-
sur -Mer

Banville

Colombiers-
sur-Seulles

Seulles

Creully

Pierrepont

FRONT LINE MIDNIGHT 6–7 JUNE

Le Fresne-
Camilly

D-DAY

716TH GERMAN INFANTRY

Carion

**CANADIAN INFANTRY & ARMOURED
ASSAULTS: D-Day, June 6, 1944**

GERMAN SEVENTH

Bretteville-
l'Orgueilleuse

Bray

0   1   2   3 Miles

Putot-en Bessin

Nue

0   1   2   3   4   5 Km

Canadian Forces
British Forces
German Forces

Norrey-en
Bessin

Car

N

INFANTRY DIV
ANTRY BDE
ARMD REGT
usiliers

8TH CDN INF BDE
10TH CDN ARMD REGT
Fort Garry Horse

ment de la Chaudière
en's Own Rifles

North Shore
(New Brunswick)

NAN

HITE B   A RED B

48TH ROYAL MARINE COMMANDOS

S W O R D   B E A C H

3RD BRITISH
INFANTRY DIV

rnières-
ur-Mer

St-Aubin-
sur-Mer

Luc-sur-
Mer

Lion-sur-
Mer

Ouistreham

Tailleville

r-Mer

Douvres-la-
Délivrande

Basly

21st PANZER DIV

nby-
haon

Anguerny

Anisy

Bénouville

River Orne

ns-les-
sons

Les
Buissons

Biéville

FRONT LINE

6TH AIRBORNE DIV

N A R E A

MIDNIGHT 6–7 JUNE

ron

Canal de Caen à la Mer

Caen

On the outskirts of the village, tank commander Bill Little felt he evened the score for the Canadians he had seen killed on the beach. As his tank broke through a hedgerow to the east of the village, he caught a full company of German troops on the move out in the open. He called for a high-explosive shell and ordered his gunner, Earl Kitching, to load and fire.

"It was like going out deer-shooting for the first time," Little said, recalling his first hunting experience with his father on the prairies, "the emotion of making that first shot. . . . It wasn't necessarily revenge, but we were there to eliminate the German army one way or another."

By the end of the afternoon, a combination of the North Shore Regiment's attacks and the Fort Garry Horse tanks' shelling had destroyed several enemy guns and forced the surrender of the German strongpoint at the Tailleville château.

Reverend Hickey caught up to the soldiers of his regiment digging slit trenches for protection against a potential counterattack in the night. Meanwhile, Lieutenant Little got out of his tank for an impromptu meeting with a fellow tank commander and a company commander of the North Shores. A German grenade suddenly came flying over a wall and into their midst. When Little tried to jump clear, the explosion propelled shrapnel into his legs, arms, and chest and burned his forehead. Within twenty-four hours he was on board a first-aid vessel on his way back to England. When his wife finally joined him in a British hospital, he learned that while he had been behind security wire and off to fight on D-Day, she had given birth to their first child.

8:30 a.m. June 6, 1944—Nan Beach, France

D-Day was also Bob Cameron's graduation day. Sometime later, he even received a mailed invitation from the University of Toronto president, who was unaware that not only was Cameron out of town but he was making history on the other side of the Atlantic.

"I had done three years of an Honours Bachelor of Arts in English and history," Cameron said, "and they gave me my [fourth] year because I was in the army. . . . The graduation ceremony was June 6, 1944, at Convocation Hall, but they never bothered to check where I was."

From as early as 1938, Cameron attended the Canadian Officers Training Corps (COTC) program that groomed young officers while paying for their university education. A teacher had suggested he study languages and join the diplomatic corps but when the war broke out, he went to Brockville and Kingston for signals training instead. During the winter of 1942–43 he learned "to climb ice-covered telephone polls and freeze to death sitting in the back of a radio truck." By March he was a full lieutenant in the Royal Canadian Corps of Signals (RCCS). He was shipped overseas as a reinforcement that spring and posted to the 3rd Canadian Infantry Division in charge of a forty-man telephone stringing section.

Cameron learned he would be Juno Beach signals master, building wire communication links from the beach to divisional headquarters and to the three battalions as well. Consequently, he took great pride in preparing his section for the coming invasion—waterproofing vehicles, loading and unloading landing craft, winding and unwinding thousands of yards of telephone wire, and preparing his two assistants for the real thing. Cpl. Leo "Buck" Grittner came from Kelowna, B.C., and Cpl. John Tolstad was originally from Bristol, England. They were older than most of the soldiers, thirty-five to forty years of age, and reasonably phlegmatic about the war, with a healthy sense of humour. During the lead-up to D-Day, Lieutenant Cameron decided that if he grew a moustache he would look older than his twenty-five years and thus worthier of their respect. The two corporals responded by holding their superior officer down and shaving off half his moustache. The unit was jelling.

Just after 8:30 a.m. on D-Day, about thirty minutes after the assault infantry, the threesome came ashore in Nan sector. Cameron recalled the horror of seeing the underwater obstacles poking up through the surf, each iron tripod armed with what looked like a magnum champagne bottle full of explosive. In spite of the early-morning bombardment, the concrete gun emplacements and pillboxes looming before them looked equally threatening. The LCT delivered the three signallers and their jeep safely into shallow water between the obstacles. As they waded their vehicle up to the seawall, an AVRE group was just blasting a hole through it.

"There were bodies in the surf," Cameron said, "so Buck and John and I dragged this one guy ashore, not knowing if he was alive or not. We found he was dead. He had a gold ID bracelet on his wrist. I turned it over to find out his name and there was an inscription on the back: 'God keep him safe. I love him so.'"

The physical test of their mettle was just as severe as the psychological. Cameron and his two corporals now had to string telephone wire from the beach area to an intended advance division headquarters inland. The problem was that if they laid it across the sand and rubble, tanks and other vehicles grinding their way through the village, or the German artillery barrages, would continually sever or blow the lines to pieces. That meant endless repairs, reconnecting damaged lengths of telephone cable. On one of his trips back to the beach to fix a broken line, Cameron met two Canadians lugging gear that did not include rifles or grenades.

"Where's Div Headquarters?" asked one of the newcomers.

"Hop in. I'm going there," Cameron answered. The two men told Cameron he was taxiing Canadian Press war correspondent Ross Munro and *Globe and Mail* reporter Ralph Allen. They carried little besides their typewriter cases and stationery valises. They were looking for Maj.-Gen. Rod Keller, commanding officer of the 3rd Canadian Infantry Division. Cameron obliged and answered some questions from the two journalists along the way.

"We had just arrived at Div Headquarters," Cameron recalled, "and [the Germans] opened up on us with eighty-eights. They were murderous. And then there were the clusters of mortar bombs called 'Moaning Minis.' . . . I had already built a dugout beside headquarters, so Munro and I jumped in."

Bob Cameron's other slit-trench mates, Corporals Grittner and Tolstad, were not as fortunate. Within a few days of his signals team's landing in Normandy, Cameron was posted to become brigade signals officer, while his two corporals stayed in the section attached to divisional headquarters. Grittner was killed in a barrage attack in July and Tolstad when American B-17s mistakenly bombed Canadians and Poles moving along the Falaise Road on August 8. He was one of sixty-five killed and 250 wounded in one of several "friendly fire" incidents during the Normandy campaign.

8:12 a.m. June 6, 1944—Nan White Beach, France

On D-Day, troops of the Queen's Own Rifles of Canada encountered their first brush with danger even before they boarded their shoebox-like landing craft. In the pre-dawn, below decks on their landing ship, members of A and B companies entered a concrete blockhouse. The area, called the "Dieppe" hold, was designed to prevent a repeat of an accident that had occurred during that ill-fated raid on August 19, 1942. En route to France, some troops were killed when a soldier priming a grenade in the open accidentally let it explode.

So, on their way to the LCAs, two men of the Queen's Own at a time went into the Dieppe hold, primed their grenades, emerged, and boarded their landing craft. Then came the thunderous pounding of beach fortifications by the 16-inch Allied naval guns, whose shells sounded "like freight trains passing overhead," followed by the delays. The LCAs of all three Queen's Own companies began to circle in anticipation of their assault led by DD tanks. But the seas in this sector were so rough that the DD-tank commanders feared any attempt to swim them ashore risked their being swamped; some tried it and sank like stones. Now twenty minutes later than the expected H-Hour, the first two assault groups, A and B companies, were ordered to land anyway. In the last few thousand yards, assault troops were both shaken and bolstered by the rounds of rocket fire swooshing over them and straight into the enemy's beach defences. Some of the Queen's Own reported seeing an RAF Spitfire that had descended perilously close to the shoreline blown out of the sky by the rockets. Finally, with heads down, the first wave of men felt that last furious adrenaline rush as they burst through the spray of water and enemy gunfire to the beachhead.

When the front ramp dropped on the LCA containing No. 12 Platoon from B Company, Corporal Fred Barnard was about halfway back. Joining him in the leap into waist-deep water in front of Bernières-sur-Mer were his younger brother, Rifleman Donald Barnard, and his childhood friend, Rifleman Gordon Arthur. The three had grown up together on the same street in east-end Toronto. But this was not Sutherland Avenue in East York.

"As we were going down the ramp," Fred Barnard said, "I yelled to my brother, 'Give 'em hell!' And the next thing I know, I'm in four feet of water."

Immediately in front of him, and his only concern in those first few moments, was the maze of obstacles that sat exposed by the low tide. Barnard quickly realized that the mines on the hedgehogs were the source of the explosions around him. There seemed to be continuous detonations as several of the Queen's Own landing craft triggered the mines. As he reached dry beach, he came upon one of the youngest men in his platoon, a nineteen-year-old whose stomach had been cut open by shrapnel. The wounded lad tried to push his innards back in place and called out in a panic for his mother. Ahead of Barnard, his chum Gord Arthur had made it to some cover.

"Then I saw my brother Don . . . lying on his back as if he was asleep," Barnard said. "There was just a black hole in his uniform right in the middle of his chest. No blood. He must have died instantly."

While he had scored best marksman in the company, twenty-year-old Don Barnard had been unable to get off a single shot. Just twenty-three himself, what Fred Barnard experienced in his first moments ashore might have been enough to paralyze him with fright on the spot. Despite his shock, though, he knew he could not delay, not even long enough to drag his brother's body with him. B Company had come ashore 200 yards east of its intended landing site, directly in front of the main resistance nest at Bernières. Within the first few minutes of the engagement, the company accumulated sixty-five casualties.

Out of the LCA at about the same time as the Barnard brothers came Joe Oggy. A photo engraver with Simpsons department store in Toronto, Oggy began as a rifleman and second-in-command of his section with the Queen's Own. Aboard the landing craft on the way to Juno Beach, a piece of Oggy's equipment got caught up on the soldier's pack in front of him, which forced him to stand nearly all the way in. Oggy made the best of his raised position by giving his buddies a blow-by-blow description of the ongoing assault. Uppermost in his mind, though, were the words of a Queen's Own officer.

"You've got fifteen minutes to live. Kill or be killed," Oggy remembered him saying. "If there's a retreat off this beach, the Queen's Own Rifles will be the last to leave."

Like Fred Barnard and Gord Arthur, Corporal Oggy managed to reach the low seawall in front of Bernières relatively unscathed. A few yards away, a Native Canadian soldier kept trying to get up and climb over the same wall until persistent German gunfire finally knocked him down lifeless. Oggy could see the tall blades of grass bending and twitching as the machine-gun bullets from the resistance nest whistled through them. He ducked down and slowly crawled through a hole in the seawall, punched out by a navy shell. On the other side, in a ditch between the sand dunes, he met another Queen's Own rifleman. "Stumpy" Gordon was preparing to attack a nearby pillbox, and he stopped long enough to ask Oggy, "What are you doing, corporal?"

"I'm scared, Stump," Oggy admitted.

"Jesus, I am too!" said Gordon and he gave Oggy a water bottle and then disappeared around a corner in the ditch to toss grenades into the pillbox. It was about eight-forty when Joe Oggy took a moment to scrape the dirt off his hands and looked at his wristwatch for the first time since he had come ashore.

"It had been more than twenty minutes," Oggy said, "and I was still alive. I'd made it past the fifteen minutes."

Even so, during its first hour ashore B Company had lost more than half its strength. When the dust settled, the lieutenant in charge of the three headquarters platoons did a roll call. Fred Barnard wrote down the names of the survivors: nine in Joe Oggy's section, seven in Gord Arthur's section, seven in his own section, and a few others. Barnard had lost not only his younger brother, Donald, but many brothers from his army family.

When the young man momentarily shed some of his gear, he realized how close he had come to losing more than that: "I'd been hit in the side with a piece of shrapnel and it was just a nick. But when I took my pack off, it was full of holes. Bullets or shrapnel must have gone right through it when I was crawling across the beach. But there was nothing left inside. Mess tins, ground sheet and rations, they were all smashed to smithereens. I just threw the pack away."

8:35 a.m. June 6, 1944—Mike Red Beach, France

Just as Bill Little's armoured squadron and the rest of the Fort Garry Horse tanks had battled the elements and an entrenched enemy alongside the 8th Canadian Infantry Brigade on the left flank of Juno Beach, so did the 1st Hussars tanks rush to support the 7th Infantry Brigade on the right flank. In fact, the Hussars motto—*Hodie non cras*, Today not tomorrow—no doubt resonated in the mind of every 6th Armoured Regiment tank trooper on D-Day. It certainly did for the Hussars' wireless operator, Bruce Evans.

"In the beginning it wasn't patriotism that drove us," Evans said. "We knew our job was to stay in close proximity with the infantry . . . get them ashore and stay with them as they cleared the town."

As a member of C Squadron, Trooper Evans also understood that he would not be ashore until three-quarters of an hour after the first troops and Hussars DD tanks had presumably touched down in the 7th Brigade sectors. Most of his squadron, including the LCT carrying his jeep and the four non-swimming Sherman tanks, was supposed to make a dry landing after the two sister squadrons of DD tanks had reached, and moved off, the beaches. Once his scout car was ashore, Evans would act as a liaison, communicating on one wireless set with tank commanders and then with the infantry on the other set.

Evans had grown up on a southern Ontario farm near Woodbridge, and wanted so desperately to serve in the Hussars tanks that he had trained on everything—gunnery, driving, and wireless. With no spots available among the invasion tank crews, he gladly took what he could, acting as the communications link between the Hussars and the Winnipeg Rifles troops. Evans took the regiment's motto very seriously.

Just after eight o'clock, Trooper Evans's landing craft bobbed in the water several thousand yards off the beach. He was still fighting off the effects of overnight seasickness from the Channel crossing. He squinted into the morning light at the objects in the distance, the DD tanks of his comrades in A and B squadrons, attempting to launch at sea and assist the first wave of Royal Winnipeg Rifles and Regina Rifles rushing the beach defences.

"The water was so rough that at first they gave the order not to launch the [DD] tanks," Evans remembered. "Finally, the order was given to launch . . . and some tanks managed to land with the infantry and they saved quite a few lives, but in the process we lost tanks in the water. They just sank."

Evans and the rest of the Hussars watched helplessly as their sister squadrons lost eight tanks on the run-in. One went down, hit by a mortar shell. The engine of another failed and the tank was abandoned. Two more sank when their flotation screens collapsed because of the rough surf and the gunfire from shore. A Squadron lost three tanks when an LCT struck and exploded a mine. Another was sunk when the wake of a rocket-launching LCT washed over its protective flotation screen. In all, A Squadron managed to land seven DD tanks, and B Squadron successfully landed fifteen Shermans.

Sgt. Leo Gariepy, in B Squadron, wrote a vivid description of his "swim" towards shore in the Hussars' regimental diary:

"After launching we found it impossible to maintain correct formation in the rough sea and each DD made for its appointed place on the beach. At about 3,000 yards, I looked around and saw Maj. [J. S.] Duncan about 30 yards to my starboard and the rest of the DDs behind us. The port aft strut broke and the crew had to wedge a fire extinguisher between the screen and the hull. We had been showered with small arms fire, but suddenly I saw two pillars to the right near Maj. Duncan's tank, the first shell fire we had received on the way in. I looked ahead again and when I turned around once more the major's tank had disappeared."

Roughly on schedule, the Sherman tanks and support jeeps of C Squadron emerged from the water on the beach to the left of A Squadron's DD-tank crews, who were now waiting for engineers to lay a scissors bridge for them so they could move off the shingled beach. As the tide continued to rise, the beach space available for the steadily arriving stream of men and equipment was shrinking. Traffic was beginning to back up in front of Courseulles-sur-Mer. Some of the tank crews had even left their vehicles to look for potential exits from the beach. Evans did the same, leaving his driver, W. B. Griffin, behind. As he climbed down from the jeep, several mortar shells slammed into the beach around them. One smashed the front windshield and critically wounded Griffin, and another threw Evans flat on his back on the ground.

"I was in such pain," he said. "I just laid there for a moment, wondering if I'd lost a leg. . . . Soon, I was coming around and I realized both my legs were mobile. Glory be, I'm alive."

When Evans shakily got to his feet he realized how badly the shrapnel had injured his driver. With shells still periodically landing on the beach area, Evans found a protected area in the sand dunes and dug a slit trench. He placed blankets in the trench and the wounded Griffin on the blankets. Evans knew medical personnel would soon land on the beach, so he reassured his friend he would be in good hands. Then he jumped back into the jeep and pressed ahead to catch up with his tank regiment. By midday, Evans's own wounds were sapping his energy and the pain in his shoulder and his hip was intensifying. One of the Hussars' officers spotted him, dressed his wounds, and directed him to a regimental first-aid post that would prepare him for the return trip to a hospital in England.

"Surely you can keep me here," Evans said to his captain. "I just got here."

"There are no facilities here for your wounds," he said.

Bruce Evans would rejoin his regiment in Europe eventually, as a tank commander in B Squadron of the 1st Hussars, but his career would indeed have to wait until tomorrow.

8:30 a.m. June 6, 1944—Nan White Beach, France

There was one additional silent witness to the Canadians' historic struggle to gain Juno Beach that morning. Positioned toward the stern and slightly to the port side of a Queen's Own landing craft, Sergeant Bill Grant watched through the viewfinder of a motion-picture camera as a platoon in the second wave debarked the LCA. The film he shot was destined to become the most famous 35 seconds of wartime movie footage of the day.*

"We scored a complete scoop," wrote Grant's commanding officer triumphantly.

Sergeant Grant was one of at least seven Canadian cameramen to accompany the assault troops that morning. Every one a volunteer and every one a trained soldier in the Canadian Army, the group operated as No. 2 Canadian Film and Photo Unit (CFPU) within the army's Public Relations Unit. Like every other invasion participant, the CFPU cameramen had prepared intricate strategic plans in order to capture as many images of the Canadian troops in action as possible during D-Day.

As the invasion force discovered elsewhere on Juno Beach that day, however, some of the best-laid plans fell short of their marks. That morning, as Sergeant Bud Roos came ashore with the Regina Rifles, his LCA struck a mine, throwing him and his movie camera into the seawater, and ruining his film. The landing craft carrying still-photographer Lt. Don Grant ashore with the Royal Winnipeg Rifles ran aground on a sandbar and tossed him and his equipment into the surf; he survived but his

---

* There is controversy about the origin of this film footage. Some skeptics contend that the famous motion pictures were captured on 16-mm film through a camera that was fix-mounted aboard the Queen's Own Rifles' LCA. They point out there was insufficient room aboard the landing craft for a Canadian Film and Photo Unit soldier to stand behind and operate a movie camera and that a crewman aboard the LCA turned the camera on to capture the sequence. Both Pte. Chuck Ross, driver with the CFPU, and Staff Sgt. Ken Ewart, editor with the CFPU, insist that an LCA crewman would have had neither the time nor the ability to operate the camera in such combat conditions and that Bill Grant wound the camera mechanism and shot the film with a tripod-mounted, 35-mm Eymo camera from the rear of the LCA. Correspondence with despatch rider Brian O'Regan verifies that he later carried Grant's three film cans (100 feet of film each) to the beach for transport to Britain. Richard Malone, head of the Public Relations Unit, further verifies this story in his book *World in Flames*.

pictures didn't. Elsewhere, Capt. Frank Duberville, Capt. Colin McDougall, Capt. Ken Bell, and Sgt. Alan Grayston came ashore to shoot stills of Canadian troops in action. But cine-cameraman Bill Grant provided what became the day's world-wide exclusive.

Tucked in behind the Queen's Own assault troops on the LCA, the lanky Grant had long since readied his movie camera for action. He had mounted the 35-mm, Bell and Howell Model-Q Eymo camera atop his tripod. ("The commanding officer was most particular that the cameramen use tripods; if not, he blew his top.") He had pre-wound the camera's clock-work mechanism and tucked the crank key back into the handy pocket for it at the top of his trousers. He had rotated the appropriate lens into position on the front of the camera. Then, with seconds to go before the LCA crew swung open the front doors of their vessel, Grant pressed the start button on the camera. He knew the device would give him about a half a minute of continuous-action exposure.

Captured on his film are the darkened, clearly visible figures of the Queen's Own troops silently exchanging last-moment instructions, moving ladders and rifles into final ready posi-tions, and patting the forward-most troops on their backs for encouragement. The doors finally open and the brighter out-side light streams in, and the first troops leap out of the LCA. Ahead of them, clearly captured in Grant's sequence, are the famous beach-resort houses that the Germans had incorpo-rated into their coastal-defence system.

In the minutes that followed, Sergeant Grant scooped up his camera, tripod, and two more rolls of unexposed film, and scrambled ashore with the troops, seeking cover among the sand dunes in front of Bernières-sur-Mer. There on the beach and then shortly afterward in the village, he shot all three rolls of motion-picture film.

The next step in the historic film's journey was left to fate.

Since there was no way that Lt.-Col. Dick Malone, in charge of the Public Relations Unit, could know which ships and landing craft would survive the landings, he had supplied each of the CFPU cameramen with canvas bags, metal tins, and strips of waterproof tape. On the exterior of each tin the words "Press— Rush by whatever means possible—To Ministry of Information, London" had been painted in red. Malone had instructed the photographers to pack the film in the cans and get them to the first landing craft they could find bound for home.

As luck would have it, CFPU despatch rider Brian O'Regan also made it safely ashore and completed the delivery of Grant's historic film.

"I picked up a white-taped aluminum can containing cine reel number one by Sgt. Bill Grant," O'Regan wrote, "and got it to the beach movement control officer for transport to England."

Overnight, officials in Portsmouth, England, eagerly took delivery of the three tins of Sgt. Grant's film and hustled them along by another despatch vehicle to the Merton Park Studios in south London. After it was developed, roughly 300 feet of raw black-and-white 35-mm movie film were delivered to the editing table of a novice film editor, Staff Sgt. Ken Ewart.

"The first thing that had to be done was censor it, keeping any [Allied] weapons in the dark," Ewart explained.

Up until 1944, the closest Ken Ewart had been to motion-picture film was in the theatre seat of a British movie house. He had completed his training with the Loyal Edmonton Regiment in Britain, during which he had exhibited both inquisitiveness and a unique knowledge of weapons—in particular the sounds they made. As a result, he was shipped off to the Canadian Public Relations Unit in early 1944 to learn how to edit motion pictures and soundtracks. Within a month he was editing newsreel movies to be shown in the British theatres. Early on Wednesday, June 7, 1944, he received the processed film that Bill Grant had shot at Bernières.

"There was footage of troops crouched down inside the landing craft . . . jumping out the front of the landing craft, rushing up the sand dunes, and into that first village," Ewart said. "Of course, for the newsreels, we took the best part of every scene. We didn't use everything. We flashed the news. That's what we did."

The scripting, dubbing, and sound-recording were then added to complete the presentation that the public would see on the movie screens around the world. Each newsreel consisted of about 1,000 feet of film footage, or about ten minutes of viewing for a theatre audience. Within forty-eight hours of D-Day, people in Britain saw Sgt. Bill Grant's film sequences, including the first images of the Allied troops, the Queen's Own Rifles of Canada, landing in Normandy. Even before that, the raw footage was flown across the Atlantic and shown to North American audiences.

"The London papers and movie houses all showed Canadian pictures that day," Richard Malone wrote proudly. "The following evening, theatres in New York were all showing the first newsreels of the landing. . . . Unhappily, the American theatres did not identify the troops shown landing on the beaches as Canadian."

SAND, DUST,
AND GRAVEL BOYS

----

6 a.m. June 6, 1944—Hampshire, England

THERE WERE PLENTY OF REASONS for a young RCAF
pilot to be excited and nervous on D-Day.
    Flying Officer Richard Rohmer from Hamilton,
Ontario, had flown with No. 430 (RCAF) Photo Reconnaissance Squadron since September 1943. He and two dozen
other pilots with the squadron conducted low-level map reading and photography from Mk I Mustangs. The work had to be
precise. These recce flights pinpointed German truck, train,
tank, and gun movements in France. Secrecy and danger surrounded some of their missions, including the "no-ball" sites,
a cricket term applied to the results if a pilot ran afoul of an
area's deadly accurate anti-aircraft guns. The Mustangs would
follow bombers over these mysterious sites and photograph the
inflicted damage. They turned out to be V-1 launch pads.
    Early in 1944, Rohmer was still relatively new to the squadron.
He was twenty, yet looked all of sixteen, a fact vividly illustrated
during an impromptu inspection of the Mustang squadron by
the flamboyant U.S. Army general, George S. Patton, Jr. This

particular morning, in May 1944, the general had arrived promptly at eight o'clock and just as promptly jumped from his jeep to review a long line of Mustangs and their pilots. Resplendent in his wedge cap, battledress jacket, tan breeks, polished boots, and ivory-handled revolvers, "Old Blood and Guts" had passed quickly in front of the precisely parked Mustangs with their pilots all standing at rigid attention on the flight line. He spoke to no one, until he suddenly stopped in front of the slight and boyish-looking Rohmer.*

"Boy," Patton had demanded, "how old are you?"

"I'm twenty, sir," Rohmer replied proudly.

The general pointed up at the looming nose of the Mustang towering over Rohmer's youthful frame.

"Do *you* fly that goddam airplane?"

"Yes, sir."

With that, the general dropped his arm, blurted out, "Son of a bitch," and turned, shaking his head, to finish the inspection.

Even Rohmer admitted that his squadron commanders were overly protective of him and kept him from carrying out certain operations until early that year. So when they had given him the chance, Rohmer had felt a little nervous. On June 5, the young pilot had joined the rest of the squadron painting black-and-white invasion stripes on their Mustangs. Their excitement heightened when the pilots gathered at Group Captain Ernie Moncrieff's D-Day briefing. Rohmer was told he would fly a tactical-reconnaissance mission at dawn, over the beachhead

---

* Mustang pilot Richard Rohmer served with RCAF fighter reconnaissance throughout the rest of the Normandy campaign and participated in the liberation of Belgium and Holland in 1944–45. His 135-mission tour of operations earned him a DFC. He retired in 1953 as Wing Commander and, in addition to his successful career in law, he became the author of a number of bestsellers, including *Patton's Gap* (quoted here).

and south to Caen to report on ground or air activity. He would fly number two to Flying Officer Jack Taylor.

Rohmer also felt some anxiety that he was not flying the most agile single-engine fighter aircraft in the Allied arsenal. The Mustang Mk I, while rugged and fast, was also large and heavy and not highly manoeuvrable in a dogfight. The Mustang would not fare well in a contest with a Messerschmitt 109 or a Focke-Wulf 190. Furthermore, while the Luftwaffe had not ventured in massive force over the United Kingdom since the end of the Battle of Britain and the Blitz, Allied Intelligence knew that it operated from strength on its own side of the Channel. On the whole western front, the Luftwaffe boasted approximately 500 serviceable aircraft, including about 160 day- and 50 night-fighters. Its operational strength in bombers was somewhat smaller, with 185 of a possible 400 Junkers 88s available on D-Day. There was genuine fear, however, that if the Luftwaffe came out in force on June 6, Allied airmen could face a titanic air battle over Normandy.

To add to any anxiety he felt about the aircraft he was flying, Rohmer also knew that the Mustang bore an uncanny resemblance to the Messerschmitt 109 and might easily attract the attention of trigger-happy Allied gunners.

However, in the end, another complication entirely almost made F/O Rohmer a war statistic on D-Day.

Earliest reports of the morning's missions boded ill. Rohmer's friend and fellow recce pilot, F/O Jack Cox, had been shot down when his formation of four Mustangs was attacked by four Focke-Wulf 190s. Nevertheless, Rohmer and Taylor took off about 6 a.m. to do a visual reconnaissance, first over Caen and then over Sword, Juno, and Gold beaches. As they approached the coast, the two encountered a wall of cloud, so they flew over it for a quick look at the roads south from the beach toward Caen, and then returned north for their reconnaissance of the landing area. They were down to about 500 feet over Juno beach and they watched as some of the first Canadians landed.

"It was euphoric, the most fantastic sight I'd ever seen in my life," Rohmer said. "Then out on the horizon we saw black smoke and blinking lights. Of course, those were the battleships firing at the targets that were right under us. What Taylor and I didn't realize was that we were flying through probably hundreds of shells that were coming in to land on the targets below us."

Rohmer was transfixed by the scene. He took it all in—the battleships, the landing craft, the rockets, the DD tanks, the assault troops coming ashore. He also kept close watch on the skies around him and his leader, Jack Taylor. In spite of the specs that did not augur well for a Mustang in a dogfight, the orders for the pilots were to defend the troops and ships on the beach from strafing and bombing should the Luftwaffe appear. Eventually, after nearly two hours in the air, Rohmer glanced across his instrument panel. His fuel gauge was registering zero. What with the length of the flight and his manoeuvring to stay close to Taylor, Rohmer suddenly suspected he might not have the gas to make it back to England. He notified Taylor and the two immediately turned north for home.

"I climbed up to fifteen hundred feet," Rohmer said. "I leaned back the engine, the mixture, to preserve fuel. . . . I had a couple of choices. I knew I couldn't ditch the aircraft. The Mustang would go straight into the water, taking me to the bottom with it. I could bail out, though, because the Channel was loaded with ships."

Meantime, Rohmer aimed for Britain's closest visible point, Thorney Island, right on the south coast. Ten miles from the RAF station, the Mustang's fuel gauge ticked below the empty mark, but the engine kept firing. He radioed the airfield controller at Thorney Island, got clearance to land, and came straight in. Barely down on the runway, on the first taxiway, the engine cut out.

"I did another D-Day sortie at about three o'clock in the afternoon," he said, "but I was much more mindful of my fuel gauge."

8:30 a.m. June 6, 1944—Nan White Beach, France

What men saw and heard all along Juno Beach on D-Day morning registered in their memories in very much the same way. The sights of other men crumpling and machinery being twisted or tossed were as horrific in Nan sector as they were in Mike. The roar of the surf and of the shelling and shooting and screaming sounded as deafening in front of St-Aubin as it did in front of Courseulles. The way Canadian troops expressed their fear was shaped by every man's individual experience. Some, driven by adrenaline, ran faster than they had ever run before. Those in shock sometimes froze in one spot for many minutes. Many cried openly. Most shouted to relieve the internal stress.

Some men around Pierre Gauthier thought he was crazy when he smirked and at times laughed out loud. Within minutes of landing with Le Régiment de la Chaudière, the nineteen-year-old private from Montreal had scampered across fifty feet of open beach and crouched, panting, behind the seawall in front of Bernières-sur-Mer. The enfilade of German machine-gun fire and the clusters of mortar bombs from well off the beach sliced into the ranks of his platoon in D Company every step of the way. By the time Private Gauthier huddled into the relative shelter of the seawall, very few in his section remained, perhaps half a dozen men. They bunched there to catch their breath, unsure what to do next.

"You're not concerned about big things when you're a private in the infantry," Gauthier said. "You're mostly interested in the sight you have in front of you . . . the section's problems or the platoon's problems. You're not interested in the war's problems."

Almost directly in line with the Chaudières' landing point sat a German strongpoint. Its blockhouse showed no access on the side facing the sea, not even a gun slit. Protected by the stone and concrete facing the sea, its guns were trained on the beach east and west of it, while gun positions off to either side poured an enfilade of fire down on the Chaudières' position. The men in Gauthier's group realized they had to find a way around the seawall and the blockhouse.

No one factor saved Gauthier and the band of Chauds around him. Some of them, he sensed, believed their religion protected them. Most men in the regiment were devoutly Catholic and no doubt prayed for a way out. The Chauds were also physically strong, many having volunteered from the farms, lumber camps, and mines of rural Quebec. They all spoke French and in the face of so many other English-speaking regiments, as then-reporter René Lévesque[*] noted in Southampton, "these men seemed to be marked with an invisible stamp that made them larger than life."

Gauthier felt the regiment's training also contributed to their survival that day. Weeks of basic training at St-Jerome and advanced training at Valcartier and then months of amphibious rehearsal in England had equipped them with the tools of war-

---

[*] Born in 1922 in Campbellton, New Brunswick, René Lévesque grew up reading and craving to write in his first language, French. When the war broke out he became a temporary wartime employee with Radio-Canada, then went overseas to take a paramilitary job with the American Office of War Information. As D-Day approached, he gathered reports on military preparations on the outskirts of Southampton. Naturally, he was particularly drawn to the francophone soldiers of Le Régiment de la Chaudière. He later became the first Parti Québécois premier of Quebec.

fare and had given their platoons and sections the cohesion and the chemistry to work together. It might even have been the tot of rum the brigadier had issued to all just before the troops shipped out of Southampton the night before. Gauthier believes, however, that what made the difference in those first, fearful moments at the seawall below Bernières was the leadership of the regiment's NCOs.

In particular, the young private remembered a Sergeant Dion, who came upon him and his section pressed up against the wall. During training, Gauthier had never given the man more than a moment's consideration. Dion was simply a senior-ranking NCO who had to be saluted and obeyed out of respect. Suddenly, in action, with the responsibility of thirty men in his hands, Dion earned that respect.

"We can't stay here," Gauthier remembered Dion telling his platoon. "There's a path off to the right. Let's see what we can do with it. Let's go."

Encouraging his small contingent of men all along the seawall, Sergeant Dion came to the west end of the barrier and found a depressed pathway. The Germans had constructed dugouts up from the beach. They had used them as machine-gun positions and for moving their men safely in and out of the blockhouse. The path the Chaudières found was wide enough for a man to pass and it wound its way up from the beach. By now, Dion was leading about a section of Chauds, about a dozen men.

"We'll climb up this path and see what happens," Dion said.

The group's first foray brought a sharp response from a machine-gun position directly ahead of them. The group edged its way forward, eventually close enough to the machine-gun nest to lob in grenades. The explosions silenced the gun, so the rest of Dion's group could move freely to the top of the path. Before them lay the seaside railway track and the coastal roadway beyond. Before long the Chaudières were advancing into the fields through the village of Bernières and by day's end as far inland as Bény-sur-Mer, their D-Day objective.

Perhaps because of the group's experience that day, Gauthier's platoon became an infiltration group within a few weeks. It was ordered to travel exclusively at night, conducting reconnaissance. It probed German positions to find out troop strength and weapon alignment, reporting back before sunrise. Like most infantry units on June 6, the Chaudières suffered losses getting ashore and inland. Gauthier felt fortunate to have survived that first day in Normandy. He also sensed that he had gained an understanding of this war.

"Sergeant Dion was afraid, the same as we were," Gauthier said, "but he had a bit more of something that we didn't have then. It must have been courage."

11 a.m. June 6, 1944—Nan White Beach, France

On paper, Operation Neptune, the assault phase of Operation Overlord, established very clear objectives in Normandy. Overall, the 3rd Canadian Infantry Division was supposed to seize and secure the beach area through sectors Mike on the right flank and Nan on the left, including the villages of Graye-sur-Mer, Courseulles-sur-Mer, Bernières-sur-Mer, and St-Aubin-sur-Mer. Intelligence suggested that the infantry could then move directly inland, so the generals anticipated that the Canadians could next capture an area extending some ten miles inland encompassing the high ground west of Caen astride the main road to Bayeux. In short, the first waves of Canadian troops—the 7th and 8th Brigades—would establish a beach-head at Juno and clear as many of the beachside villages of German troops as possible. As soon as the code word "Catnip" was transmitted back to the waiting landing craft, the second, or reserve, waves, made up of the 9th Brigade, would come through the first waves, secure the inland villages as far as the Caen-Bayeux road, and ultimately reorganize to face an anticipated German counterattack. Speed would be essential.

That last detail, the need for speed, translated into additional physical baggage during the landing for the Stormont, Dundas and Glengarry Highlanders, who came ashore in the 9th Brigade.

"We trained for six months on bloody bicycles," said John McDonald of the Glens. "We had two bicycles each. We had an ordinary civilian bike and then we had the little airborne ones that fold up, collapsible bikes. . . . Once we were in France, we were supposed to ride fast and get to the Carpiquet airport."

John Angus McDonald knew a fair bit about transportation. In 1935, the year after his father died, he had left school in Cornwall, Ontario, to find work at age seventeen. To help support his mother and four siblings during the Depression, he found a job at a bottling works, eventually driving a truck and selling Orange Crush soft drinks on commission. All winter and summer he drove and sold throughout eastern Ontario. He joined the Highlanders right after they mobilized in June of 1940. So did his older brother James and his younger brother Francis, whom the recruiters would not accept until he had put on a bit more weight. An older brother, Donald, later joined the air force.

The three McDonald brothers in the Stormont, Dundas and Glengarry Highlanders excelled at every aspect of their training. John had been an army cadet and was extremely fit from "tossing all those Orange Crush cases on and off the truck," and all three brothers were pretty good marksmen having acquired the skill shooting groundhogs with a cousin's .22 on the farm.

The regiment spent three years in England preparing for the invasion on hillsides, beaches, and roadways, and in woods and swamps, living up to its complimentary moniker, "the sand, dust, and gravel brigade." Then to make things interesting, in early 1944 the Glens' officers integrated bicycle drill with regular marches and manoeuvres, "to test the speed and mobility [of the regiment] in action and to practise the carrying of bicycles in landing craft."

John Angus McDonald was a product of his generation. He worked hard. He felt fierce loyalty to both his family members and his regimental brothers. He volunteered for service immediately, out of a sense of duty to Canada, as if not doing so would be letting down his family and neighbours. If he had a credo, it was contained in his comment "We lived life as it came." During the long lead-up to D-Day, John McDonald met a woman in Manchester, England. They were married in February 1944. When he came ashore with his two brothers and the rest of the Glens at Bernières-sur-Mer on D-Day, John McDonald was a corporal.

"We landed at about eleven a.m.," John McDonald said. "They hadn't been able to clear all the guys off that part of the beach. When I saw half a dozen bodies it struck me that things are going to happen here."

Charles Cline went in as a reinforcement with B Company of the Glens. He was still seventeen, having signed up underage. Naturally, everything he witnessed made a deep impression on him, including every item in his combat kit. As a rifleman he wore an assault jerkin with pockets that contained two Bren gun magazines, two No. 36 grenades, one No. 74 anti-tank grenade, two smoke grenades, one No. 69 grenade, and three bandoliers of rifle ammunition. Besides his socks, towel, gas cape, respirator, ground sheet, and commando knife, he carried two twenty-four-hour ration packs. Each contained a chocolate bar, a block of porridge, a block of liver, pieces of toilet paper, a waterproof case with nine British cigarettes, seasickness tablets, and a vomit bag. The average Highlander pack weighed nearly eighty pounds.

For Cline, the longest-lasting impression was that of his dash ashore: "When the LCA dropped its ramp, I remember running up onto the beach. . . . I saw another landing craft with a man's torso wrapped around the propeller. There were other body parts on the beach. . . . I vomited and cried and tried to figure out what was going on. . . . Nobody who was there came back the same."

Another reinforcement to the Glens was Jimmy Wilson, who came ashore aboard LCI 1709 in the second wave. During training he had specialized in Bren guns, hand grenades, and Projector, Infantry, Anti-Tank weapons (PIATs), and of course, collapsible bicycles. Like all the Glens' bikes, Wilson's had a butterfly nut under the seat and another in the crank case. When the nuts were loosened and the handlebars turned, the bike collapsed on itself so that the two wheels folded together, side by side. The bikes were compact and light. On board the LCI, the regiment had constantly rehearsed loading and unloading them, so that each man could claim his bike in orderly fashion during the landing. As for packing personal effects, the troops proved very innovative.

"Some of the guys put all their belongings in condoms," Wilson said. "Money, rings, wristwatches were dumped in to keep them dry."

Wilson had a calm stomach during the Channel crossing. In fact, he sat back and read a paperback edition of Edgar Allan Poe's *The Murders in the Rue Morgue* on his way over. But when he saw the assault landing craft going in and the heavy shelling of the beaches in front of him, he paused.

"I was standing there at the back of the landing craft, just looking around and thinking, 'You're part of history.'"

Congestion greeted the troops in front of Bernières-sur-Mer. Each minute, the tide continued to rise, reducing the size of the beach. Routes into and out of the town were few and any available roadways quickly clogged with men and equipment disgorged by the steady stream of landing craft arriving in the sector. Carrying their bicycles, the Glens began backing up in front of the seawalls. And with little room to manoeuvre on dry land, the entire 9th Canadian Infantry Brigade suddenly became easy targets for the German artillery and mortars randomly firing into the beachhead. Fortunately, most of the shells exploded out of harm's way. What became abundantly clear to the Glens' rank and file, though, was that their "speedy" form of two-wheeled transportation had become a hindrance rather than an asset, especially as they tried to move quickly through the crowded village.

"Pushing and carrying those damn bikes," John McDonald said, "we knew we were never going to use them. They were just slowing us down. So we dumped them in an orchard. That's the last we ever saw of them."

Meanwhile, residents of the village of Bernières-sur-Mer ventured out of their homes for the first time since the invasion had begun. They shouted and waved at the Canadians. Some unfurled French tricolour flags they had kept hidden throughout the four years of German occupation. John McDonald spoke no French, but one of his platoon mates translated for him that the townsfolk wanted to salute their victory with a drink. Out came bottles of what looked like apple cider.

"It was Calvados, their local drink," McDonald said. "It was hot. We were thirsty and we drank it. It was a liqueur, distilled apple cider, 40 percent alcohol. . . . Before long my head was just bouncing from this drink. It was powerful!"

The Glens had little time to recover. The regiment pushed inland two or three more miles toward the village of Bény-sur-

Mer, where the men would dig in for the night. During his first hours inland, Corporal McDonald witnessed his first combat massacre. In the confusion of attack and counterattack along the roads and hedgerows of Normandy, McDonald's platoon spotted another unit of Canadian troops ambushing a German patrol comprised of motorcycles and a truck carrying a dozen troops. The Canadians nearly wiped out the patrol.

"Bodies were lying all over the road," McDonald recalled. "The driver, the co-driver, and those twelve guys, all knocked off. They looked like they'd just gone to sleep there. Then, there was this one German soldier alive and he's shouting, 'Wasser! Wasser!'

"Jesus, what the hell does he want? We'd been training for four years and all the time we had on our hands, and we'd never been taught one word of German. We didn't know this guy was only asking for water."

The Normandy campaign proved extremely disheartening for John McDonald. In July he saw three Glens accidentally killed by Canadian artillery fire. He barely missed injury himself during the errant RAF bombing of the Stormont, Dundas and Glengarry Highlanders in August. But the death of his younger brother, Francis, from wounds during the push to liberate Caen left him totally "demoralized."

9 a.m. June 6, 1944—Bernières-sur-Mer, France

While citizens in many of the liberated villages of Normandy had reason to celebrate on June 6, for some French families the euphoria was short-lived. Later in the day, tragic news arrived from Caen. Within the precincts of the stone prison there, Gestapo jailers had been holding scores of French Resistance fighters. Since they realized they had no time to transfer the prisoners to camps in Germany, the Gestapo had ordered that

they be eliminated. Many of the prisoners, who had been captured only recently, belonged to local resistance organizations
in the Calvados region. That very morning, eighty of them
were marched from their prison cells and executed by German
firing squads. Then the Gestapo removed the bodies without a
trace.

A month later, when Caen was liberated by the Allies, the
ledge from a prison window was salvaged. The image of a freedom fighter had been etched into the stone. Carved next to the
figure was the emblem of the French Resistance and the date,
June 6, 1944.

Nineteen-year-old Jacques Martin knew some of the French
Resistance fighters in his village of Bernières-sur-Mer. One was
a family friend arrested in April of 1944 and quickly shipped to
Germany, where the man died of typhus. During the night of
June 5 and the early hours of June 6, Jacques had been hiding in
a backyard bunker that he and his father, Paul, had dug when
the Allied bombings began earlier in the spring. In that darkened trench, roughly three yards long and three yards deep, the
Martin family waited out the bombardments, and early in the
morning watched soldiers and vehicles passing back and forth
in front of the entrance to their bunker.

"Suddenly we heard an enormous noise. The ground was
shaking," Jacques Martin said. "We came out of the bunker and
saw an army tank with a huge drum in front with chains that
were rotating and hitting the ground to explode mines. It was
coming right at us and we thought we would be crushed in our
trench."

The commander of the Royal Engineers' flail tank spotted
them in time and veered off in another direction. That was
when father and son decided to venture out into the streets to
find out what was happening. The two set out, Jacques taking in
all the activity and his father pulling a wagon containing what

few belongings he had salvaged from their bombed-out home. Since their yard was within a block of the beach, the Martins soon met the first of their liberators, an officer with the Queen's Own Rifles of Canada.

"Go down to the beach," the officer told them.

"No," said Paul Martin who knew some conversational English. "We are French. We have waited for you for four years. . . . See, I am with my family."

"Go to the beach," the Canadian soldier insisted.

"No. The Germans shells are still falling on the beach," Martin said. "Look, our house has been destroyed. On top of that you want us to be killed?"

The Canadian officer had orders to round up anyone he suspected might not be sympathetic to the invasion forces, so he told Martin and his son that they were now in his custody and began leading them to the Bernières train station for further questioning. Jacques spotted another soldier with a shoulder patch he could read, "Le Régiment de la Chaudière."

"Are you French?" Jacques asked in French.

"Hello," the sergeant replied in kind. "We are French Canadians. We have come to free France."

"Yes, but we are prisoners," Jacques told him.

With that, the jovial expression of the Chaudière sergeant changed to one of concern. He explained to Jacques and his father that his regiment was from Quebec, and that he was a reconnaissance sergeant and would investigate their arrests. Before long, Sgt. Rosaire Gagnon had cleared up the misunderstanding and had freed the Martins. The sergeant led the two civilians back up Rue de la Mer to l'Hôtel Belle Plage, which had been converted from a café hangout for German troops to a communications centre for the Allies. By ten-thirty that morning, the hotel was bustling with British and Canadian photographers, cinematographers, and journalists, all trying to write their latest takes on the invasion at Juno Beach. While the Martins were there, the British released several hundred homing pigeons, to quickly carry messages back to England about the progress of Operation Neptune.

Writing and recording some of his first impressions of the Canadian assault for later broadcast on CBC Radio was French-Canadian war correspondent Marcel Ouimet. In his *actualité* he had painted a word picture of the Chaudières' first encounters with the citizens of Bernières. He described the women showering the troops with flowers and unfurling a multitude of flags: British, American, and the French tricolour. And he told his listeners about the shouts of "Vive le Canada!" and "Vive la France!" that the citizens and soldiers exchanged.

In a subsequent report, Ouimet recounted an interview with one Bernières-sur-Mer citizen, Paul Martin. He preferred not to disclose the Frenchman's identity because Martin's elder son, a former French artillery officer, had been captured early in the war:

"From a Norman I will not name because he has a son imprisoned in Germany," Ouimet's broadcast began, "I learned how it had been impossible for the civilian population to evacuate the area, despite the warnings of the BBC. . . .

"'The Germans forbade us to do so,' my informer tells me. 'And furthermore, for more than a month and a half, all our radio sets were confiscated. . . . But I kept telling my friends that you would be coming. I tried to encourage them because a lot of them had lost hope.'

"I could only admire this man, who once had known wealth, but who was today financially ruined. . . . A man of sixty, straight as the letter 'I,' wearing dirty clothes because he spent the night in a shelter. He had lost everything during the bombardment. . . . But for him the loss didn't mean anything. For four years he had meditated and understood that freedom is even more valuable."

During those later morning hours, Jacques Martin stayed close to the young Chaudière soldier who had helped him and his father regain their freedom. He and Sgt. Rosaire Gagnon were nearly the same age; Gagnon was about twenty. Before the Chaudières pushed inland, Jacques watched Sergeant Gagnon speak with other Bernières townspeople. A member of the Canadian Film and Photo Unit, Captain Ken Bell captured the moment as Gagnon stood near the railway station and regaled the civilians about the part of Canada from which his regiment came and about why his comrades felt compelled to liberate France. Bell's photo was perhaps the last taken of the young sergeant. A week later he was killed by a German sniper further inland near the village of Rots.

"There was an area called the Kill Club," Jacques Martin remembered. "It was a cemetery where about one hundred [Canadian] soldiers were temporarily buried near the blockhouse on the beach. The German prisoners were ordered to wrap the bodies in blankets for burial. . . . There were Queen's Own and Fort Garry Horse and Chaudières."

In the days that followed, a hilltop near the inland village of Bény-sur-Mer became the official Canadian D-Day burial ground. Pte. Osborne Perry, a despatch rider with the Queen's Own Cameron Highlanders of Canada, remembers his "first job was being assigned to burial detail . . . burying the first Canadians at Bény, one hundred and twenty bodies in four-foot graves." In all, 2,043 Canadians would be interred there.

Noon, June 6, 1944—Nan White Beach, France

When Canadian Intelligence Officer Reg Weeks came ashore with the Stormont, Dundas and Glengarry Highlanders, the assault troops already "owned" the beach below Bernières-sur-Mer. The twenty-two-year-old lieutenant landed in water but barely got his feet wet. He had to navigate around a few remaining beach obstacles—Element C, as Intelligence referred to them—and several floating bodies of those assault troops who had not even made it ashore. The scene did not particularly frighten him.

"The thing I remember most was not the ones who had been killed, but those who had gone ashore ahead of me," he said. "There was a look in their eyes I've never seen since . . . a combination of fear, uncertainty, and disbelief all in one heap."

Unlike his infantry mates aboard the landing craft, Weeks didn't have to lug a collapsible bicycle past the seawall and into the village. Instead, he wore his regular survival pack and carried a cloth map sewn into his battledress and a compass disguised as a jacket button. One personal possession he considered an essential part of his gear was a flat, metal cigarette case that he had tucked into the breast pocket of his battledress, "in hopes it might deflect a bullet should it come my way."

He also carried a Sten gun, a weapon notorious for misfiring or jamming.* Before he had ventured very far up the beach that midday, he came across a slit trench in the sand. He pointed the Sten into the trench to fire off a few trial rounds, and the gun jammed. In frustration, Weeks pitched it into the trench, where it promptly began firing on its own. Fortunately, the dancing Sten chopped up the sand and nothing else. The only serious injury Weeks sustained during the landing was a broken nose when he fell face first on the hard ground. The only other casualty on landing was his cigarette case, which likely fell out of his pocket and disappeared into the sand when he took that first tumble.

---

* The Sten gun, named for R. V. Sheppard and H. J. Turpin, the inventors, and *En*gland, was a lightweight 9-mm calibre submachine gun of relative simplicity produced in vast numbers during the Second World War.

When Lieutenant Weeks and his intelligence group got to the house chosen as their divisional headquarters in Bernières, they found it already humming with activity. Maj.-Gen. Rod Keller and a number of his staff officers were busily establishing communications and dealing with such war correspondents as Ross Munro and Ralph Allen. Weeks knew the work ahead would be important inside the new HQ, so he set about finding a suitable spot for his first night's sleeping accommodations. He explored the yard near a stone wall adjacent to the house and among some blooming daffodils, he found soft soil deep enough to dig himself a trench for shelter.

D-Day strategists most feared when and how the Germans would counterattack during the Allied invaders' first hours ashore. Although he was an intelligence officer, Reg Weeks did not know that some of his colleagues in Operation Fortitude were trying to fool the Germans into thinking the main Allied invasion force would attack in the Pas de Calais area. Using full-size inflatable Sherman tanks, artificial landing craft, and fake aircraft, British spoofing specialists had given German reconnaissance the impression of a large military buildup near Dover, in southeastern England. Fortitude's objective was to keep Hitler's strongest forces, the panzers, away from the Normandy beachhead as long as possible.

Fear of the panzers was legitimate. Hitler had decreed that the strength of the Wehrmacht, the German army, be reinforced beginning in November 1943. Fortunately for the Allies, however, of the ten panzer or panzer-grenadier (armoured infantry) divisions in France, only six were battle-ready. In fact, some of the German army's crack armoured divisions remained on other fronts. The 9th and 10th S.S. Panzer divisions were fighting on the eastern front in Russia; the Hermann Göring S.S. Panzers were engaged in Italy; and the Panzer Lehr Division, stationed near Le Mans, had been until recently in action in

Hungary. Another important battle-ready group close by was the 12th S.S. Panzer Division, with its fanatical *Hitlerjugend* (Hitler Youth), just fifty miles from the Normandy beachhead, and the 21st Panzer Division, under Rommel's direct control, in the Caen area. The trick for the Allies, then, had been to keep such tough opposition out of the picture as long as possible.

As it turned out, Lieutenant Weeks was among the first to prove that Operation Fortitude had succeeded. Since he spoke German, soon after he landed in Normandy on D-Day he began conducting interrogations of enemy soldiers captured in and around the Juno beachhead. It wasn't long after June 6 when Weeks interrogated a German sergeant who carried a slip of paper apparently promising him he would have his confiscated wristwatch returned to him at some point. Weeks acknowledged the paper and then interviewed the man for about fifteen minutes, trying to determine his home regiment.

"I asked him his name, rank, and number, which was legitimate," Weeks said. "Then I talked to him a while and he told me quite openly that he was with an armoured division. . . . Here was the first evidence that the Panzers were moving in strength into the invasion area. . . . Days into the invasion, it looked as if the Germans still thought there was going to be another, bigger invasion at Calais and had left the majority of their tougher forces a long way from Juno Beach."

Noon, June 6, 1944—Nan White Beach, France

Initially, where and whom his opposition might be in Normandy had never occurred to Cpl. Gordon Drodge, a wireless radio operator and loader in the 27th Armoured Regiment (the Sherbrooke Fusiliers). After a year and a half of workups on Salisbury Plain in England, he was thrilled to get a chance to fight. Until they received word the Fusiliers would be part of D-Day,

Drodge and his best buddy, Sgt. Jim Parsons, had spent most of their time training and the rest pooling their pay and relying on Parsons's uncanny ability to win dice games.

"Our regiment was finally picked to go ashore in the second wave," Drodge said. "We were told the choice was made on the basis of checking the abilities of gunners, wireless operators, and drivers. They gave us all a test and we were told that we had been picked to go in with the 1st Hussars and the Fort Garry Horse. . . . I think it had something to do with politics too. We were a Quebec unit."

About noon, the Fusiliers made a successful dry landing in support of the 9th Canadian Infantry Brigade, the divisional reserve. Their objective, with the Stormont, Dundas and Glengarry Highlanders, was the airport at Carpiquet, but like the infantry, the Fusiliers also found the beachhead congested in front of Bernières-sur-Mer and the roadways through the village choked with vehicles and people. That's where Corporal Drodge first witnessed townspeople shaving the heads of young Frenchwomen whom they suspected of collaborating with the Germans. Many of the villagers had little to eat, so Drodge and the Fusiliers offered them some of their own canned rations and white bread, "which everybody just sort of stood and looked at in amazement." In return, some of the civilians offered the tank crews sample after sample of Calvados liqueur, which the men eventually mixed with juice to reduce its potency.

"We found that in the vacant spots where ammunition had been, a bottle fits very well," he said. "We got some of this Benedictine. Drink enough of that stuff and we felt terrible."

One other detail crossed Gordon Drodge's mind as he landed in Normandy on June 6, 1944: it was his birthday. He had actually lied about his age when he joined the Canadian Army in Newfoundland three years before; on D-Day he turned nineteen. Corporal Drodge received no birthday present, however, until the next day. During the regiment's advance toward Authie with the North Nova Scotia Highlanders, Drodge's B Squadron encountered stiffer resistance than they had on D-Day. His tank commander had just ordered him to load the Sherman's 75-mm gun. As he bent over to reach for his own shell, a German 88-mm shell pierced Drodge's tank wall, literally putting a crease down his back without breaking the skin. It ricocheted off the radio at the back of the tank and hit the gunner, Cpl. John Kachor, killing him and severely wounding the tank commander with shrapnel. Bruised, in shock, and momentarily blinded by the smoke inside the tank, Drodge found himself otherwise unharmed.

"There was a fire in the radio," Drodge said. "We had an asbestos glove we used for removing hot shells, so I used the glove to smother the fire. . . . The crew commander [Major Mahon] was moaning down on the tank floor, so I took a wad of gauze and bandaged the hole in his arm."

In the confusion, Dusty Rhodes, the driver, along with Jim Parsons and Drodge, managed to turn the tank around and steer it away from the battle. In the rear-echelon area, medics attended to the tank commander and examined Drodge's creased back and bruised arm. Since he had been checked at a regimental aid post, the army documented Drodge's non-life-threatening injury and then mailed his mother a "wounded in action" notice, with no other details. That night, Parsons scrounged some Scotch whisky and the two tank crewmen belatedly celebrated Drodge's nineteenth birthday and his survival at Authie.

"I woke up the next morning with not only a bad back and a bad arm; I also had a bad head."

"A SPLENDID BODY OF MEN"

9:25 a.m. June 6, 1944—Nan White Beach, France

AMONG THE WEAPONS that Lt. Garth Webb carried with him to Juno Beach on D-Day was the inspiration supplied by Gen. Bernard Montgomery. The twenty-five-year-old gun-position officer with the Royal Canadian Artillery (RCA) particularly remembered Monty's lectures and inspection visit in the days just before June 6.

Often portrayed as a cautious general with an excessively prickly ego who was at times abrasive and aloof, Montgomery nevertheless understood the value of good publicity. Just as important, he recognized the value of troops who trusted him. In his signature woollen sweater and beret, the general appeared to favour informality, and all the while expected fierce loyalty from the rank-and-file soldier. Lieutenant Webb recalled both qualities.

"We all went to a theatre meeting with Montgomery about two months before D-Day," he said. "He lectured us, and it's pretty well known that you go in there, you don't cough, you don't make a sound. He's in charge. . . . Later, he inspected our artillery regiments in a big parade square. He's out in the middle and he's lecturing us there. But then he says, 'Around me, move.' And everybody charged in there. He was a very inspiring leader."

Atop a parked jeep and using a loudspeaker, Monty first told the artillery troops to sit down. Once they were settled, he addressed each regimental group for about fifteen minutes. Then he addressed several more groups, as many as five regiments a day, and ultimately spoke to more than 100,000 soldiers in those crucial countdown days. All the while he complimented his soldiers, suggesting "you would not see such a splendid body of men in any other army in the world."

Not that Garth Webb relied completely on Monty's encouraging words to get him ashore at Nan White Beach on D-Day morning. The Queen's University graduate, originally from Calgary, Alberta, remembered both the preparation and the landing as one of the busiest times of his life, so busy that he had time only for the job at hand and certainly no time to be afraid.

From the moment his 14th Field Regiment gave up its traditional 25-pound field-artillery pieces in favour of the Priests, or SPs, the 105-mm guns mounted in pulpit-like fashion atop each self-propelled vehicle, Webb had immersed himself in the retraining. Since the guns were now mounted on Sherman-tank chassis, he had taken special tank-driving courses and then had taught others the same techniques. He had also practised waterproofing the vehicles for the Channel crossing aboard tank landing craft (LCTs). Then, most critical to the run-in to the beach, he had studied and rehearsed the new Fire Plan technique of firing the guns while the SPs were still strapped to the LCTs and sailing in toward the beaches.

"I'm [officer commanding] troops in this landing craft," he said. "So all night long I was working on the planning and handing out 'don't get sick' [anti-nauseant scopolamine] pills. Guys that waited all night wondering, 'Am I going to live through tomorrow?' They had more concern and fear than I did. I was too busy."

It was H-Hour-plus-90 when Lieutenant Webb and the rest of his C Troop landed at Bernières-sur-Mer. By comparison, the 14th Field Regiment's troops of self-propelled artillery enjoyed a relatively orderly and problem-free arrival. German mortars and machine-gun fire inflicted a number of casualties as the RCA landing craft hit the beach, but Webb "waltzed right over it."

Bill Warshick was a signaller who operated wireless radio for the regiment. He remembered coming ashore in an LCT piloted by a Royal Navy man. A veteran of several previous landings in North Africa, Sicily, and Italy, the skipper promised he would land the Canadian gunners and their equipment high and dry. All went well as he navigated the ungainly craft through the obstacles close to the beach. Then, as the ramp went down, it hit an underwater mine, flinging a jagged steel obstruction in the way of the gunners' intended exit.

"The first vehicle just rolled forward," Warshick said, "pushed the obstruction down so all the vehicles and all the men landed safely. . . . The Royal Navy captain kept his word, too. We had maybe three or four inches of water to wade through. . . . He had put his landing craft so high and dry, it was apparently thirty days before they could get it back off the beach."

More lethal than German shore mines and gunfire, it turned out, was something inherent in the 14th Field gun crews' invasion preparations. The tank-like SPs were designed for the efficient delivery of 105-mm shells in battle, whether during the amphibious run-in or on land to support infantry firefights. However, with space in short supply during the landings, each SP came ashore carrying additional arms and ammunition. Slung between each SP's tracks and secured to its chassis, for example, was a sixteen-inch-high "stone boat" containing .303 rifle ammunition. Not a problem during straight-ahead travel, the stone boat seriously reduced the SP's manoeuvrability when backing up or making sharp turns. In addition, the crews had strapped canvas-covered cases full of mortar bombs and land mines to the rear deck of each Priest. Sgt. Wesley Alkenbrack, a twenty-four-year-old gunner with "Dog 4" Troop, recalled the SP's surplus and volatile baggage.

"In the desperate emergencies of the moment and our haste to get clear of the beach and the town," he wrote, "no time or thought was given to relieve us of these deadly loads. And it was in this awkward and perilous condition that we crossed the beach, made our cumbersome way through the breach in the seawall and moved through the town."

Just as the Queen's Own Rifles, the Chaudières, and the Stormont, Dundas and Glengarry Highlanders had run into traffic problems trying to negotiate their way through Bernières-sur-Mer, so the Canadian artillery crews became stuck in crowds of vehicles and swarming citizenry in the village. Alkenbrack recalled that the guns of three batteries, packed nose to tail, slowed to a crawl. Helplessness and anxiety washed over him as he and his fellow gunners sat waiting their turn to move forward through the narrow streets.

The first four SP guns of the RCA batteries finally emerged from the southwest part of the village at about 11:30 a.m. Alkenbrack envied the Chaudière infantrymen who were able on foot to begin probing the orchard of young trees on the outskirts of town. He noted that the height and foliage of the trees would not likely impede crest clearance; that is, his gun would be able to fire shells over the treetops to provide cover for the advancing Canadian troops should it be necessary. The gunners soon discovered that the crest clearance made them targets at the same time.

Four self-propelled guns now moved out from behind a wind-wall, long since erected to protect nearby farm buildings on the outskirts of town. A command-post officer and Lieutenant Webb, the gun-position officer, crouched in the field at the edge of the orchard. They began calculating the aiming mark and plotting the firing line so that all four arriving guns would be in sync at that position. Meanwhile, Art Evans's "Charlie 2" SP moved past the wall first to begin setting up a gun position. Then the officers directed the next three guns into position—Ed Crockett's "Able 3" SP, Bob Sciberas' "Able 4" SP, and Wes Alkenbrack's Dog 4 SP. The Charlie 2 crewmen had almost reached their position when the first German 88-mm shell slammed into them.

"Above the sound of our labouring engines and clanking tracks came the grinding screech of an armour-piercing shell meeting steel at high velocity," Alkenbrack wrote. "As smoke and dust billowed up from the stricken vehicle and the gun crew leapt from the deck to hit the ground, with incredible swiftness the second gun, Crockett's, was struck and similarly abandoned."

Some 700 yards directly ahead of the four Canadian gun crews, strategically sited to cover all exit from the village, the German 88 was deeply dug in with its barrel at ground level and skillfully camouflaged with earth and brush. The gun had been there for some time, but in the excitement and revelry of their new-found liberation the townspeople had neglected to warn the Canadians of its existence. The four Priest crews discovered it the hard way.

With two guns crippled and burning, the 14th Field deployment quickly fell into disarray. Sergeant Alkenbrack's Dog 4 SP pressed on to a firing position, but the stone boat still strung beneath its chassis made a sharp turn impossible. Strangely, although the first two guns had taken direct hits, neither shell explosion had ignited the two guns' extra stone boats or the cases full of mortar bombs and land mines. That quickly changed. The 88's third shell scored a direct hit on Sciberas' gun and it erupted in a massive explosion. The concussion knocked down anyone who was standing and paralyzed all the gunners with shock.

"One moment there was flame," Alkenbrack wrote, "and the next moment revealed the stark and utter disintegration of what had been 30 tons of moving steel, now strewn on the ground like scattered garbage, the gun barrel and bits and pieces of steel plate and the remnants of tracks and heavy castings blown here and there, and not the slightest evidence that six men had stood on the deck of that SP when sudden destruction came."

Every man in Sergeant Alkenbrack's crew was transfixed by the horror of what had just happened. The spell was broken only when the D Troop commander shouted to get Dog 4 out of the line of fire. Not sure that any action could prevent further disaster, but shaken back to his senses by the shouting, Alkenbrack leaped to the front of the vehicle to guide the way. He stared into the ghost-white face of his SP driver, Bruiser Burke, and motioned to him to back up the vehicle. The SP's tracks churned without effect against the stone boat, emitting the grinding squeal of steel on steel. The gun was going nowhere. Burke jerked the tank forward and tried desperately to reverse the SP again, while everyone waited for the next 88 round to strike.

By this time bullets were "sizzling across the field like a swarm of bees" as the stone boats and canvas cases exploded into blazing fires aboard the Charlie 2 and Able 3 gun vehicles. Amid the noise and chaos, a fourth shell from the German 88 glanced relatively harmlessly off the left rear corner of the Dog

4 SP and smashed into the nearby wind-wall. Meanwhile, Lance/Bombardier Buck McDonald from Dog 4's crew had crawled under the SP and hurriedly unhooked the stone boat from beneath the chassis. That allowed Burke, the driver, to quickly back his SP behind the wind-wall.

The German gun fired no more. In the time it took the 88 to fire four rounds into the Canadian guns, the Chaudière infantry had pinpointed the enemy position and overrun it. In the meantime the damage was done. Six gunners had died in the 14th Field's first action above the beach. Five more were wounded. As inspired as the RCA crews had been coming across the Channel to Juno Beach, to know that three of their original eighteen guns and eleven of their fellow gunners were already casualties in the first day's action was very dispiriting to those who remained.

"Everybody knew some of us would be killed," Garth Webb said. "Then the 88 blew up three of our guns and two of the guns, the crews, were all killed. And that was just the first day, the first two and a half hours into the first day. . . . A lot of us wondered, 'What the hell are we going to do?'"

Noon, June 6, 1944—Bernières-sur-Mer, France

As the remaining guns of the 14th Field regrouped in a church courtyard, about three blocks away Lieutenant Webb attended to one of his wounded men, Bill McFeat. All officers had been equipped with medical syrettes, small needles containing morphine. If a medic was not present, the officer could administer a dose of the drug by inserting the syrette just under the skin of a wounded soldier in pain. Just before he jabbed McFeat with the syrette, Webb spotted another man then with the troop, a decorated veteran of the Italian campaign, and consulted him about how to insert the syrette.

"You're pretty experienced," Webb said. "You give it to him."

"No, no. There's nothing to it," the veteran told him. "Just jab it wherever."

McFeat was Webb's first patient. The lieutenant forgot the last step in the process—attaching the used syrette to the wounded man's shirt collar, to prevent overdosing. Webb later learned that when they saw no syrette on McFeat's collar, one or two other members of the troop had given McFeat morphine shots, too, making him "probably the best morphine patient returning to the brigade dressing station."

McFeat's impromptu first aid was the exception rather than the rule on D-Day. The mortality rate during the Second World War was 66 soldiers per 1,000; by contrast, a decade later in the Korean War, thanks to medical advances, only 34 per 1,000 would die. In preparation for the Normandy landings, the Royal Canadian Army Medical Corps organized units of doctors, nurses, and support staff to come ashore as soon as the assault troops established a beachhead. Eventually, RCAMC personnel organized makeshift operating rooms that ran twenty-four hours a day, admitting and treating more than 500 wounded each day and evacuating patients from France twice a week.

In the Normandy battlefields, every regimental aid post (RAP) had its medical officers and NCOs as well as twenty stretcher-bearers, all trained in first aid. Medical staff at the RAP conducted triage. The medical officer in charge and a sergeant would record the names of all casualties and their treatments and dispositions. The staff dealt with emergencies first. The stretcher-bearers applied dressings and splints. Where possible, the RAP staff bandaged and transported those casualties who could travel by field ambulance to a casualty clearing station further behind the lines. Ultimately, if wounded men needed serious surgery and treatment, Allied aircraft or hospital ships transported them back to England.

As complicated as treating limb and internal body wounds proved to be in the field, working with head wounds required special medical teams. Pte. Tony Burns came ashore at Courseulles with such a group, No. 1 Canadian Mobile Neuro-Surgical Unit (CMNSU).

"The saddest head wounds," Burns remembered, "were the ones in which the face and head were sprayed with tiny pellets only skin deep. The patient could maybe talk, but his sight was gone or his face and lips damaged . . . leaving an ugly mess."

One of nine children from a Cape Breton Island family, Burns had come to the medical corps instinctively and out of tradition. His father, formerly an engineer who administered first aid to injured men at a Nova Scotia coal mine, had served overseas in the Royal Canadian Army Medical Corps during the First World War. So, in May 1942, when Tony turned eighteen, he went to Halifax to join the army and particularly to serve in the medical corps. He learned how to operate a Lee Enfield .303 and went out on schemes and route marches, yet when the first opportunity came along to train as an operating room assistant (ORA) he jumped at it. At the Cogswell Street Hospital in Halifax he was immediately exposed to the realities of the operating room.

"They gave me a mask and a pair of rubber gloves," he said, and right away he was front-row witness to "seeing the incisions, the inside of a stomach, the blood, the stopping of bleeding, the sewing up and bandaging. After the successful operation, we all thanked each other." He could hardly wait to tell his father how proud he felt to be part of the Canadian medical corps.

In 1943, Private Burns crossed the Atlantic aboard the *Louis Pasteur* and was immediately assigned to Basingstoke, the neurological and plastic surgery hospital in Hampshire, England. In the next few months, he attended all kinds of surgeries, familiarizing himself with the instruments of his wartime trade:

aneurysm needles, forceps, drills, scissors, retractors, saws, scalp clips, traction tongs, suction tubing, and anesthetic gases. Then, like most Canadians who came ashore after the initial push on D-Day, he still had to wade waist-deep through those last few yards of surf at Juno Beach.

"The first action I witnessed was a German plane heading towards us strafing the beach with bullets," he recalled. "We just stood there in a stupor watching this plane coming at us, until a British [sergeant major] yelled at us to duck. . . . From then on, we knew we were at war."

At No. 1 CMNSU, Private Burns was immediately assigned to work in Courseulles at No. 77 British General Hospital. He worked with C.O. Major W. S. Keith, anesthetist Major R. S. Daymond, surgeon Capt. Norm Delarue, neurologist Capt. Cam Gray, nursing sisters Lieutenant K. E. Zeagman and Lt. Dusty Miller, and a fellow ORA Cpl. Jerry Street. The unit eventually worked in a hospital tent mostly treating the wounded from Canadian outfits.

The work was both physically and emotionally taxing. When Burns and Street received a soldier with a head wound, they had to shave his head despite the victim's writhing. If surgery was required to remove shrapnel from the skull or brain, they assisted the surgeons in cauterizing the bleeding or suctioning the blood while the doctors cut the scalp or used surgical pliers to find and remove the fragments. After surgery the ORAs would cauterize the bleeding again, pour sulphur powder on the wound, and help with suturing and bandaging. In the first month of the unit's operation, Burns recalled that it handled more than 200 cases. Of that number, a dozen or so died. Yet the volume of patients they treated was not what he found most remarkable.

"To my deep surprise, when the wounded soldiers closed their eyes," he said, "they sobbed and asked for their mothers.

Yes, their mothers, whether the seventeen-year-old recruit or the veteran trained officers."

As thorough and dedicated as he was in his work, Pte. Tony Burns became the CMNSU's own first casualty. During one of the unit's busiest days of the Normandy campaign, surgeons, nurses, and the two ORAs laboured feverishly to keep up with the incoming wounded. At about noon, the trailer in which they were working came under enemy fire. One of the explosions nearby capsized an instrument sterilizer full of hot water onto Private Burns, scalding him across his back and arms. The surgeons immediately anesthetized him to treat his burns, but they feared serious infection might set in. Accordingly they arranged to fly him to England.

"I fell into a coma," Burns said. "My eyes were closed. I couldn't move a muscle, but I could hear everything being said. I even felt the chaplain near me giving me last rites."

They shipped Tony Burns back to Basingstoke Hospital where he had trained to become an ORA. Many months later he recovered, and he returned to No. 1 CMNSU, by then with the Canadians fighting in Holland. The unit proved itself so successful in treating head wounds that its staff received numerous awards of merit.

8 a.m. June 6, 1944—Gold Beach, France

Nearly 15,000 Canadians landed on Juno Beach on June 6. As far as Allied strategists were concerned, however, the Canadian Force J of Operation Neptune was a component of the larger British assault force. They considered the 3rd Canadian Infantry Division and the 2nd Canadian Armoured Brigade part of the 70,000-strong British Second Army; Juno Beach was merely the middle sector of three British assault beaches, Sword to the east, Juno in the centre, and Gold to the west.

In the same way, Canadian Lt. Don Kerr suddenly found himself in the middle of a British assault group on the eve of the invasion. "The [British] suddenly needed a signals master, so the day before D-Day I got transferred to go in on Gold Beach."

Kerr's first language was French. He was born in Montreal and later moved with his family to Toronto, where he attended the University of Toronto Schools. There he enrolled in the UTS cadets, where the rifle drill, marching, and discipline invigorated him. In 1939 Bell Telephone hired the young man to repair telephone lines, experience the army would exploit when Kerr enlisted the next year. His training led him into the Royal Canadian Corps of Signals (RCCS). By 1944 he was overseas preparing a fifty-four-man Canadian line section for D-Day.

His signals troops learned everything they needed to know about communications—from placing poles to stringing wire to troubleshooting telephone systems—and on top of that they all learned waterproofing. For two weeks, Kerr rigorously drilled each of his four line crews to seal their jeeps and trucks from bumper to bumper. By the time the signallers had finished their training, a two-man crew could waterproof an entire vehicle in less than three hours. The D-Day strategists gave waterproofing top priority, believing that when the signals group went ashore at Juno Beach, the men would land in sea water up to their chins. On June 5 the whole game plan changed. Lieutenant Kerr and one of his RCCS sections were quickly transferred to the British Force G landing group. Kerr's dozen-man section and their eight waterproofed vehicles would now go ashore at Arromanches on Gold Beach.

"After all this waterproof training, of course, we could have driven factory-made vehicles off the landing craft," he said. "They never even got their axles wet."

While Kerr was ready for the deep water he never encountered, he was not ready for the overwhelming noise, the destruction, and the confusion of war. The sky seemed alive with falling shells, the water was churned up by landing craft and vehicles, and the sands lying ahead of him heaved with gunfire and bombs exploding. In those fearful few minutes, Kerr said he truly saw his life pass before him. Orders and instinct told him and his line section to race as quickly as possible off the landing craft and up the beach. Training told them otherwise.

"You can't drive fast in the sand," Kerr had warned his men. "If you gun it in the soft sand, the first thing you know you'll be grinding the sand under you and you'll just stay there. Imagine you're driving in a snowstorm in Canada. Drive in third gear, nice and slow. They're going to shoot at you whether you're doing fifty miles an hour or fifteen."

With his line section safely ashore and convoying for cover, Kerr then got on his means of transportation, a Norton motorcycle, and with head down began making his own way up the beach. He stopped next to a jeep with a British captain slumped in the driver's seat. The dead man had taken a sniper's bullet through the head. Hearing the "Keep moving" order in his head, Kerr paused only long enough to gently lift the captain from the driver's seat, stow the Norton quickly in the back of the jeep, and drive off. Soon the Canadian signals section had rendezvoused above the beach and taken cover in the wooded areas south of the village of Arromanches. Kerr's entire section had survived its baptism of fire.

Their luck ran out sooner than they expected after that. In the next few days, Kerr's signals group rejoined the rest of its Canadian regiment and commenced operations, advancing toward Caen. They installed land-communication lines between infantry and artillery batteries and between divisional headquarters and brigade headquarters. Of necessity, the signals crews often found themselves perilously close to front-line combat. On one memorable occasion, Don Kerr said his signallers were operating within a few hundred yards of the fighting. Suddenly, he heard bombs exploding close by. He looked up to see coloured smoke in the distance and recognized some of his men running away from it.

"What the hell's going on?" Kerr shouted to them.

"Look up!" the man exclaimed, pointing skyward at incoming bombers. "They're bombing us!"

As part of Operation Tractable near Falaise that day, Bomber Command had despatched 417 Lancasters, 352 Halifaxes, and 42 Mosquitoes to strike six targets at 2 p.m. Seventy-seven of the aircraft bombed short of their targets and hit Allied troops. Under orders issued by SHAEF, one of the recognition signals the Allied troops were to use to identify themselves to friendly aircraft was yellow smoke or flares. Remarkably, neither SHAEF nor Allied Expeditionary Air Force headquarters had notified the RAF, RCAF, or Bomber Command of the procedure. In fact, Bomber Command had, until then, used yellow smoke itself to mark enemy targets. So, the British and Canadian bombers misinterpreted the yellow smoke Allied units burned while under attack as target, not friendly-troop, identification.

"We buried twenty-two guys that afternoon," Kerr said, while in total 65 Canadians died, 241 were wounded, and another 91 became missing-in-action statistics. Don Kerr summed up the work of his comrades: "We didn't shoot anybody. We didn't liberate anything. We just did our job and did it well."

Noon, June 6, 1944—English Channel

Several hours had passed since HMCS *Prince David* and HMCS *Prince Henry* had participated in Operation Neptune. After their early-morning role, off-loading hundreds of assault troops onto Juno Beach, the Canadian troopships and their crews had one final duty to carry out: they awaited the return of landing craft with D-Day wounded. Beginning about midday, *Henry* took fifty-six aboard and *David* fifty-eight. Two physicians, Dr. John Beggs and Dr. Paul Schwager, worked aboard *Prince David*.

"Around noon, landing craft came by bringing casualties," Schwager wrote. "They were [British] Royal Marine commandos. . . . in spite of being wet, dirty, chilled, and in severe pain, not one of them complained."

Getting the wounded aboard proved more complicated than expected. Of necessity, during invasion exercises, training had concentrated on getting the assault troops over the side and into the landing craft rather than on receiving casualties. And since the craft ferrying the injured troops had not originated from *David*, the ship's crew could not simply latch onto the craft to hoist it and its cargo of wounded aboard. They had to improvise. Able Seaman John Gorsline said he was detailed to help out. The crew ultimately secured the wounded Marines in wire baskets, which were held horizontal as each man was raised to the ship's main deck and transferred to sick bay.

"All types of wounds were encountered," the doctor wrote, "including seven abdominal, five penetrating chest wounds, and four neck wounds. By far the greatest number were extremity wounds. . . . One Marine had over 100 of them. One soldier with multiple gunshot wounds of the head failed to regain consciousness and died in spite of shock-therapy given."

Schwager worked rapidly to clean wounds, slow bleeding, and ease pain among the wounded men; he also noted the enthusiasm of *Prince David*'s crew. Each sailor seemed to voluntarily adopt a patient and monitor his pulse, keep track of his morphine doses, and report his progress back to the overworked doctors. By early afternoon, the troopship received orders to steam at top speed back through the Channel's mine-swept approach lanes, straight for Southampton. Gorsline recalled that as the *David* began to move away, all on board were shaken by a sudden jolt.

"There was a hell of an explosion," according to Gorsline. At the time, he was at his locker, seconds away from a passageway that led to the main deck outside. "If there's any explosion and you feel the concussion, you wonder, 'Is it us or somebody else?' You're never quite sure. But in the time it took me to go from my locker to the after-gun deck, I looked out and saw a minesweeper going down about four hundred yards astern of us. . . . It was disappearing, going down headfirst and its propeller was still going around."

As had been the order of the day, *David* carried on without stopping. Gorsline later found out the culprit was probably a floating mine that had bumped into the minesweeper; the ship's onboard magazine of shells, in the bow or bottom of the vessel, had torn the ship apart in one massive explosion. From a crew of about eighty, only three men in the bridge area were thrown clear by the explosion and survived the sinking. It was the only vessel that Gorsline saw sink on D-Day.

By about nine o'clock, around dusk and a mere twenty-four hours after HMCS *Prince David* had departed Southampton for Juno Beach on June 5, the ship redocked in England. Port authorities must have been expecting the hospital ship *St. David*, because the Canadian troopship found a huge convoy of ambulances lined up to receive the wounded onshore. Also in the mooring area, hundreds of American troops stood waiting to board ships and landing craft bound for the D-Day beaches. Dr. Schwager noted that for the Americans, watching the procession of scores of "patients dangling in stretchers . . . presented quite a gruesome sight."

Gorsline faced the anxious Americans as well. This time he had been detailed as a stretcher-bearer, carrying the wounded Marines down gangways to the waiting ambulances.

"What's it like over there?" one of the American soldiers asked him.

At first Gorsline hesitated, but gave the man the only truth he felt he could offer. "It's noisy" was all he said. To himself, he summed up his experience as so many did: "It had been a very exciting day."

Evening, June 6, 1944—Bernières-sur-Mer, France

For officer Garth Webb of the Royal Canadian Artillery, June 6 had also been a long and busy day, from enduring a rough Channel crossing to landing under fire on Juno Beach to tangling with German 88-mm gunners above the beach the same morning. The young lieutenant's introduction to war had been thorough. The first twelve hours of the Normandy campaign had tested his entire 14th Field Regiment to its marrow.

At day's end, however, things reverted to a routine that every soldier, rookie, or veteran understood—digging in for the night. Each took his trenching shovel and excavated a foxhole or slit trench deep enough to keep himself out of the way of incoming gunfire or exploding shells. If he collaborated with a section mate, he might build it long and wide enough for one man to sleep while the other stood watch. As his troop of guns formed a diamond configuration and dug in, Lieutenant Webb remembered that a Canadian not connected to the 14th Field had approached him. It was Captain Ken Bell, still-photographer with No. 2 Canadian Film and Photo Unit.

"Okay if my sergeant and I sleep in this gun position?" Bell asked.

"Sure," said Webb, tossing him a shovel, "but you'll have to dig your own trench."

Captain Bell chose what seemed the most protected spot in the area, right in the centre of the gun formation. Bell had come ashore that morning with the 9th Canadian Infantry Brigade. Like all members of the CFPU, he was a volunteer, trained and ready to fight if necessary, but primarily he would record on film indelible images of Canadians battling their way through France throughout that Norman summer. He would also find civilians eager to give him personal snaps of life during the German occupation.

"The experience of fighting in western Europe . . . for me, began on D-Day," the photographer later wrote. He never thought of himself as a hero getting those dramatic shots by the hundred, but he considered "my Rolleiflex camera" his principal weapon throughout the campaign.

D-Day had begun for American and British troops very much like it had for the Canadian invasion forces.

About midnight on June 5, members of the 1st Canadian Parachute Battalion jumped with the British 6th Airborne Division into drop zones to secure the left flank. During those first hours in France, the Canadians successfully captured their assigned bridges east of the invasion beaches, while the British units took care of their appointed bridges and then set out to destroy or neutralize the coastal battery at Merville. Ultimately, the 6th Airborne had orders to secure the area between the rivers Orne and Dives and to operate defensively to delay any movement of enemy reserves east or southeast of the invasion beaches. Of all the Allied divisions fighting in Normandy on D-Day, the British 6th Airborne proved the most successful in seizing and holding its intended ground. There wasn't one objective that it failed to take.

When the joint British and Canadian paratroop effort was about two hours old, two airborne divisions of American paratroopers began dropping into the eastern side of the Cotentin Peninsula to secure the right flank of the invasion area. The 82nd and 101st Airborne divisions sustained heavy casualties as they hit the ground, but by the evening of their first day in

France, the American paratroopers had secured much of the territory between Ste. Mère-Eglise and Carentan.

By the time Canada's J Force began landing assault troops at Juno Beach, just before eight o'clock, American infantrymen had been storming ashore at Utah and Omaha beaches for nearly ninety minutes. Of all the seaborne assaults, the American U Force, consisting of the U.S. VII Corps with the U.S 4th. Infantry Division, met the least resistance that morning at Utah Beach. Effective pre-invasion bombing had softened beach defences and by evening the Americans had established a substantial beachhead. Those assault troops landing with O Force, however, had a tougher time of it. At Omaha Beach, the U.S. V Corps and the U.S. 1st Infantry Division faced some of the strongest German defences and higher ground than at any other invasion area. The Americans at Omaha had to fight desperately just to maintain a foothold, and even after a full day's fighting held a beachhead only 2,000 yards deep.

On the right and left flanks of the main Canadian assault at Juno, the rest of the British Second Army landed at approximately the same time. West of Juno, the 50th British Infantry Division came ashore as G Force at Gold Beach. They experienced much the same landing conditions and progress as did the Canadians, penetrating to just short of the Bayeux–Caen highway and linking up with the 3rd Canadian Infantry Division by nightfall. There was, however, no link-up between the British at Gold and the Americans at Omaha by day's end.

Similarly, to the east of Juno, where S Force landed at Sword Beach, German resistance had slowed progress of the British 3rd Infantry Division, whose objective was to seize the city of Caen, but achieving this quickly was now out of the question. By the end of fighting on D-Day, no contact had been made between the British Sword sector and the Canadian Juno beachhead. Making matters worse, the British troops had faced an afternoon counterattack on their western flank from the 21st Panzer Division, and the German commander claimed that one group of his tanks had even reached the sea at Lion-sur-Mer.

When full darkness fell over Normandy, at about 10 p.m., Canadian, British, and American assaults had put nearly 175,000 men ashore. Total losses on D-Day, including fatalities, wounded, and prisoners, amounted to about 9,000 men. From the American airborne sectors in the eastern Cotentin Peninsula to the British airborne holdings east of the rivers Orne and Dives, the Allied invasion front occupied about fifty-five miles of Normandy coast. A ten-mile gap (with the exception of the cliffs desperately held by the U.S. 2nd Ranger Battalion atop Pointe-du-Hoc) lay between Omaha and Utah beaches. Another seven-mile stretch between Utah and Gold beaches also remained unoccupied by Allied troops. And a three-mile gap between Juno and Sword beaches separated British and Canadian troops on the extreme left flank. The widest beachhead was only six miles (at Juno), and the narrowest (at Omaha) was less than one mile.

On the other hand, by sunset on June 6, 1944, at every Allied landing point in Normandy, Hitler's Atlantic Wall had been breached. The German defence system that had consumed thousands of tons of concrete and hundreds of thousands of reinforcement rods, and had taken four years, nearly round-the-clock, to construct—a latter-day Maginot Line—had been penetrated and overrun in a day, in some spots within a matter of hours. German infantry and armoured divisions still held the territorial advantage even though they would be fighting a defensive action. But their intricate network of fixed fortifications, reinforced pillboxes and bunkers, extensive trench systems, communication lines, and artillery emplacements—their first line of defence on the western front—was largely kaput.

TUG OF WAR

Midday, June 6, 1944—off Île de Vierge, France

N O QUESTIONS were asked more frequently on D-Day than "Where are the panzers?" In the air: "Where's the Luftwaffe?" And at sea: "What happened to the German navy?" With all the dire predictions that had preceded June 6—losses of two-thirds of the invasion fleet, half the airborne troops, several thousand Canadian assault troops—the absence of German air and naval forces, particularly near the invasion beaches, was conspicuous, to say the least. Conspicuous, yet no accident.

Aside from the general element of surprise the Allied forces enjoyed along the Normandy coast, Canadian naval groups carried out several safety measures that ensured the seaborne invasion would not be molested. Operation CA established a series of naval protective screens at the eastern and western entrances to the English Channel. Some forty ships organized into six escort groups, two of them Canadian, were assigned the task of preventing U-boat penetration across more than 56,000 square miles of sea stretching from the Île de Vierge on the northwestern French coast to a point in the Atlantic south of Ireland. Five Canadian frigates, including HMCS *Waskesiu*, comprised Escort Group 6 patrolling the westernmost waters of the Channel. George Devonshire, torpedo man aboard *Waskesiu*, had first-hand U-boat combat experience. He operated the frigate's Hedgehog (mortars) the night *Waskesiu* caught and sank *U-257* a few months before D-Day.

"The submarine was earlier reported on the surface trying to attack a convoy," Devonshire wrote in his diary. "We attacked with Hedgehog first, then made two attacks with depth charges. The sub was damaged and she finally broke the surface ahead of us. . . .

"We illuminated the target with star shells and searchlights and commenced firing. . . . The submarine crew struggled to get out of the conning tower and from the deck hatches. Most were killed by our fire. The survivors were the ones who stayed below until after we checked fire and those lucky enough to leave the sub just before she sank. We saved four of them by helping them up the scramble nets. . . . The rest died by our gunfire, drowning or exposure. . . . We could not see them in the dark, but I could hear them calling out as we got underway."

Waskesiu's job as part of Escort Group 6 proved less hazardous but no less intense. Along with frigates *Outremont, Cape Breton, Grou*, and *Teme*, Devonshire's ship and crew patrolled the assigned western approaches to the Channel from June 3 through D-Day. From his action station at the Hedgehog located on the fo'c'sle of the frigate, Devonshire recalled the relatively calm seas and clear skies. Throughout June 6, while he was constantly on the alert, he saw only Allied aircraft, with their familiar black and white invasion stripes. Nonetheless, the escort group considered any naval contact in the Channel hostile and fired mortars and depth charges at the slightest indication of U-boat presence.

"We killed thousands of fish," Devonshire wrote, "rather than take a chance."

Ashore in Normandy, the strategy to keep the panzers from action on D-Day had consumed the 1st Canadian Parachute Battalion and the aircraft that delivered the paratroopers to the Drop Zone east of the rivers Orne and Dives. Keeping the German defenders off balance also preoccupied most of Bomber Command's operations overnight on June 5 and throughout the day of June 6. Russell McKay piloted one of 1,300 bombers to German targets in France those two nights. He remembered reading Gen. Dwight Eisenhower's "We will accept nothing less than full Victory" despatch to all members of the Allied Expeditionary Force on June 5. Then he and the rest of his No. 420 (RCAF) Squadron joined a sortie to bomb German coastal batteries at Houlgate, on the left flank of the invasion beaches.

McKay's Halifax III took off from the station at Tholthorpe in Yorkshire just before 2 a.m. Somehow, these operations seemed more critical than most. While he always wore his air-force blues and his Canada shoulder flash with pride, McKay recalled that the nose art on the panel below his cockpit made him feel particularly patriotic on these nights. His ground crew had painted a cartoon character of the day, a large ape named Alley Oop, swinging a club, as well as the crew's nickname for their aircraft, "Xterminator." More important, they had also painted a prominent Canadian maple leaf.

"This was no ordinary op," McKay wrote. "It was special. We were in direct support of our army. We had to do better than our best to help them get a toe-hold on the beaches."

Back at Tholthorpe by 6:30 on D-Day morning and running on little or no sleep, McKay's crew was sent up again during the day with sights set on a bridge at Coutances, France. The enthusiasm and precision of Xterminator's crew was typical of the station. The blackboard on the wall of the operations room showed bombers from No. 420 Squadron and its sister

No. 425 Squadron taking off and landing within minutes of each other.

Flying toward the Continent, McKay reported seeing so many ships that "one could step from ship to ship to France." As soon as his crew had successfully bombed the bridge at low level and turned for home, the Halifax met another armada of American B-17 Flying Fortresses with their navigation lights on, looking "like a Christmas tree," bound for Normandy. While his final entry on D-Day brims with pride over the BBC report describing "one of the greatest military feats in history," it is also punctuated by the ironic conclusion ". . . and so to bed. Our losses were very light—only ten aircraft missing."

7 p.m. June 6, 1944—Keevil, England

As it had begun, the D-Day invasion in the skies closed with a glider lift into Normandy, inland of the beaches. The evening airborne operation, code-named "Mallard," launched 256 gliders full of paratroops and stores to reinforce the 6th British Airborne Division, which included the 1st Canadian Parachute Battalion. Fifteen squadrons of fighter aircraft assembled to escort the multi-engine tug planes and the Horsa and Hamilcar gliders they towed to landing zones (LZ) in the farmland north of Ranville and between Ouistreham and Caen.

Tugging his allotted glider to France on the evening of June 6 was, in fact, Flying Officer Walter Schierer's second major sortie of D-Day. Just after one a.m. earlier the same day, he and his five-man crew had flown their "J for Jig" Stirling to a Drop Zone near Caen. In the dark, they had safely dropped twenty British paratroops and about dawn returned to their station at Keevil in south-central England.

"I was coming back when the Americans were going in," he said. "They were dropping gliders in Cherbourg when I turned for England. And their stream still hadn't cleared the English coast when I arrived back in England. . . . It was the greatest armada I'd ever seen."

Had the army not lost track of him, Walter Schierer might well have gone ashore in Normandy aboard an infantry landing craft. Born and raised on a mixed farm outside Ponoka, Alberta, he finished high school in the mid 1930s, travelled with his family in the United States for a while, worked his way up from baker to assistant chef at a hospital back home, and in 1940 decided to volunteer for the army before the army conscripted him. But what he really wanted was to join the air force. The problem he and his buddy Milton Gilchrist faced was how to get out of the army.

"All we have to do is put on civilian clothes," Schierer said, "walk into the air force–recruiting station, and join."

"That won't work," Gilchrist said. "They'll cross-check your name."

"What'll we do?"

"Why not change our names?" Gilchrist suggested.

So each man borrowed the name of a real person from his past. They both chose men whom they knew were visually impaired and would never have been accepted into the services, let alone the air force. Gilchrist became Leading Aircraftman Ganzer while Schierer became LAC Robert Holmes. Both men went through the entire British Commonwealth Air Training Plan in Canada under their assumed names, until they graduated and received their wings in October 1942. That was when Schierer's conscience got the better of him. He confessed to his commanding officer and legally changed his identity from Flying Officer Bob Holmes to Flying Officer Walter Schierer before going overseas that winter. Throughout 1943, Schierer built up his flying hours doing operational training and piloting various aircraft from stations around the United Kingdom.

He was finally sent to a heavy conversion unit and learned to fly the four-engine Short-manufactured Stirling bomber.

"They were a terrific aircraft," Schierer said. "When we were doing drops of supplies for the French Underground, we had an air speed that was superior to either the Halifax or the Lancaster. Stirlings were faster at lower altitudes."

Stirlings also turned out to be the best-powered aircraft for tugging Horsa gliders. Beginning in February 1944, Flying Officer Schierer flew more tugging exercises than just about anything else, sometimes three lifts a day. It was clear that, in addition to the frequent supply drops he made that winter and spring, tug missions would become his key function as an invasion plan evolved. During those months, D-Day planners began pairing tug pilots and glider pilots. Schierer was teamed up with a nineteen-year-old glider staff sergeant in the British Army, Fred Sampson.

"We met in a briefing room," Sampson said, "I thought his name was Bob."

While the confusion about Walter Schierer's name followed him right up to D-Day, Fred Sampson's history was equally revealing of him. A product of a grammar school in Brighton, England, Fred had run away from home at age fourteen and taken a job as an attendant aboard the Pullman trains assisting in the evacuation of children from London. He too had risen in the hospitality business, supervising the staff of a forty-room hotel on England's south coast when he was only fifteen. During the Battle of Britain, in 1940, he decided he would join the forces. He had gone to a recruiting office in Worthing, West Sussex. He was very tall, six foot three inches, but still only seventeen years old.

"Date of birth?" asked the recruiter.

"May 16, 1923."

"You're too young."

"How old do you have to be?"

The man said he had to be eighteen.

So Sampson left the army-enlistment office, walked around the block, approached the same recruiter a few minutes later, and announced, "I made a mistake. I was born in 1922. I'm eighteen," and he was immediately signed up.

He joined the Royal Sussex Regiment, and, like Schierer, had always wanted to be in the air force, in part because his father had flown with the Royal Flying Corps in the First World War. He eventually got his chance as a corporal in the Glider Pilot Regiment in 1942. The training proved rigorous (every order had to be carried out in double-quick time); the instruction was comprehensive (recruits learned engineering, gunnery, mortars, and parachute-jumping); and the discipline bordered on the neurotic (everybody slept in tents, yet had to have a sharp crease in his trousers the moment he got up in the morning). This was the Glider Pilot Regiment's method of weeding out the weak and ultimately creating "the total soldier" to fulfill any role required of him in the front line once the pilot landed his glider.

"I even used to do my own needlework," he said. "So when I got my wings [in August 1943], I sewed them on myself. My wings had to be perfect. My [sergeant] stripes had to be perfect. Everything had to be perfect."

Staff Sergeant Sampson's drive for perfection, whether innate or instilled during training, probably saved his life on more than one occasion. It certainly paid off during the series of exercises leading up to D-Day. Each was code-named: "Exercise Bizz One," "Exercise Sailor," "Exercise Exeter." The regiment even performed one in front of the royal family. The one Sampson considers himself fortunate to have survived, however, was the mass nighttime landing at Netheravon in Wiltshire, southern England. No lights were permitted during "Exercise

Gunner One" as four squadrons conducted a tug-and-cast-off exercise at one o'clock in the morning. More than 200 tug planes and gliders converged on the historic Salisbury Plain aerodrome that night. Then the winds suddenly shifted and only two of the four squadrons were notified and altered their courses to compensate. As a result, half the gliders found themselves racing head on toward the other half across the moonlit sky.

"You could suddenly see other gliders coming at you," Sampson said. He resorted to a quick evasive manoeuvre and "I got down quickly. . . . Every few seconds the silence was broken when you heard the splintering of wood, thirty or forty gliders crashing into each other. . . . A lot of casualties that night; I think seventeen died."

Perhaps a reflection of Sampson's skill as a pilot, but as much for fun, his co-pilot, Frank Powell, had the nickname "Shytot" painted on the fuselage of their Horsa. For the evening mission on June 6, Staff Sergeant Sampson would fly his glider loaded with a 6-pounder anti-tank gun, a padre, his jeep and trailer, a signals officer, and five troops. His four-and-a-half-ton Horsa, fully loaded, weighed eight-and-a-half tons. Personally, Sampson carried five francs—so-called escape money—a silk map sewn inside his uniform, a state-of-the-art Swiss watch, an American carbine, a rucksack with survival gear and grenades, and, contrary to the Geneva Convention, a fixed-blade commando knife strapped to his thigh.

By June 1, Sampson had been confined to quarters at the Keevil station, where all the glider crews watched movies and surveyed maps and models of the landing zone. Among other things, reconnaissance photography revealed an LZ feature that caused Sampson some sleepless nights. As part of their ground-defence system, the Germans had erected anti-glider poles, which the Allied airmen nicknamed "Rommel's asparagus." Pilots were told that these wooden poles, about the height and width of telephone poles, filled many of the open fields north of Caen. They were also informed that the British and Canadian paratroops already on the ground would have destroyed them by the time the gliders arrived late on D-Day. Sampson and the other glider crews absorbed these details under a veil of absolute secrecy.

"A military policeman went to the toilet with us," he said, "because we weren't allowed to talk to anybody, not even our tug crew, about the mission. . . . Even my tug pilot [Schierer] didn't get a briefing of our lift until he got back from his early-morning mission just in case he got shot down and taken prisoner."

Meanwhile, F/O Walter Schierer had wakened from a few hours' sleep. He had attended his briefing for the new op. About midday a driver transported him to the flight line where his Stirling tug plane was being bombed up, or prepared, for the evening operation, which he was about to discover involved more than simply towing Sampson's glider over the landing zone.

"Boy, I wouldn't want to be flying this one tonight," the driver told him.

"Why not?" Schierer asked innocently.

"This guy's going to be carrying twenty-six canisters of gasoline in his bomb bay."

H-Hour for Operation Mallard takeoff was seven o'clock. When it was his turn, Schierer taxied his J-for-Jig Stirling to the centre of the runway. With the one-inch-thick hemp tow line (containing an intercom for cockpit-to-cockpit communication) already attached to Sampson's Horsa, Schierer slowly picked up speed. He held off full throttle until a green light on the runway signalled that the tow line was taut and the glider was actually in tow. Keevil station had two miles of runway, which gave the pair plenty of time to get airborne. Presently, forty-three tug-plane-and-glider combinations began to rendezvous and form up over southern England for the trip to Normandy. It would be daylight until well after the operation was complete, two hours later.

Schierer levelled off his Stirling at 3,000 feet, towing at about 165 mph. The formation crossed the Channel three abreast and about 500 feet apart. Both Schierer and Sampson described the weather as clear and the winds calm. Closer to the invasion beaches, the formation dropped to under 1,000 feet. Because it was still daylight both pilots noticed people below looking up at the approaching aircraft. They also took in the carnage of the day's battle for the beachhead. Minutes after passing over the coastline, at about 800 feet, Sampson spotted his landing zone and prepared to release his Horsa from the tow line.

"Casting off," he said into the intercom. "Cheerio!"

"Good luck, Sammy," came back from Schierer just before he disconnected.

Sampson drifted slightly below the tug plane and looked down to plot his glide path. In the instant he looked away, however, the sky ahead of him suddenly filled with an unexpected obstacle: the first of the twenty-six containers of gasoline were falling and their parachutes were opening directly in Sampson's glide path. Apparently, Schierer's bomb-aimer, anxious to complete the second phase of the mission, had opened the Stirling's bomb-bay doors and released all of the forty-gallon canisters. Both they and their chutes blossomed open right in front of Sampson's glider. He had no choice but to dive and bank away from the falling payload. In seconds, his Horsa had dropped to less than 200 feet above the landing zone.

Then Sampson saw them: Rommel's asparagus dead ahead. The wooden anti-glider poles completely filled the field in which he was to land. Despite the Horsa's speed, Sampson had very little altitude within which to manoeuvre. He stared at the poles erected in perfectly straight rows, "like lines of German soldiers," and figured there was just enough space between them for the Horsa glider's fuselage to fit comfortably. Sampson would have to set the Horsa down between two lines of poles even while he realized the poles would shear off his wings as he landed. Then he spotted the other feature the recce photos had not shown: wires were also strung between the poles. The next instant, the Horsa's fuselage and wings were stretching and snapping the wires like the strands of a spider's web.

"I'm pulling back [on the control column] to drop the fuselage into the gap," Sampson said, "when I see one pole right in the middle of the lane. Who's the bloody fool who put that one there? I burst out laughing and my second pilot, Powell, thought I'd gone off my head. I thought if the poles are lined up perfectly this way, they must be lined up if I go forty-five-degrees. I kicked rudder to the right forty-five degrees and went down between the poles the other direction."

When the racket of the Horsa wings disintegrating and the pole wires breaking finally stopped, Staff Sergeant Sampson's Shytot was down, its fuselage perfectly in line between two sets of poles and, more important, (except for the wings) perfectly intact. Within minutes, Sampson's passengers had removed the rear section of the glider and were able to drive the jeep, the anti-tank gun, and their remaining equipment out of the fuselage without delay. It was just after nine o'clock and the Horsa was on target and on time. As he made his own getaway in the direction of the beach, Sampson no doubt recalled his close call at Netheravon and his sleepless nights inside the security wire at Keevil.

"The reason I didn't sleep any of those nights," he said; "I wondered if, on the mission, I was going to be a coward."

He soon found a hedgerow and dug a slit trench in which to hide from German patrols during the night. Again, he slept very little. The next morning, as he made his way back toward the beaches, however, he came across the bodies of two fellow glider pilots from the same mission. Both had been shot. Of the 240 glider pilots on Operation Mallard, 39 died. Still, the RAF planners considered the operation "singularly successful" since 95 percent of the gliders had reached their landing zones.

The statistical assessment of the mission omitted the details of F/O Walter Schierer's return trip to Keevil station that evening. Unlike his relatively trouble-free paratroop drop in the early hours of D-Day, his way home from the tug operation proved as gruelling as any the twenty-five-year-old pilot had faced. Much as Sampson had expected that the paratroops would have taken care of the anti-glider poles, Schierer believed that the territory he had to cover heading back toward the coastline was firmly in Allied hands. He did not expect to encounter any hostile ground fire.

Following the premature gas-canister drop, Schierer maintained his 800 feet of altitude and then manoeuvred his Stirling just to the right of his wing commander to fly in formation back to England. Their flight path took them across the coastal village of Lion-sur-Mer, and directly over the steeple of the village cathedral. Sensing that his wing commander had not left enough room for both aircraft to pass comfortably to the left of the obstruction, Schierer veered to the right of it, and directly into the path of a lone German anti-aircraft gun positioned on the right side of the steeple.

"Go down, right!" shouted Sergeant Seedhouse, the Stirling's rear gunner.

Schierer took every direction his gunner gave him as he

threw the bomber around the sky, trying to evade the cannon fire from below.

"Now up, left," Seedhouse ordered.

Despite his quick reactions, however, the pilot could not quite remove the bomber from the enemy fire and J for Jig took a raking fire along its port side, including several shots into its outer port engine. Sadly, the Stirling immediately astern and to Schierer's right failed to recognize the sudden threat in time, too.

"He just came right along into the same line of fire," Schierer said. "The [German] gunner must've killed the pilot, because the plane gradually rolled over, left wing down, and went straight into the sea. Everyone was lost."

Schierer's troubles continued out over the water. Several of the remaining Stirlings in the squadron saw Schierer take the cannon shots in the engine and they moved in around him as he limped back across the Channel. He struggled to keep the aircraft straight and level, figuring it better to bail out over friendly territory than to ditch in the sea. He managed to fly directly north for the British coast and straight home to Keevil. Only when he throttled back on his final approach did the stricken outer port Hercules engine refuse to respond. He shut it down and landed on three engines.

"When we got down and looked, there were one hundred and forty-two bullet holes in the plane," Schierer said. "The anti-aircraft shells had blown three cylinders [of fourteen] right off the top of the engine and it still ran all the way home.

"I flew twenty-two missions . . . and it's only when I have time to think that I realize how scared we were. . . . I mean, there's nobody there to tell you what evasive action to take. You're by yourself and you learn. But after about six or seven operations, you kind of look forward to the next one because you like the adrenaline. You like the high."

On June 8, Fred Sampson and Walter Schierer were reunited at Keevil station. Since the Canadian was an officer and the Briton still an army staff sergeant, they could not share a drink in the same mess as their fellow pilots. Sampson took the time to thank his tug pilot—despite the peculiar timing of the canister drop—by giving Schierer a memento, the fixed-blade commando knife that had travelled to Normandy and back.*

"It was the kinship you felt," Sampson said, "because your tug pilot towed you better than anybody else."

2 p.m. June 6, 1944—Portsmouth, England

While the Canadian frigates of Escort Group 6 patrolled the western approaches to the Channel invasion area throughout D-Day in search of U-boats and German destroyers that never appeared, the eight boats of the 29th Canadian Motor Torpedo Boat Flotilla had engaged with German military vessels in the eastern Channel almost every night. They expected business as usual on June 6 and were not disappointed.

When they opened their Confidential Books with their orders for D-Day, four of the Canadian MTB commanders— Lt. Tony Law on MTB *459*, Lt. Dave Killam aboard MTB *460*, Lt. Charlie Chaffey on MTB *465*, and Lt. Barney Marshall of MTB *466*—found they would comprise one of two striking forces from the 29th assigned to join other warships and British MTBs protecting the eastern flank of the British assault area in Normandy. The Canadian MTBs would be facing their wartime nemesis, the crews of German gunboats based at the occupied

---

* On Feb. 19, 2003, the author arranged to bring together Sampson and Schierer for interviews in Port Hope, Ont. The two veterans had not seen each other since 1944. Following an emotional reunion, Schierer announced he had a gift for Sampson to mark the occasion. After 59 years he was returning Sampson's commando knife.

French port of Le Havre. To that end, unlike the days leading up to D-Day, when the MTBs were allowed to keep one or two craft at a time out of circulation for damage repairs, maintenance, and crew rest, the 29th Flotilla was ordered to remain 100 percent operational on June 6. Allied Intelligence estimated that the Germans still had an active naval force of fifty E-boats (*Schnellbootes*) and sixty R-boats (*Raumbootes*).

"It was our job to intercept them and sink them if possible," recalled MTB Petty Officer Fred Walden. "We worked mostly at night."

As recently as the autumn of 1943, the twenty-four-year-old motor mechanic had been on a course in Detroit at the Packard plant that manufactured the MTBs' twelve-cylinder engines. With three years' service in the volunteer navy, Walden had shovelled coal aboard a steam-driven minesweeper off Halifax, served in the engine room aboard a Fairmile launch, and become acting petty officer motor mechanic on convoy duty in the Gulf of St. Lawrence. Walden admired "the speed and power" of the motor torpedo boats most of all, so that spring when the navy asked him, he quickly volunteered for overseas service in the 29th Flotilla. By May 15 he was assisting the chief engineer aboard MTB *460*.

The Canadian MTB striking force left its HMS *Vernon* mooring about two o'clock in the afternoon on June 6. Each boat had crews of a dozen or fifteen men, fully loaded machine guns, pom-pom guns, Oerlikons, and depth charges, and the fuel tanks brimmed with 2,800 gallons of hundred-octane gasoline for several days on the Channel. As the crews left Portsmouth they observed the usual formalities—leaving the harbour in line-ahead formation, officers and men lining the fo'c'sle as the admiral's flag was piped—and then ships' companies moved to action stations as the MTBs left the Solent and the Isle of Wight heading for Normandy. P/O Walden was at his post in the engine room of *460* that afternoon as the fast-moving boats of the 29th Flotilla shifted to full speed across the Channel.

"You couldn't stand up and walk around in the engine room those [three] engines were so powerful," he said. "We used to plug our ears with cotton batting, the noise of the engines was so loud. . . . It was just something to endure, that's all."

The motor torpedo boats moved so quickly through the mine-swept approach channels that afternoon that they passed scores and scores of the 7,000 other vessels still making their way to the Normandy beachhead. They passed Liberty ships full of troops. They overtook convoys of merchant ships, the first vessels to establish a continuous supply line for the invading troops. They spotted a barge outfitted with a boxcar-like structure that turned out to be a self-propelled floating kitchen. Every half mile they passed the Dan buoys that the flotilla of minesweepers and trawlers had laid in the night. Partway through the approach lanes they met the northbound Canadian troopships *Prince David* and *Prince Henry*, transporting casualties from the beaches back to Britain. The MTBs spotted the green maple leaf on each ship's funnel and signalled "Well done" as they raced south.

Before nightfall, the four MTBs reached a light vessel anchored within view of the Canadian landing sector. The small red ship flew an Ensign and had "JUNO" painted in white across its hull. The striking force moved on to rendezvous with its mother ship, HMS *Scylla*, a cruiser acting as the flagship of the Eastern Task Force commander. Nearby, several British and American battleships were still firing shells at targets above the Normandy beaches. Tied to the stern of *Scylla*, the four MTBs paused in the rough water to feed their tired crews and receive the night's briefing. The Assault Area control officer literally shouted the orders through a megaphone from *Scylla*'s stern to the officers of Tony Law's MTB *459* and then repeated the process, passing the specifics on to the others as the four MTBs bobbed in the water like corks.

On D-Day night the Canadian foursome was ordered to patrol the Channel about twelve miles off Cap Le Havre. In this they would be assisted by the 55th British MTB Flotilla and backed up by Allied destroyer patrols. They were to shift their position every hour to counteract the strong Channel currents. The MTBs were the advance ears and eyes of the Allied naval force, waiting for the German convoys and gunboats to leave the shelter of Le Havre.

"We would be directed to a certain position, stop engines, and just drift there in the dark," said Jack Foote, sub-lieutenant aboard MTB 459. "If there were enemy ships in the area, we would be directed toward them. If our own radar operator picked up anything, we would head towards them."

The Canadian MTBs had watched and waited from a couple of different positions before the darkness was suddenly illuminated by tracer shells and searchlights on shore. An air battle had begun over Le Havre, although the lights revealed no enemy ships for the moment. A short time later, another volley of tracers and then starshells, designed to light up the night sky, showed the British MTB Flotilla moving into action. It also revealed to the Canadian MTB crews that, 3,000 yards ahead of them, six German R-boats were hurrying east, away from Le Havre.

"Maximum speed," 459 radioed to the flotilla. "Going in to attack."

The four Canadian boats raced forward in battle formation, gaining on the R-boats, which were now all strung out in a line. At 700 yards the four MTBs began firing pom-poms and continued until they had closed to within 150 yards of the enemy gunboats.

Gunners aboard the German boats had determined the range of the oncoming MTBs. Their return fire damaged all four of their Canadian pursuers. The R-boat shells struck and wounded two gunners aboard MTB *466* as well as Able Seaman Bill Bushfield, the gunner feeding shells into the forward two-pounder on MTB *459*.

In the engine room of MTB *460*, motor mechanic Fred Walden tended the gun hydraulics and helped the chief engineer maintain the boat's three screaming engines. He stuck his head up through an open hatch as Lieutenant Killam ordered his gunners to illuminate and open fire on the grey object about 500 yards ahead of them.

"The first starshell must have ricocheted off the water," Walden said, "but it seemed to splash and then light up the R-boat. Then 'Bang!' Everybody hit it at once and it just blew up. It must have been carrying mines."

Sub-Lieutenant Foote could not see the R-boat explode, because about that time he was carrying *459*'s gunner Bushfield below decks for medical assistance. Foote settled his patient in a spot near the first-aid cabinet in the coxswain's cabin. He was about to administer a syrette of morphine when he paused.

"I can do this," he assured Bushfield, "but we've got to move closer to the light."

The gunner was in a lot of pain, but did not object to moving. The two men turned away from the one side of the boat toward the light on the other and a German shell came through the wall of MTB *459* precisely where they had been seated moments before. The shell punched a hole in the boat's wooden hull above the waterline, so there was no serious damage to the vessel. Foote remained stunned by the incident long after. "I am alive today because I made that one move," he said.

The battle hastened to a close. Suddenly mines were exploding in the water all around the Canadian flotilla. Lieutenant Law realized that the engagement had carried the gunboats of both sides into the British minefield known as the Area Scollops, just outside Le Havre harbour. He ordered the boats to disengage, lay down a smokescreen, and steam northward out of the area. The ten-minute firefight had ended abruptly with one R-boat destroyed and another in flames. The 29th Flotilla striking force had suffered only a few wounded and shaken crewmen. Its D-Day war diary recorded success, though every man in the flotilla knew the final battle was still a long way off.

P/O Fred Walden survived his own close call during his time with the motor torpedo boats. Several weeks after his baptism of fire on D-Day aboard MTB *460*, he received word that another boat needed a chief engineer. Since he served as second engineer aboard *460*, Walden asked his skipper, Lt. Dave Killam, if he could leave to apply. Despite Lieutenant Killam's attempts to keep Walden aboard *460*, the petty officer decided to take the chief's job on MTB *464*. On her very next trip, MTB *460* ran into mines in the Channel and blew up. Only six sailors survived.

"The whole engine-room crew was gone," Walden said. "It could have been me."

4 p.m. June 6, 1944—English Channel

Motor Torpedo Boat skipper Lt. Tony Law witnessed a number of extraordinary things that first day of the invasion. The skirmish off Le Havre left him with vivid first impressions of close-quarters combat with German gunboats. The severe weather tested the Canadians' mettle and their concentration too. Perhaps most of all, the armada of D-Day vessels churning up the ninety miles of English Channel from Portsmouth to Juno Beach impressed him. In addition to his recollection of the returning Canadian troopships *Prince Henry* and *Prince David* and the lonely kitchen barge, he had also noted with curiosity "a congestion of cement blocks . . . and barges and strange pontoon bridges, being towed at caterpillar speed by puffing tugs." He later discovered he had been observing another of the D-Day marvels, the Mulberry harbours, being towed to Normandy.

None of the beachheads that the invasion forces had secured by the end of D-Day included a natural port through which to feed the tons of munitions and supplies the troops would need to push farther inland. Consequently, the Allies had had to improvise. If there were no harbours, the Allies would bring harbours with them. The plan was to assemble prefabricated Mulberries at Gold Beach at Arromanches and offshore at St-Laurent in the American Omaha Beach sector. The process would begin as forty to seventy ships, dubbed "Gooseberries" and "Corncobs," were scuttled about a mile offshore to create a breakwater against the rough waters of the Channel. Next a series of concrete caissons, known as "Phoenixes," each weighing 660 tons, were floated into position and sunk end to end to create a solid barrier for the new harbour. Then pierheads, or "Spuds," with legs positioned on the seabed, would provide the framework for piers, wharfs, docks, and a network of floating roads to link the floating harbour to shore.

These historic pieces of engineering, created by Commodore John H. Hallett and prefabricated in secret by tens of thousands of workers around the British Isles during the previous year, all had to be towed to Normandy. That process began early on D-Day under an escort group of Canadian corvettes. Writer Scott Young had just been posted to the corvette HMCS *Mayflower*. Formerly an overseas war correspondent for Canadian Press at its London bureau, Young had been feeding stories back to Canada since 1942. However, wanting to contribute in ways other than reporting, he had returned to Canada in 1943 and joined the Royal Canadian Navy. Almost immediately he was posted to its public relations branch. He accepted

(RIGHT) He missed his graduation day at the University of Toronto (June 6, 1944) but because Juno Beach signals master Bob Cameron met correspondent Ross Munro (below) on the beach and drove him to divisional headquarters Munro interviewed him.

(ABOVE) His editors at Canadian Press said Munro "yearned to park his typewriter" where Canadian soldiers served their country and so witnessed their landings at Dieppe, Sicily, Italy and Normandy.
(RIGHT) *Maclean's* war correspondent Lionel Shapiro (right) confers with his two Canadian Press colleagues William Stewart (centre) and Munro.

(TOP) This image came from one of several thousand frames of 35-mm motion picture film that Canadian cameraman Sgt. Bill Grant (above) shot on the way in to Juno Beach on D-Day. A member of No. 2 Canadian Film and Photo Unit, Grant landed with the Queen's Own Rifles that morning. His fellow cameraman, Pte. Chuck Ross (left), arrived soon after with the standard CFPU issue Bell and Howell Eymo camera and tripod. Grant's unique footage was a worldwide scoop, seen in newsreel theatres just days after the event. Canadian cameramen paid a high price for getting unique wartime film; four cameramen and two drivers of the CFPU were killed in Italy and Northwest Europe.

Unlike the U.S. "Saving Private Ryan" concept, in the Canadian Army Cpl. Fred Barnard (left) could "claim" his brother Donald (right) into his regiment, the Queen's Own Rifles, the theory being that brothers fighting side by side inspired solidarity. This telegram, received by their mother, Janet, on June 17, 1944, reveals that the reunion didn't last long.

CD1X

CANADIAN PACIFIC
TELEGRAPHS
World Wide Communications

W D NEIL, General Manager of Communications

RNA63 46/43 2 EX DL GB REPORT DELIVERY=OTTAWA ONT 17 1111A

=MRS JANET BARNARD

1944 JUN 17 PM 1 10

=16 SUTHERLAND AVE TORONTO 13

=5207 MINISTER OF NATIONAL DEFENCE DEEPLY REGRETS TO INFORM YOU
THAT B137985 RIFLEMAN DONALD MCKAY BARNARD HAS BEEN OFFICIALLY
REPORTED KILLED IN ACTION SIXTH JUNE 1944 STOP IF ANY FURTHER
INFORMATION BECOMES AVAILABLE IT WILL BE FORWARDED AS SOON AS
RECEIVED=

:DIRECTOR OF RECORDS=

Four McDonald brothers from Cornwall enlisted, Donald, the eldest, in the airforce while (l to r) James, Francis, and John Angus all joined the local eastern Ontario regiment—the Stormont, Dundas, and Glengarry Highlanders. All waded ashore in front of Bernières-sur-Mer on June 6, but not all survived the 9th Infantry Brigade's objective of solidifying the D-Day beachhead.

(LEFT) By this point on D-Day, the frontline fighting was inland several miles, but on Juno Beach reserve units of the 1st Hussars armoured regiment battled the congestion of landing craft delivering reinforcements, engineers clearing debris, and the order ringing in their heads, "Keep moving!"

(RIGHT) Welcoming French civilians and the narrow streets of the coastal villages made matters worse as tanks, trucks, and troops negotiated their way to the frontlines farther inland.

(LEFT) Members of the Stormont, Dundas, and Glengarry Highlanders offered an "Up the Glens" toast to the day's successes with tots of the local Calvados liqueur.

(LEFT) For a generation artillery crews hauled their 25-pounder guns by truck, tractor, or jeep. For D-Day, they learned to fire a 105-mm howitzer mounted on a self-propelled SP vehicle (a tank chassis); the gun's pulpit-like firing position earned it the nickname "Priest."

D-Day night Capt. Ken Bell (right) gave his camera a rest and dug in among guns of the 14th Field Regiment. He snapped this shot of a nearby gun crew: (l to r) Doug Allen, Ken Darling (under table), Garth Webb, and gunner Cowie. It was one of the first D-Day photos published back in Canada, seen within several days on the front page of the *Calgary Herald*, in Webb's hometown.

(LEFT) Second World War mortality rates of 66 per 1,000 were cut dramatically on D-Day because Royal Canadian Army Medical Corps units came ashore on the heels of invasion troops.

(RIGHT) Tony Burns, an operating room assistant with No. 1 Canadian Mobile Neuro-Surgical Unit, attended to the most severe head wounds.

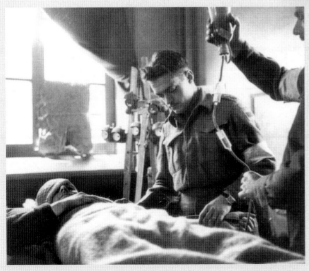

(LEFT) Sgt. T.F. McFeat and Pte. J. Viner (with the 23rd Field Ambulance) administer plasma to a Normandy casualty.

Members of ground and aircrew at Keevil station in England pause during pre–D-Day training. Pilot Fred Sampson, in the doorway of his Horsa glider, nicknamed "Shytot," was paired with Stirling bomber pilot Walter Schierer (left). They would be one of the 256 glider–tug plane combinations of Operation Mallard, late in the afternoon on June 6. By day's end 95 percent of the gliders would have successfully crash-landed in Normandy.

(LEFT) Sub-Lieutenant Jack Foote said of the motor torpedo boats, "The speed was wonderful and the power . . ." As they crossed the Channel, their MTBs hit top speed of 41 knots, or nearly 50 miles an hour.

(RIGHT) The crew of MTB 459 (l to r on bridge) Lt. John Shand, S/Lieut. Jack Foote, Lt. Tony Law, L/S Cyril French; (second row) Tel. T.O. Donald McCallum, Tel. T.O. Patrick McAuley, A/B James Beyea, Sig. Robert Lovelock, A/B William Dublock; (front row) A/B Harold Seaton, A/B William Bushfield, A/B Roland Stevens, Sto. M. Jack McMahon, L/S William Reid, A/B Herbert Simpson, Sto. M. James Roberts, P.O. M.M. Edward Dawson.

(RIGHT) Tony Law, commander of MTB 459 and leader of the 29th Motor Torpedo Boat Flotilla, wrote up and sketched this baptism of fire, an engagement with six German R-boats off Le Havre after dark on June 6, 1944.

The first contact with the enemy on the ground in Normandy unearthed dozens of unexploded land mines (below, right), yielded hundreds of prisoners (top) and unveiled a first look at the sand tables and strategic maps the Germans used to defend Hitler's Atlantic Wall (below left).

(TOP) During a theatre performance in London, the Tin Hats posed for a "V for Victory" photo: (front row l to r) Ronnie White, Johnny "Triby" Heawood, Wally Brennan, Joe Rocks, Norm Harper, Bill "Trixie" Dunstan, J. E. "Spud" Cooper; (band members l to r) Charlie More, Eric Halsall, Les Abraham, Harry Connolly, Stan Stevenson, Bert Churchill. (LEFT) In a day and a half, Sherbrooke Fusiliers tank crewman Hubert Thistle went from the relative peace of a security-transit camp in Britain, through a rough Channel crossing onto Juno Beach, to a near-death experience at the hands of Kurt Meyer's S.S. *Hitlerjugend* troops in Normandy. (BELOW) It took 15,000 workers at 240 different British companies to construct the components of the artificial Mulberry Harbours that were towed by 200 high-sea tugboats to two locations off Normandy even as the battle on the beaches raged on.

(TOP LEFT) When he raised the idea for the Juno Beach Centre, D-Day artilleryman Garth Webb told his granddaughter that he wanted to lead a march of veterans when it opened. On June 6, 2003, he did just that. (TOP RIGHT) Fearing that his emotions might get the better of him, D-Day signaller Don Kerr avoided a return to Normandy after 1944. When he decided to return in 2003, he wasn't afraid to show his emotions as a proud Canadian. (BELOW) Its design like a maple leaf, its appearance a glass and titanium wave rising from the sea, its symbolism a partnership between two nations that began with "a war of deliverance," the Centre, with its Remembrance and Renewal sculpture in front, opened on the 59th anniversary of D-Day.

the assignment on condition that he be out covering the navy's fighting men at the front, not stuck behind a desk. On D-Day he found himself aboard *Mayflower* as it escorted the Mulberry-towing flotilla.

"On the way over, a pigeon landed on one of the tugboats pulling the Mulberries," Young said. "The bird was so tired, somebody walked up to it and found a little note on its leg. So the captain of our corvette, [Lt. D. S.] Martin, signalled to England indicating the pigeon had a canister on its leg and what were we supposed to do?"

Young and the corvette captain soon learned that before D-Day, RAF planes had dropped as many as 500 homing pigeons across France. The hope was that members of the French Underground or average citizens might find the birds, scribble down German gun positions or troop movements on slips of paper, insert the papers in the canisters on the pigeons' legs, and release them for their flight back to England. Having intercepted one of the messengers, Young and Martin were therefore instructed to contact the local army headquarters when they got to Arromanches and to deliver the bird to British Intelligence officers there. Meanwhile, Young recalled that the pigeon was kept in the ship's wardroom; the creature barely moved, and it never relieved itself during the entire Channel crossing.

At Arromanches, Royal engineers immediately began assembling the massive Mulberry harbour components. Sub-Lieutenant Young and Lieutenant Martin came ashore with the pigeon stowed in a cotton bag. They made their presence known in the town and arranged for their transportation by jeep to the recently established British headquarters at a nearby château. There they were ushered into a briefing room for an audience with British army, navy, and air force Intelligence Officers. Young was impressed with the walls of the room, which were completely covered in top-secret maps of the area with the names of area spies and their information meticulously displayed. Salutes and greetings were exchanged.

"I understand you've brought a homing pigeon with information," said the senior officer present.

Martin acknowledged that he had the pigeon in the cotton bag he carried.

"We'll be very interested to see it," the officer said.

The corvette captain then reached in, seized the pigeon, and pulled it from the bag. Whether the pigeon was excited about being brought out and into the light or the skipper gripped the bird too tightly, Young has never been sure, but the bird let fly several days' worth of pigeon manure. It spattered the officers, it blotched the maps, it sprayed everything and everyone in the room. Young and Martin chose not to wait around to see if the note on the pigeon's leg revealed any vital enemy secrets. They beat a hasty retreat.

Scott Young returned to his typewriter to continue his service in the navy as a probationary sub-lieutenant. Faithful to his wish to report primarily about the average seaman at the front, he covered the invasion of southern France from aboard one of HMCS *Prince Henry*'s assault landing craft and later aboard HMCS *Prince David* during the liberation of Yugoslavia and Greece. Never shying away from difficult assignments, Young had reported on the dangerous Newfoundland-to-Londonderry convoy missions. He had covered missions with the Canadian motor-torpedo-boat flotillas and scooped all other correspondents by getting quotations from Buzz Beurling, the famous Canadian fighter pilot, from his hospital bed in London in 1942. He believed that he saw more of the war in half a year than many other reporters did in five years.

Perhaps most troubling of the wartime images for him was what he saw in the immediate aftermath of D-Day. "There were a lot of bodies floating in the Channel," he said. "By being in the water so long and it's summer, it was just grotesque. Soldiers just floating and their bloated bodies are as big as a hippopotamus. None of us knew what to do. We were always doing something, going somewhere, and we couldn't start hauling bodies in. . . .

"These were the leavings of D-Day."

Noon, June 6, 1944—Bernières-sur-Mer, France

When he finally got his feet onto dry land in Bernières-sur-Mer, about midday on June 6, the tall, dark, and moustached Lionel Shapiro carried only a typewriter as he made his way up the beach. The thirty-six-year-old correspondent for *Maclean's* magazine and stringer for the North American Newspaper Alliance made his way to the makeshift press quarters, about 300 yards into the village.

There, in the dining room of l'Hôtel Belle Plage, Shapiro typed out his first, and quite poetic, take on the invasion: "History is standing astride these rolling Norman fields and resolving its own direction for perhaps a thousand years to come. We mortals who sit below can only be awed by its mighty presence."

In his first words about the Allied accomplishment that day, correspondent Shapiro was, of course, mocking Adolf Hitler's 1933 claim that his Third Reich would endure for a millennium. Originally from Montreal, Shapiro had written reports and commentary for the Montreal *Gazette* from London throughout the Blitz. Partly because of his growing reputation, the CBC and BBC had also contracted with him to do some voice reports while covering the Allied campaigns in North Africa, Sicily, and Italy. Then, just before D-Day, *Maclean's* asked him to write about the significant steps leading to the invasion.

Described by his editors as "a seasoned correspondent with a vivid pen," Shapiro also illustrated his "burning Canadianism." So, when he wrote about events of June 6, he also reflected on the courage and resilience of the Canadian citizen soldiers.

"Between the little seaside town of Bernières-sur-Mer and the Caen battle front, Canadian troops have written an immortal history," he wrote.

Like the other war correspondents who waded into Normandy that day—William Stewart, Ross Munro, Ralph Allen, Charles Lynch, Matthew Halton, and Marcel Ouimet—Shapiro wrote stories about as many of the home regiments as possible, interviewed the obligatory number of officers, and tiptoed around the Allied censors. He wandered as far afield within the secured beachhead as he dared and then returned to that hotel dining-room table to finish his story. Shapiro also mentioned that the daughter of the hotel proprietor brought out wine that the family had "hidden from the hated Boche." He watched Canadian soldiers march scores of German prisoners back to Juno Beach as the French residents jeered and gestured at the former occupation troops.

Shapiro's wartime reporting would earn him an Order of the British Empire, and in 1955 his D-Day reflections would emerge from the typewriter as *The Sixth of June*, a tremendously successful romantic novel set in wartime England. The book would sell more than two million copies, earn him a Governor-General's Literary Award, and be adapted into a hit Hollywood movie. And though he would go on to a prolific writing career, D-Day remained a most powerful moment in Shapiro's life.

"Darkness was falling now and German aircraft were beginning to drop bombs on the beach," he concluded in his report of D-Day. "I went to a field and fell into a sleep of exhaustion. A great and historic day in Canadian history was ended."

THE LONGEST DAYS

_____

"THIS IS A NATIONAL NEWS BULLETIN. A summary of the day's news . . ."

That's the way announcer Earl Cameron began reading CBC Radio news copy as night fell in France on June 6 and the new day dawned in Canada.

"The dagger pointed at the heart of Berlin has been driven into the side of Nazi Europe," he continued. "The first news of the mightiest military operation of all history came at thirty-eight minutes past midnight Eastern Daylight Time last night, when the Germans broadcast a report that Le Havre was being bombarded. The official account is rounded out by despatches from correspondents. They say that Canadian, American, and British troops have landed on the Normandy coast of northern France. One report indicates that the Canadians may be among the troops fighting in Caen, but the report is not confirmed. . . ."

In fact, Canadian troops were not in Caen. No Allied forces had penetrated that far inland. They and their allies would take another six weeks to achieve that objective. However, the Canadians—as well as the British and the Americans—had breached Hitler's Atlantic Wall and, if they could, were certainly resting on ground that the Germans had occupied for four years until that day.

Canadian medic Ernie Jeans hardly slept at all that first night, as he steadily gave first aid to fellow paratroopers near the crossroads at Le Mesnil. Intelligence Officer Reg Weeks had dug a slit trench next to the garden of daffodils outside the divisional headquarters in Bernières-sur-Mer for his first night's stay in Normandy. Meanwhile, Canadian Press correspondent William Stewart slept on white sheets, thanks to a grateful French couple who opened their home to him in Graye-sur-Mer. Padre R. M. Hickey shared a can of self-heating soup and a slit trench with two members of the North Shore (New Brunswick) Regiment near Tailleville the night of June 6. Queen's Own Rifleman Fred Barnard, still in shock from having seen his brother dead on Juno Beach, found a former German trench in which to rest that night. Artillery commander Stanley Todd slept on the ground under the signal truck so he could hear any radio reports of the expected German counterattack. Wounded and later evacuated back to the beach, wireless operator Bruce Evans and the 1st Hussars got as far as the Caen-Bayeux railway line; theirs was the only element of the entire Allied invasion force to reach their D-Day final objective before backtracking and settling on high ground southwest of Pierrepont.

Meanwhile, Field-Marshal Erwin Rommel was at his home in Herrlingen, Germany, when he received a telephone call from Maj. Gen. Hans Speidel in Normandy. His chief of staff offered Rommel a first full briefing on news of the Allied invasion that day. Rommel was stunned by the report. He admitted it was a day he had expected, one he had warned would be "the longest day."

In twenty-four hours of their longest day of the war so far, the Allies had managed to land about 130,000 soldiers along fifty-five miles of Normandy beach, plus drop 24,000 paratroops inland from the beachhead. Across all five of the assault beaches the invasion forces had suffered nearly 9,000 casualties, far fewer than any of the pessimistic Allied strategists had predicted. On the other side of the equation, however, few units had reached the D-Day objectives that were key to the Allies' securing a toehold in France. The British 3rd Infantry Division, coming ashore at Sword beach, had not taken Caen. The American soldiers who landed on Utah Beach had pushed a few miles on to link up with hard-pressed airborne comrades, but the situation at Omaha Beach, where the bridgehead was about half a mile deep, was cause for concern. In the middle, the 3rd Canadian Infantry Division had firm control of Juno Beach, but it had not captured its objective, the airfield at Carpiquet. The momentum of Operation Overlord therefore depended on the reserve energy and initiative that the landing troops could muster in their next hours ashore. Consequently, D-Day-plus-1 and D-Day-plus-2 proved terribly long days too.

Canadian orders for June 7 called for the 7th Canadian Infantry Brigade to move forward from its positions—the Royal Winnipeg Rifles from Creully pressing forward on the right, the Regina Rifles from Le Fresne-Camilly advancing on the left, and 1st Canadian Scottish from Pierrepont providing a firm base. In contrast to the brigade's early-morning casualties the day before, by noon the three regiments had moved forward to Putot-en-Bessin, Bretteville-l'Orgueilleuse, and Secqueville-en-Bessin, respectively, with little resistance.

In the eastern sector of the Allied bridgehead, the 9th Canadian Infantry Brigade had orders to begin advancing southward from its D-Day stop point. So the Stormont, Dundas and Glengarry Highlanders moved from Colomby-sur-Thaon, and both the Highland Light Infantry and North Nova Scotia Highlanders from Anguerny. The Sherbrooke Fusiliers were to provide armoured support for the day's action, heading toward the brigade's original D-Day objective, Carpiquet. Attaining it would prove to be a bloodier challenge than anyone expected.

Normandy was a long way from Ayre & Sons department store in St. John's, Newfoundland, but up to that point it had been no greater threat. A former hardware sales clerk and now Sherbrooke Fusiliers crewman, Hubert Thistle had come ashore on D-Day without a scratch. Landing at Bernières-sur-Mer in C Squadron of the 27th Armoured Regiment, Thistle was just twenty and a wireless radio operator in a Sherman Firefly tank, under its troop commander, Lt. Ian MacLean. When darkness closed in around their position, Thistle and the other four men in his tank crew had dug in a mile south of Bernières and considered their first twenty-four hours in France pretty uneventful. In fact, the start of D-Day-plus-1 proved extremely routine for them too.

Just before eight o'clock the morning of June 7, the combined infantry and armoured operation began. A Fusiliers' recce troop in four Stuart tanks led the way along with North Novas aboard Universal Carriers. Also in the battle group's vanguard were the Fusiliers' heavier weapons, the Sherman Firefly tanks with their long-barrelled, 17-pounder guns. For the first mile or so of the advance, as well, the North Nova Scotias combined the operation literally.

"As we were moving up, the infantry started clambering up onto the back decks of our tanks," Thistle said. "But I told them we were moving up as a troop . . . so they began jumping off. . . . The four tanks in our troop continued advancing quickly, one tank forward, two to the flanks and one to the rear. . . . We were probably a mile ahead of the rest of the squadron . . ."

About noon the column of Fusiliers' recce tanks and North Novas' lead infantry platoons reached the village of Buron. There they drew machine-gun and sniper fire from the long grass beside the road as well as mortar and artillery shells from a greater distance. The assault group split into three prongs, one on either side of the village and one through the centre of town, and passed through Buron quickly. A mile farther down the road, the lead tanks and infantry entered Authie, where the return fire grew more intense. By advancing so quickly, the Canadian soldiers and tanks had drawn out their advance into a long column, exposing its flanks. It was now too far inland for effective artillery support from the day's starting point.

"The next thing I knew," Thistle said, "the other three tanks in our troop had disappeared. They had turned and high-tailed it back. . . . I said to the crew commander [MacLean] that we were running into anti-tank fire. His last command was 'Driver, advance' and 'Gunner, range . . .' and I think we hit three of their tanks. . . . But in the next moment, we were hit by an eighty-eight right under the turret."

What Bert Thistle and the rest of the advance group of the 9th Canadian Infantry Brigade did not realize was that at Authie they had run smack into the first major German counteroffensive, spearheaded by the 12th S.S. Panzer Division. Its ranks contained crack troops of the *Hitlerjugend*, young soldiers fresh from the Hitler Youth military-fitness camps in Germany and full of Nazi ideology. While two-thirds of them were only eighteen and had not fired a shot in battle, nearly all would soon display reckless courage and a degree of barbarity unknown in any other enemy formation. What the Canadians also did not know was that their every move that day had been scrutinized from a chapel tower of the Abbaye d'Ardenne by the commander of the 25th S.S. Panzer Grenadier Regiment, Col. Kurt Meyer.

Standartenfuhrer Meyer ordered his men to "attack the landed enemy and throw him back into the sea. . . . Objective: The beach . . ." From his elevated vantage point Meyer decided that retaking Authie and Buron was the first step in that process, so he waited patiently for the forward units of the North Novas and the Sherbrooke Fusiliers to fully expose their eastern flank to the Panzers' guns and soldiers. As the German troops opened fire and advanced, the Canadians recognized the counter-attack taking shape against them, and were unable to bolster their position with artillery, naval gunfire, or troop reinforcement quickly enough. They tried to pull back and consolidate, but the Hitler Youth, in their baptism of fire, fought ferociously. At times the battle became hand-to-hand combat. In the villages of Authie and Buron, the North Novas were overwhelmed. In the fields between, the increasing number of disabled Fusiliers tanks spelled an armoured defeat as well.

The 88-mm shell that struck Lieutenant MacLean's lead tank penetrated more than the turret's armour plating; it ignited the fuel in the engine compartment. When his commander ordered the crew to bail out, Bert Thistle quickly crawled through the turret and jumped. He twisted his ankle on landing, but was otherwise uninjured. Meanwhile, on the other side of the tank, the driver, a trooper named Redman, managed to crawl back into the tank and help the gunner and the loader escape. By now German sniper fire was pinging off the tank and through the tall grass as MacLean's crew crawled away on their bellies in different directions. Before long they heard a thunderous explosion as the ammunition and fuel ignited and blew their tank apart.

"That was the end of the road for me as a fighting man," Thistle said. "These young SS captured us and took our watches, cigarettes, things like that. . . . And they took us to Abbaye d'Ardenne."

The 9th Brigade's advance and the panzers' counteroffensive on June 7 had cost both sides severely. The Canadians claimed the destruction of thirty-one German Mark IV tanks, effectively taking that panzer-grenadier regiment out of action.

Meanwhile, the North Novas had suffered 242 casualties, eighty-four of them fatal; and the Fusiliers had lost twenty-eight tanks and suffered sixty casualties, twenty-six of them fatal. More than 120 Canadian infantrymen and tank crewmen were taken prisoner and herded in groups through the afternoon and evening to the panzers' regimental headquarters at the Abbaye d'Ardenne.

A number of the Canadians captured during the battle, however, never made it to the makeshift prison at the Abbaye. Most had their hands tied behind their backs. Many had been wounded in the fighting. En route to the Abbaye, several S.S. troops periodically drew their weapons and shot individual Canadian soldiers on the spot. In some cases the bodies of the murdered men were not buried or were deliberately tossed onto the roadways so that passing German vehicles would grind their remains beyond recognition. In the chapel yard, the surviving prisoners had most of their identification—tags and paybooks—removed and then faced individual interrogation. At dusk German guards began demanding volunteers and leading the men away. That night the soldiers of the 12th S.S. Panzer Division executed twenty-three Canadian prisoners, including North Novas and Sherbrooke Fusiliers.

"They took us into this barn, five of us, and lined us up. We were next," Thistle recalled. "They had a sniper in front of us, ready to go. We shook hands, you know, like it was the end, when in came some high-ranking [German] officer and stopped him. . . . Just a split second and another five would be among the dead."

Bert Thistle spent the next ten months as a prisoner of war. A few months after the Americans liberated the Newfoundlander and the authorities repatriated him to Canada in 1945, his captor, Col. Kurt Meyer, went on trial for war crimes stemming from the events of June 7. The German officer was found guilty, yet had his death sentence commuted to life imprisonment about the time Bert Thistle returned to his job at the Ayre & Sons department store in St. John's.

Mark Lockyer's brush with death at the hands of the S.S. on D-Day-plus-2 was equally chilling.

The private in the 1st Canadian Parachute Battalion had jumped from a Dakota transport plane into the darkness and, as it turned out, straight into flooded pastureland around Robehomme when the D-Day invasion began. Through the pre-daylight hours of June 6, he had waded and probed his way alone to his rendezvous point, the Robehomme bridge over the River Dives. There he had joined other Canadian paratroops whose first D-Day mission was to blow up the bridge to protect the eastern flank of the invasion beaches from a German counter-attack. When engineers and their explosives did not appear to carry out the mission, Lockyer and his fellow paras had impro-vised by packing all their plastic explosive around the support-ing girders of the bridge. By 3 a.m. Lockyer was ready and pushed the plunger, crippling the bridge until the demolition experts finally arrived to finish the job.

On June 7, Private Lockyer and other members of B Com-pany who had gravitated to the Robehomme bridge moved west toward the battalion's headquarters at Le Mesnil cross-roads. Their initial job as commandos parachuting into drop zones to carry out hit-and-run attacks against the Germans now shifted to regular infantry duties—conducting night recon-naissance patrols, digging in and establishing firm defensive bases, and participating in full-fledged ground attacks against enemy positions. One such strongpoint existed at Le Mesnil, a large farmhouse set in an apple orchard and surrounded by a stone wall. A skirmish with German infantry on the morning of June 8 had forced the enemy units of the 857th and 858th

Grenadier Regiment to retreat into this strongpoint, and brigade headquarters decided to clear it. B Company of the paras was chosen to carry out the attack.

Like so many of the paratroopers dropped on D-Day, the Canadians had not slept since reveille in England three days earlier. They were grimy, weary, and hungry. Many were angry at the loss of comrades during the first assaults. Their commanders must have sensed all that, as they explained their mission to them at Le Mesnil. Private Lockyer described Capt. Peter Griffin assembling nearly forty men and drawing a plan of attack in the sand, a frontal assault on the German gun positions dug in and around the farmhouse. The Canadian paras would gather in a ditch in front of the strongpoint and, with the battalion's mortars and Bren guns covering them, then dash with fixed bayonets straight at the German position.

"Two Bren gun units, one on the left flank and one on the right flank, will keep firing to keep the enemy's heads down while we're on the way in," Griffin told his men.

With battalion mortar-shells raining down on them, the Germans abandoned their machine-gun positions outside the stone wall. Moments later, German guns farther back began returning the fire and pinning down the Canadian Bren guns on the flanks. Rather than the attackers distracting the defenders with their fire, the defenders were distracting the attackers. Lockyer was just feeling the initiative was lost when he heard his commander bellow, "Charge!"

In Lockyer's platoon, Sgt. Cliff Huard took several steps beyond the ditch and was cut down by the machine-gun fire. Corporal O. M. Bastien was next to fall. Then Private M. Lanthier. Lockyer remembered zigzagging to try to avoid the continuous German fire, but was knocked down moments later with a burning pain in his chest, a bullet through his right lung. A few paces beyond him, Private W. W. Shwaluk dropped. Around Lockyer now lay Privates Robinson, Shwaluk, and Baynes, moaning. The attack had faltered and those paratroops not yet hit by the German gunfire quickly withdrew.

The battlefield fell silent. Lying perfectly still, Lockyer saw two enemy soldiers approaching, one a private and the other an S.S. officer with a chevron on his sleeve and epaulettes on his shoulders. The officer approached the wounded Private Shwaluk first, pulled out a revolver, and shot him dead. Lockyer knew his turn would come. He reached into his tunic, rubbed his hand in the blood from his chest wound, and smeared it over his own face, just as the S.S. officer shot Private Robinson dead.

The German private approached Lockyer and kicked him three times in the stomach. Lockyer did not respond and the German said, "Soldat kaput," and moved on to Private Baynes.

"No! No! Don't!" Baynes pleaded. The S.S. man shot him too.

Again, the battleground became quiet. The Germans began a counterattack against the Canadian positions. A mortar exploded near Lockyer and ruptured his eardrum. On came their infantry. By that time, the Canadians had re-formed their line and they began cutting down the German soldiers with Bren guns as they ran. Two men collapsed near Lockyer and they groaned for a time and then were silent. When Lockyer tried to move, a German sniper spotted him and tried to finish him off. The pain in his chest was excruciating. Eventually he found his first-aid pack and a syrette of morphine to stab into his arm. Finally, under cover of darkness he began pulling himself, bit by bit, in the direction of the Canadian line.

Hours later he heard a voice say, "There's something out there."

Lockyer knew the password, but it was a day old so he just called out, "I'm a Canadian! Don't shoot!"

In the gloom ahead, he could see a rifle pointed at him. "Don't move." Lockyer obeyed. As soon as the man had inspected him thoroughly he shouted, "Somebody get a stretcher!"

Over the next several days, stretcher-bearers and ambulances carried Mark Lockyer down to the beach, from which a tank landing craft ferried him to England.

Back at the farmhouse near Le Mesnil, the German Grenadiers were eventually forced to withdraw. Of twenty-five men in Lockyer's assault group, eight had been killed and thirteen wounded in that one operation. Lockyer took months to recuperate in No. 11 Canadian General Hospital at Taplow. The 1st Canadian Parachute Battalion wisely promoted him to sergeant in charge of training paratroop recruits, never posting him back to the front. Time healed his punctured lung, but never his horrific memories of D-Day-plus-2.

For the crew of Ed Aveling's Halifax bomber, D-Day must have felt like a day without end. In good flying conditions and bad, No. 517 (RAF) Squadron in South Wales despatched a meteorological reconnaissance aircraft twice a day, once at midnight and again at noon. It was Flight Lieutenant Aveling's turn for the midnight operation on June 5/6, one that could take him hundreds of miles out over the Atlantic. No matter. Coming from Saskatoon, Saskatchewan, Aveling was very comfortable with wide open spaces. Just before they departed, he and his crew assembled for the routine Coastal Command briefing. The intelligence officer presented them with a picture of all the Allied shipping they might encounter around the British Isles and out in the Atlantic that particular night. The IO's map was absolutely bare. Not a ship or convoy showed on it.

"Anything you see out there," he said, "consider it to be ours!"

Aveling's weather-recce trip proved uneventful until after daybreak, about the time when Canadian assault troops were landing at Juno Beach. At that hour, his Halifax had reached its farthest point from home, about 700 miles from Land's End. Aveling's plane was ticking along at 18,000 feet early D-Day morning when it developed a mechanical failure. A breakdown in the constant-speed unit of his outer port engine made the propeller "windmill," or rotate in full fine pitch at high speed. The windmilling in turn made the aircraft vibrate so severely that his navigator's instruments and map were scattered.

Worse, the same vibrations cracked an oil line in the inner port engine, so he had to feather and stop that engine. Then a fire ignited in the outer engine, which was quickly extinguished. That left the bomber flying with only its two starboard engines functioning. Pilot Aveling struggled vainly to keep the Halifax aloft. The aircraft continued to lose altitude and the crew prepared to ditch in the ocean. The wireless operator barely managed to send off three signals of "Engine trouble. . . . Returning to base" as well as the Hally's exact position before the radio itself was shaken apart.

When the bomber finally hit the surface of the water, it broke in two with the nose section ahead of the wing posts rapidly sinking. F/L Aveling still sat in that section, in the cockpit at the controls. The crew deployed a dinghy and pulled their skipper into the life raft. Aveling vomited for hours afterward from the salt water and aircraft fuel he had swallowed. Nearly twenty-four hours later, on June 7, a Catalina from No. 202 Air/Sea Rescue Squadron located Aveling and his crew. The sea was too rough for the amphibious plane to land, so another day passed before a destroyer from an American task force took the dinghy survivors aboard. The U.S. ships were headed in the opposite direction, however, in anticipation of a rendezvous between a U-boat and a Japanese sub. Accordingly, the task force sank the Japanese vessel and later docked at Norfolk,

Virginia, where the RCAF airmen debarked with the rest of the U.S. Navy crew.

It was by then mid August, some ten weeks after they had ditched in the Atlantic, before F/L Ed Aveling and his crew finally arrived back at their South Wales weather-recce station, certainly one of D-Day's longest and most circuitous operations.

The day after Ed Aveling's crew went down in the Atlantic was the day the Luftwaffe seemed to awaken to the invasion threat and re-engage Allied airmen over the Normandy beachhead. Early on the morning of June 7, in one instance, the leading edge of a squadron of Junkers 88s emerged from clouds above St-Aubin-sur-Mer, and the first aircraft immediately struck an anti-aircraft balloon cable and crashed near the beach. The Spitfires from Nos. 401, 411, and 412 (RCAF) Squadrons, which were providing air cover over the beaches, responded to the rest of the attacking German squadron, and brought down eight more Ju 88s. Other Spits destroyed three Focke-Wulf 190 fighter-bombers and two Messerschmitt 109 fighters shortly thereafter.

That same morning, the first RCAF ground officer of 126 Wing, Senior Intelligence Officer Monty Berger, came ashore at Ver-sur-Mer, slightly west of Juno Beach. When the landing craft let his jeep down the ramp about a hundred yards from shore, his vehicle promptly sank, submerging Berger up to his neck. Unperturbed and determined to prove the effectiveness of his waterproofing job, the intelligence officer drove the jeep through the waves and onto dry land, and lost only his personal kit as a result. Berger was the vanguard of the 2nd Tactical Air Force's (TAF) vital ground crew, made up of (air-frame-maintenance) riggers, (air-engine-maintenance) fitters, armament specialists, and all the other aircrew tradesmen who would keep Allied fighter planes in the air.

"Most people in the air force don't fly," Berger wrote. "These poor unfortunate birds are called 'penguins.' . . . These penguins lived with the 'pigeons,' their pilots . . . and helped to make this most modern weapon—a mobile wing [of the air force]—one of the greatest fighting machines in history."

Berger sensed the urgency of his mission to establish the first of numerous TAF air bases in Normandy. He carefully steered his waterlogged jeep around the engineers defusing mines and the sappers bulldozing damaged vehicles on the beach and moved steadily inland. At Ste-Croix-sur-Mer, he and his advance party of intelligence officers made their way towards B3, where plans called for the construction of an advanced airstrip for Allied fighter aircraft. He suddenly noticed sniper fire popping around his group. A despatch rider raced up to him, calling for the officer and his men to stop.

"What do you mean, 'stop'?" Berger asked him. "I have to get to our airstrip in a hurry."

"Well, sir," the rider said, "the ground isn't captured yet."

Berger and his party had nearly run headlong into a pitched tank battle between the 1st Hussars and German panzers. Consequently, armed with just a pistol, the senior intelligence officer retreated to Ver-sur-Mer to wait impatiently for the land intended for airstrip B3 to be liberated. Meanwhile, more members of the TAF ground crew came ashore, one of them aircraft-maintenance mechanic Richard Brown. Leading Aircraftman Brown, with 127 Wing, landed at Arromanches, where the Mulberry harbour was being constructed. He particularly remembered the welcome his group received from German aircraft in a strafing-and-bombing attack on the beach.

He thought to himself, "We tried. Now let's go home."

LAC Brown and the rest of his No. 421 (RCAF) ground-crew comrades spent a sleepless first night of fireworks and thunder courtesy of the Luftwaffe night-fighters. The next morning they trekked their way south of the beachhead. Near Crépon, between Bayeux and Caen, the No. 421 Squadron ground crews began preparing for the arrival of their Spitfire aircraft and pilots. The airstrip area "looked like the Sahara Desert, dust and sand all over the place" as the engineers laboriously cleared pastureland and laid down wire-mesh tracking to create an area hundreds of yards wide and thousands of yards long. There followed another night without sleep as rigger Brown and his fitter counterpart, LAC Cliff Robb, erected tents and dug slit trenches to protect themselves from further bombing attacks. The Spitfires finally arrived, but the dust clouds were so thick with each landing that those waiting their turns had to circle the airstrip three or four times to let the dust settle before coming down. Finally, the ground crews took over.

"If you were on duty crew," Brown wrote in his diary, "every third day you got up at 3 a.m., de-camouflaged the kites [planes], ran them up and gassed them. About 4 a.m., the pilots would be out and at 4:30 the flying circus would be in the air. At 8:00 the other two crews would take over. We'd go to breakfast and be off until 9:30. From then on you worked steadily till midnight. . . ."

Naturally, the building of airstrips such as B3 and the resulting concentration of Spitfire, Typhoon, and Mustang fighter aircraft attracted a lot of attention from the enemy. Within three days of its completion, B3 was handling more than 125 sorties daily, 146 by June 11. Field-Marshal Rommel noted with disdain that "the enemy is strengthening himself visibly on land under cover of very strong aircraft formations." He therefore stepped up night-fighter counterattacks, which made Allied landings on the pockmarked runways treacherous and continued to keep the ground crews awake and fearful.

"We worked hard," Cliff Robb said. "Our work was different than the aircrew's. We were the men behind the men behind the guns. And we threw around gasoline and ammunition and worked way into the night. The odd time when we were strafed or attacked, this was exciting. We faced death. But we didn't face it everyday, not the ground crew."

For meals, ground crew gathered in the middle of the cow pasture with "the sky for a roof and the tables were the green grass of the field." In their earliest days in Normandy, LACs Brown and Robb and the rest of Monty Berger's penguins survived on stew and hardtack three times a day and, as long as rations were available, one chocolate bar a day. For the first month and a half the fare did not change. There were one or two exceptions, such as the evening the No. 421 Squadron ground crew heard great excitement around the mess. Some thought the shouting meant the war was over, and soon discovered that the commotion was sparked by the arrival of the first white-bread rations since the beginning of the invasion.

Flight Lieutenant Charley Fox's arrival one day caused another stir at the 126 and 127 Wing airstrips. He had flown several air-cover operations on D-Day with No. 412 Squadron and, like his fellow fighter pilots, when he moved permanently to France, seemed to be in the air constantly helping to secure the bridgehead in Normandy as well as firing on "targets of opportunity"—any German trains, trucks, and officer staff cars he could find. Under normal circumstances the aluminum slipper tank that Fox's Spitfire carried up between its landing gear gave the fighter aircraft an additional ninety gallons of fuel and consequently more time in the air for long-distance flights. On this one occasion, however, TAF brass had dispatched F/L Fox back to Tangmere station in England to retrieve a slipper tank full of beer for the refreshment of air and ground crews in France.

"When we lowered the slipper tank and opened it up, there was nothing but foam and the taste of aluminum," Fox said. "So, not to be discouraged, I flew back to Tangmere. Only this time they lashed an actual beer keg to the bomb rack under each wing of the Spitfire. I took off, gained altitude, flew back across the Channel and landed. We put gunny sacks over the kegs, poured water over them for the evaporation and cooling effect and then we drank cold British beer, the first in France."

Though the TAF ground crew might have considered that flight Charley Fox's greatest, the young flight lieutenant from Guelph went on to fly 234 operational missions—the equivalent of two tours—and earn a DFC and bar as part of the highest-scoring wing in Europe during the Second World War. The pilots of 126 Wing eventually flew 22,373 sorties and claimed 361 enemy aircraft destroyed, twelve probable, and 156 damaged. The Wing also destroyed or damaged 493 locomotives and 1,569 railcars, and cut 426 railway lines. By VE Day, May 8, 1945, 126 Wing had also lost ninety-eight pilots and 131 Spitfires.

For some soldiers, it seemed, the war had come along at just the right time. Whether he was stuck without a job or stuck in one with a built-in dead end, whether he had a family with too many mouths to feed and not enough breadwinners, or whether life had very little rhyme or reason at all, joining up solved some men's problems and answered many prayers.

That certainly appeared to be the case with Charlie More. One of eight children born to a Toronto labourer, Charlie never finished school and drifted from one blue-collar job to another, driving for Acme Farmers Dairies and delivering for the Brighton Laundry Company. Nothing seemed to motivate him, except music.

"I remember when he won the Silver Trumpet competition at the Canadian National Exhibition about 1926 or '27," remembered his brother John More. "That was pretty important to him."

Not that music was terribly foreign to Charlie More at all. Part of family folklore was the story that when his parents were courting in Scotland, she played the euphonium (tuba) and he played the trumpet in the local Salvation Army band. In fact, just about everybody in the family played some musical instrument. With father Robert conducting, the Mores used to play for the Earlscourt Brotherhood in Toronto. Through the 1930s, when he had time between his odd jobs, Charlie More worked hardest at landing gigs with his horn. He played his trumpet as a sideman some nights at Toronto's Granite Club, then weekends in the city's dance bands, summers in the resort halls along the Lake Erie shoreline, and he occasionally performed with the Toronto Symphony Orchestra. Nicknamed "Dinty" after an American comic-strip character, Charlie More was fairly well known among musicians around southern Ontario. Despite all his efforts, though, music never became his vocation until the war began.

"Charlie had been in military bands all along," John More said, "but as soon as the war broke out, he enlisted. . . . Here was something that was certain. And when he was suddenly responsible for a band in the military, everything had a purpose."

Based on the belief that "where there were the warriors there were also the minstrels," the D-Day planners had arranged for entertainers to follow on the heels of the assault troops going ashore into Normandy. The American GIs had their United Service Organization (USO) with such entertainers as Bing Crosby, Jack Benny, Ingrid Bergman, Glenn Miller's Army Air Force band, Martha Raye, and, of course, Bob Hope. The British Tommies had the Entertainments National Service Association (ENSA) featuring favourites such as Gracie Fields, Noel Coward, George Formby, and the forces' sweetheart, Vera Lynn. Meanwhile, homesick Canadian troops enjoyed performers such as Johnny Wayne and Frank Shuster, Alan and Blanche Lund, John Pratt, Robert Farnon and his orchestra, Jimmy Shields, and Mildred Morey.

What set the Canadian wartime shows apart from other Allied efforts, and perhaps made them that much more appreciated by their uniformed audiences, was that they were not only *for* the troops, they were *of* them. Whereas the American USO and the British ENSA hired civilians, Canadian entertainment units were made up of men and women in uniform. Every singer, dancer, actor, musician, and even backstage-support person was a member of the forces. Canadian sailors flocked to the "Meet the Navy Show." Air force crews got to see such RCAF entertainers as The Blackouts, The Tarmacs, The W. Debs, and "The Swingtime Show." Meanwhile, Canadian Army troops were entertained by the Soldier Concert Parties, featuring such performers as The Kit Bags, The Invasion Revue, and The Tin Hats.

On paper, Charlie More was a sergeant with No. 3 Detachment in the 15th Canadian Auxiliary Services Section of the Canadian Army Overseas. Actually, he played trumpet with The Tin Hats and, according to most, was "the band disciplinarian," keeping the twelve members of the troupe in tempo and on time. Beginning about 1943, The Tin Hats Concert Party toured among Allied troops in North Africa, Sicily, Italy, and after D-Day duty in northwestern Europe. Music formed the core of the group's repertoire, thanks to pianist Bert Churchill, drummer Les Abraham, sax players Stan Stevenson, Eric Halsall, and Harry Connolly, and trumpeter Charlie More. And "Dinty" relished playing trumpet.

"We'd go on leave, take some time off and visit a pub," Les Abraham used to say, "and after a couple of beers, Charlie would get out his horn and he'd have the place really going."

The Tin Hats claimed more than instrumental virtuosity. Their act included blackface tunes, Norm Harper on his mandolin playing cowboy songs and sketches, and featured comedians Wally Brennan and J. E. "Spud" Cooper. The Hats' all-male cast also boasted several female torch numbers. That is, despite billing "Trixie" and "Triby" as the girls fronting the band, there were no women in the cast, just female impersonators. These were not of the broadly comical variety, men who stuffed grapefruits inside tight sweaters, then smeared on lipstick and rouge and tottered around on high-heeled shoes. No, The Tin Hats' torch singers were so thoroughly convincing that Sgt. Ruth Carmichael, reviewing the group for the Canadian Army newspaper *The Maple Leaf*, wrote:

"While I sat there rocking with laughter at the gags, swooning to the baritone voice of Frank Elliot and the tenor of Norm Harper, and trying to convince myself that Jack Phillips, Bill Dunstan and Johnnie Heawood were guys not gals, I began to wonder just what makes a show without gams and G-strings click so well with the troops."

Buoyed by that kind of accolade, soon after D-Day The Tin Hats troupe of performers and musicians packed up for the Channel crossing aboard the steamship *Empire Beatrice* and a series of shows behind the Canadian lines in Normandy. The *Beatrice* left the Thames Estuary on a Wednesday afternoon as part of a supply convoy with full naval escort. On board the ship all went through the obligatory lifeboat and action-stations drills, with no indication that they would face any trouble crossing to France. That night, however, the convoy witnessed a naval engagement between the escorting warships and a flotilla of German E-boats, a confrontation that soon involved the unarmed passenger vessel.

"At approximately 0045 hours, the action station alarm was sounded from the bridge," reported the 15th Canadian Auxiliary

Service Section war diary. "Due to the terrific noise [of the naval battle], it was not heard by the majority of personnel on board."

The Tin Hats cast members were quartered in the stern of the ship, so a corporal ran aft to rouse the performers from their beds. Most of them left their sleeping quarters immediately and ran to the sides of the ship in action stations readiness. Before the remainder of the cast could be alerted, the *Beatrice* suddenly found itself completely illuminated by a starshell fired by an attacking E-boat. Almost immediately the vessel shuddered as a German torpedo struck her stern section. The explosion destroyed the lifeboats there, disintegrated the stairways leading from the hold up to the deck, and collapsed the deck where the cast had been sleeping.

"The fact that the majority of the men were standing near the sides saved nearly everyone from falling into the hold and the bottom of the ship," the diary continued. "Several did fall, but managed to scramble to safety. Pte. H. Van Buskirk was pinned in the hold by debris and was rescued. Privates Harper, Phillips and Miskelly all fell through, but eventually reached the deck . . . and left the ship by raft and lifeboat. . . . Sgt. More was seen on deck, but was later reported killed."

The forty-one-year-old trumpet player and band leader, trying to ensure the welfare of his fellow performers amid the confusion aboard the stricken ship, was apparently caught in the torpedo explosion and the collapse of the aft deck. His loyalty to the end was noted in the sympathy letter his wife and three sons received back home in Uxbridge, Ontario. Lt. J. B. Hay commended More's willingness "at all times to do anything he was called upon to do. . . . Both on and off the stage his services were invaluable."

The attack on the SS *Empire Beatrice* did not sink the vessel. It killed four men on board, including Sgt. Charlie More, a man who in wartime had found a purpose to his life and a structure that earlier experience seemed to deny him. In perhaps its final photo opportunity, The Tin Hats ensemble had been photographed on a British theatre stage sometime before leaving for France. All the performers were standing at attention. Upstage were the six members of the band dressed in dark blazers and white pants, while downstage in front were the six actor members of the cast, including the two female impersonators in costume. All were flashing Churchill's V for Victory.

"Leading the band was probably the best time of his life," said Charlie's brother John More. "Maybe he was chasing the discipline, but he certainly shone more in the military life than he did before he joined it. . . . In the end he was being responsible and putting himself together. The military and the music had been a steady source of fulfillment."

Exactly seven days after D-Day, Germany unleashed the first so-called vengeance weapon in its arsenal against the Allies. On June 13, 1944, *Vergeltungswaffen-1*, the V-1 flying bomb, a pilotless airplane with a nose containing 2,000 pounds of high explosive, appeared in the skies over London, England. With a range of less than 185 miles and a speed of about 400 mph, the V-1 contained a mechanism that at a given point pushed the aircraft into a steep dive, cut off its fuel supply, and stopped its engine. Thirteen seconds later the bomb exploded on impact, causing massive damage. The flying bombs rained down on Britain from that point until the end of the war, and the period from June through August 1944 proved the worst. In those three months, the Germans launched 8,000 V-1s, of which 2,300 reached the London area. They killed about 5,500 people, injured 16,000 more, and damaged one million buildings, mostly in London.

CBC recording engineer Lloyd Moore happened to be recording a message from Haakon VII, king of Norway, to his subjects soon after D-Day. The king spoke from his refuge study in London, while Moore sat in a recording van parked outside on the street. The king's speech acknowledged the success of D-Day and promised the inevitable defeat of Germany. In fact, the king was just telling his people that their liberation was imminent when a V-1 exploded nearby, interrupting the monarch's speech and ruining the recording. As Moore prepared a new disc the king remarked in an aside, "Doesn't sound much as if we're winning, does it?"

It was also exactly one week after D-Day that Lloyd Moore's press-corps colleagues in Normandy survived an even closer call. Immediately following the invasion, Canadian Army officials assigned the Canadian war correspondents and army public-relations staff to a concrete bunker that the Germans had constructed adjacent to a school in Courseulles-sur-Mer. Partially underground and fortified, the premises proved to be a perfect shelter for the reporters and recording engineers against German artillery and snipers by day and bombers by night. One of the correspondents, William Stewart of Canadian Press, described the nighttime attacks: "A half-hour or so after last evening light, when patrolling Allied fighters were back on the ground, the enemy bombers arrived," he wrote. "One attack was delivered shortly after midnight and a second followed before dawn."

One such attack scored direct hits on the press quarters, which were not as impenetrable as first thought. While no one was killed, all of the CP equipment Stewart and Ross Munro were using was destroyed. Lionel Shapiro, contributor to *Maclean's* magazine, lost his gear as well, while the CBC's Matthew Halton and the *Globe and Mail*'s Ralph Allen managed to save some of their equipment.

Marcel Ouimet happened to be at the front when the attack occurred, and in his message to London for replacement and repairs he itemized the priorities of a warco at the front:

"Send us some paper and carbon. Also some hair brushes, shoe brushes. . . . I haven't had a shave in two days because I lost all my toilet articles. . . . This war is a hard war to cover. Much more difficult than Italy, but we are doing our best. . . . Need cigarettes badly."

Nevertheless, CBC correspondent Matthew Halton returned quickly to a microphone to deliver his final reflections on June 6: "By the night of D-Day, the Canadians had taken nearly all their objectives, and that night, already, the conquest of Germany had begun." He went on to comment on the ferocious counterattacks of June 7 and 8.

"The German storm troops included the 21st Armoured Division, famous in the old desert campaign, and the 12th S.S. Hitler Youth Division, a formation of cunning and ferocious young Germans who'd been indoctrinated since childhood with the most fanatic Nazism and with only one idea—to fight like devils and throw us back. That's what the Canadians faced on the first night and every hour through the next bloody three days. That was their initiation into the horrors of war, but they never budged."

The destruction of the correspondents' first press quarters on June 13 hardly fazed thirty-year-old Ralph Allen. Like Halton, Ouimet, and Munro, he had covered several Canadian military campaigns of the war by then. In Italy he had travelled roads known to be mined in pursuit of stories. He thought nothing of writing his copy in the back of a moving jeep. One night, after dark in the Italian hills, he had typed out a story with one finger by the fitful gleam of a dynamo flashlight held in his free hand. The tall redheaded journalist was moody, stubborn, and not much of a conversationalist, though he could quote Shakespeare flawlessly. What he refused to reveal verbally, he stated in his unique warco attire—beret, rumpled battledress blouse, faded turtleneck sweater, oxford shoes rather than boots, and a pair of yellow-corduroy breeches.

He was, however, a soldier's war correspondent, having enlisted originally with the Royal Canadian Artillery before signing on with the *Globe and Mail* in 1942. Consequently, said his colleagues, he brought a non-commissioned outlook to the war. He claimed that war correspondents too often wrote about themselves and felt sorry for themselves when, for a jolt of reality, all they had to do was look closely at the lot of the lowly Canadian infantryman.

"I never see or talk to a front-line soldier without being amazed by the boundless store of greatness that is wrapped up in the human race, often hidden and unsuspected, but still there waiting to be tapped," Allen once wrote. "The person who can discover precisely what makes soldiers such great human beings and devise a method of organizing or channeling their greatness in peace will have the basic blueprint for that fine new world."

With Operation Neptune virtually complete, Winston Churchill's promise, offered to the people of Europe during the dark days of the retreat from Dunkirk, seemed fulfilled. "In God's good time, the New World, with all its power and might [will] step forth to the rescue and liberation of the Old."

On D-Day-plus-3, General Montgomery reported to the British prime minister that the Allies were sufficiently established ashore that Churchill could visit the area in person. The latter immediately took a train from London to Portsmouth, crossed the Channel aboard a British destroyer, and met General Montgomery on Juno Beach. Churchill reported that all was calm there, the day was brilliant, and everything seemed under control. From Juno Beach the two men were driven to Montgomery's headquarters, Creullet Castle, a château with lakes and lawns surrounding it. They lunched in a tent facing south.

"How far away is the actual front?" Churchill wanted to know.

"About three miles," replied Montgomery.

The prime minister asked the general if the Allies had established a continuous front yet.

"No."

"What is there, then, to prevent an incursion of German armour breaking up our luncheon?" the prime minister asked.

Montgomery said simply that he doubted they would come.

In fact no one ashore in Normandy was perfectly safe no matter how far they were from the front lines. The night before Churchill's visit, the Germans had bombed Montgomery's château headquarters. Bomb craters on the lawns surrounding it gave evidence of that. Following their meal, the two men conducted an inspection of the bridgehead. Churchill showed particular interest in the activity at the local ports of Port-en-Bessin, Courseulles, and Ouistreham, where Allied shipping was already discharging 2,000 tons of supplies a day. At these locations, and eventually at the Mulberry harbour at Arromanches, munitions poured ashore. Here, the men known simply as "service guys" worked almost invisibly supplying the fighting forces ahead of them.

These were the men who transported the food rations, repaired the broken-down engines in mobile workshops, treated troops with dental problems, delivered the mail, policed behind the lines, drove the ambulances, supplied the cases of ammunition, built and rebuilt roads, erected and repaired telephone lines, and constantly worked to clear the massive paper backlog of an invasion army on the move. These were the soldiers backing up the soldiers doing the fighting. These were the troops establishing the supply lines of an invasion army already breaking out of the beachhead and pushing the Germans farther inland.

On D-Day-plus-2, a twenty-five-year-old corporal stepped ashore on Juno Beach. Wally Filbrandt had grown up on a farm not far from Leross on the CNR line in central Saskatchewan, but he joined up in Regina in 1940. Because he had worked at a stationery company in Regina, he had office skills—typing, report writing, documentation work—and the army had streamed him into its clerical section. In England, he had risen through the ranks to take charge of a reinforcement unit whose responsibility was to assign men to replace the casualties in the front line. In the early days of June, like the thousands of other Canadians packed into ships in the Channel on the eve of D-Day, Filbrandt waited for his unit to be shipped to France.

"Our vessel was tied up to a buoy in the Channel and I was sick as a dog," Filbrandt said. "I had a hand on each side of the sink and I stayed that way until we landed."

When he came ashore on June 8, Filbrandt carried the requisite ninety pounds of field gear and rations. By day's end he and his Canadian Section, H.Q. 2nd Echelon, attached to General Montgomery's 21st Army Group, had erected their tents, dug their slit trenches, and set up shop in an apple orchard near the town of La Délivrande, the very base from which William the Conqueror had launched his successful invasion of Britain in 1066. There they gorged themselves on the fresh local fruit, the Calvados apples, hanging just yards from their tents. Most developed stomach aches the first night and had diarrhea the next morning. Filbrandt might have seemed lost in this massive bureaucracy handling the day-to-day running of the military, yet each records clerk fulfilled a vital function in the smooth running of the invasion army.

"There were reinforcement companies, battalions, and brigades all ready to jump into action," he explained. "Each one of us had a unit we looked after. We would receive casualty returns and then assign reinforcements where they were needed."

Filbrandt's efforts to replace wounded driver mechanics with driver mechanics and Bren gunners with Bren gunners became just as desperate a struggle as the fighting at the front line. The section always seemed to have more of those giving orders than those carrying them out. And as the Germans mounted every new counterattack, the demands for replacements steadily grew. The days proved difficult and draining. Every cog had to function properly or the machinery of war would have broken down. And life behind the lines was not entirely out of harm's way. Filbrandt and his clerk mates regularly sought cover from German-artillery barrages during the day and at night had to contend with air attacks.

"The Germans would fly over and drop parachute bombs at random," Filbrandt said. "We had a NET [Non-Effective Transfer] unit next to us, shell-shocked people who'd come out of the lines. They were supposed to be sent back farther to safety. The Germans dropped a bomb right in the middle of their tents one night . . . and finished the job."

Cpl. Wally Filbrandt fought in the clerical trenches from D-Day to VE Day, from Normandy in France to Alost in Germany. He moved with the army, always behind the front and of necessity prepared for the army's everyday needs. He rarely took furloughs with his buddies in the taverns and R-and-R centres provided; instead he used the time to study and upgrade his skills with university-level courses. And when his rest time was over, he eagerly pressed himself back into the job of winning the paper war. In his own efficient way, Filbrandt fought the battles of D-Day, Falaise, the Scheldt, and beyond with a typewriter and a pen, and won.

Much has been said about the significance of the battle at Vimy in the First World War as a defining moment in Canadian history, a milestone along Canada's road to nationhood, because Canadian troops won victory there as an identifiable army. So it has also been said that Canada took its place in the world on June 6, 1944, when its soldiers came ashore in Normandy as full partners in the Allied breaching of Hitler's Atlantic Wall. Both claims may be true. To those Canadians aboard bombers and fighters en route to D-Day targets, at battle stations in ships guarding or moving through the invasion channels, parachuting behind German lines to secure the approach bridges, dashing from assault landing craft desperately seeking out any sign of cover on Juno Beach, supplying artillery and tank support to push the invasion inland, and even those pushing the paper that replaced the casualties at the front, D-Day wasn't about nationhood or world status. It was about survival. It was about the war several feet in front of and on either side of them. None of them knew whether they would be alive or not when June 6 was over. Few even recognized the full risk of the endeavour until they were in the middle of it. Most were citizen soldiers who considered themselves well trained, motivated, scared by the death and destruction around them, yet driven by a sense of commitment, a need to reach the day's objective.

"I was proud to be a Canadian soldier, proud to be a volunteer," Cpl. Wally Filbrandt, the records clerk, said finally. "We did what we truly believed had to be done. We believed we had to make the world safe for democracy."

"What had to be done . . ."

The D-Day success signified more than a moral imperative—meeting the enemy, smashing his will to win, reaching the day's objectives. The breaching of Hitler's Atlantic Wall, at least in the Juno Beach sector, confirmed the Canadians' battle readiness, or as war correspondent Lionel Shapiro described it, "an appetite for battle." Granted, Canadians had previously participated in the liberation of Sicily and the march to free Italy. But in northwestern Europe, the return to France (particularly after Dieppe) and the opening of the second front had great significance for Canadians on D-Day. For the troops fighting as equal partners with the Americans and the British, securing a beachhead in Normandy was a matter of pride and a partial settling of scores. One Canadian signaller reported in a letter home to his sweetheart, "we've been paying our respects to Jerry." For Canadian media, politicians and the soldiers' families too, victory on D-Day resonated at home.

Not only could CBC and Canadian Press correspondents reporting to home-front radio stations and newspapers brag that Canadian ground forces had advanced farther inland than any other Allied troops that day, but there was much else that Canadians could boast about that first Tuesday in June.

On D-Day, Canadian crews of Bomber Command had helped deliver the largest bombing payload of the war—more than 5,000 tons of bombs were dropped that night, the greatest tonnage in one night to that point in the war, with losses of less than 0.5 percent. Meanwhile, Canadians completed their fair share of the 14,674 sorties by the 171 squadrons of Fighter Command in the air on D-Day, and participated in the successful delivery of several hundred gliders full of men and munitions to drop zones in Normandy, again with minimal casualties. Losses proved higher among Canadian paratroops—113 of 543 killed, wounded, or taken prisoner—but the Canadian battalion seized or destroyed all its major objectives on the extreme left of the Allied bridgehead according to plan.

Despite predictions of 60 percent losses, most of the 110 Canadian ships survived the Channel crossing and Normandy assault. Together the 7,016 vessels of Operation Neptune succeeded in moving five divisions by sea against a fortified coastline in total secrecy, achieving both tactical and strategic surprise, which historians Jack Granatstein and Desmond Morton called "an astonishing feat of arms."

In the waters off Juno Beach, Canadian armoured crews had transformed one of Hobart's theoretical innovations—the DD tanks—into an effective element of surprise by swimming a majority of their tanks ashore in tandem with infantry assault troops. Similarly, Canadian field regiments had taken Stanley Todd's fire plan—firing artillery accurately from the decks of heaving tank landing craft—from the drawing board to the Normandy beaches; Montgomery's chief artillery officer said their D-Day achievement "set a standard for the rest of the seaborne artillery."

To ice the cake of Canadian achievement on D-Day, members of the Canadian Film and Photo Unit had recorded, on both still and 35-mm motion picture film, troops touching down at Juno Beach. With the co-operation of their countrymen, the cameramen then managed to get the film off the beach, back to Britain, developed and printed within hours of the beginning of the invasion. In fact, just forty-eight hours after D-Day, Sgt. Bill Grant's movie sequences of the Queen's Own Rifles landing in Normandy dazzled newsreel audiences in British, American, and Canadian theatres. Just 75 days later, at the end of the Battle of Normandy, Canadian ground forces had defeated and virtually destroyed two German armies in France, what historian Terry Copp later described as "one of the most remarkable military victories of the Second World War."

That Norman spring of 1944, about one million Canadian men and women were active in the three services, from a population of about eleven million people. Of those, 100,000 Canadians were directly involved in the preparations for D-Day and the invasion of France. A majority were volunteers, men ranging in age from eighteen to twenty-five. Few had graduated from high school. Most had, at best, a primary-school education.

Contrary to myth, most had left employment to enlist in the services. Whether it was a clear understanding that Hitler's armies posed a threat to Canada and Canadian values, a sentimental attachment to Great Britain and the Commonwealth, or, in the minds of some, a belief that their own father's sacrifices in the First World War might have to be repeated, they readily joined up.

Paratrooper de Vries, as a child in Holland, understood the meaning of foreign occupation. Naval radar operator Gorsline became emotional whenever he saw the Canadian maple leaf emblem. Fighter pilot Fox had the utmost respect for his father's military service dating back to the Boer War. They were all sons of democracy. And while days of setbacks and loss lay between them and final victory in 1945, the thousands of Canadians at D-Day gave their comrades-in-arms, their families, and their country great reason to be proud and full of confidence on June 6, 1944.

"THAT GENERATION
OF YOUNG MEN"

T HERE WERE TOO MANY SCARS left from D-Day and the days immediately after to allow Don James to forget Normandy and the war completely.

Part of a reinforcement group for B Company of the Royal Winnipeg Rifles, Captain James came ashore on D-Day in the second wave at the Mike Red sector of Juno Beach with two other officers and about eighty-five troops. He and his men were welcome replacements, since four of five officers in the original Winnipeg Rifles' assault group had never made it off the beach; one was shot through the eye, another two killed at the entrance to German pillboxes, and the fourth shot through the spine and paralyzed.

On D-Day-plus-1, James and his men advanced inland to Putot-en-Bessin and dug in at the edge of an apple orchard. They knew that the Germans, across a set of railway tracks south of them, were preparing a counterattack. The next morning, June 8, the 2nd Battalion of the 26th S.S. Panzer Grenadier Regiment stormed the Winnipegs' defensive area, and by early afternoon captured Captain James and a number of others in his regiment. The Germans separated James and another officer from the rest and the two men had to watch the S.S. troops shooting their comrades as they sat in a field.

During one of several escape attempts, James took a bullet through his neck and jaw, which oddly may have saved his life. The lieutenant who was with him, Duke Glasgow, administered first aid to stop the bleeding, but the two Canadians were captured again.

"A cart came along and they picked me up with a lot of German wounded and took us to the Château d'Audrieu," James said. "They carried me in and put me with the German wounded. . . . They only had candles, so they couldn't tell whether I was a German or not, because everything was dark. . . . At that time there were about twenty of our fellows who'd been taken there as prisoners. The Germans took them out and shot them individually. . . ."

Evacuated to a prison hospital in the city of Rennes in the Cherbourg peninsula, James was nursed back to health by some Frenchwomen working at the facility. By early August, the Americans began liberating the city and Captain James managed to make contact with them. He was soon transferred to British Intelligence for interrogation, treatment, and eventually embarkation back to England on August 12, "from the very same beach that I landed on."

During the post-war trial of S.S. Col. Kurt Meyer, the Royal Canadian Mounted Police visited Captain James and he gave them his account of the executions of Canadian soldiers at Château d'Audrieu in June 1944. That was virtually the last time Don James spoke publicly about his wartime experience. Little, if anything, was ever discussed of D-Day or those horrific early days of the Normandy invasion in front of his family. Not until after his death in May 1999 did James's two grown daughters begin piecing together their father's wartime story. Initially, all that Beverly, born in 1936, and Penny, born in

1940, could recall about their father and the war was that the family had moved in with their grandparents in Winnipeg.

"I remember in school we always used to go out in the hall before classes started," Beverly (James) Vasey said. "They played the national anthem and God Save the King. Then they would list the fathers and uncles who were serving in the war."

"Every night, we'd go through this sort of ritual too," Penny (James) Adair added. "My mother had us kiss the picture of my father. That's all I knew of my dad."

Not until they were adults did they two sisters investigate their father's career as a Royal Winnipeg Rifles captain in Normandy. In a strange reversal of his self-imposed silence about the war, in 1994, during a fiftieth anniversary return visit to France, Captain James agreed to an interview aboard a ferry crossing the English Channel. Penny and Beverly eventually obtained a transcript of the interview. Then they discovered diary notes that their father had written as well as newspaper clippings and photographs from D-Day and afterwards. Not until June 2003, however, did the two women know instinctively what they must do with their father's story. They would incorporate it into their planned trip to France and Normandy, where their father had landed with his regiment on June 6, 1944.

Crossing the ocean no doubt lost its charm for nineteen-year-old Hallett Whitten during the naval war that Winston Churchill named "the Battle of the Atlantic." The German attempt to stem the vital trans-Atlantic flow of men and supplies to Britain between 1940 and 1943 would cost the Allies more than 2,600 merchant ships, the lives of 30,000 merchant seamen, 5,000 aircrew, and 2,500 aircraft. More than twenty Royal Canadian Navy warships would also be lost. Able Seaman Whitten of the Royal Canadian Naval Volunteer Reserve survived sixteen round trips on the famous "Newfie-to-Derry" (St. John's and

Londonderry, Northern Ireland) convoy run aboard an RCN frigate, HMCS *Prince Rupert.*

At his depth-charge battle station, late in the winter of 1944, Whitten recalled his ship's participation in a typical "hunt to exhaustion" battle with a U-boat in the mid Atlantic. In the course of the engagement, the *Prince Rupert* joined an American flotilla of escort ships, the carrier USS *Bogue,* and aircraft from RAF Coastal Command to sink *U-575* on March 13. In late May, his ship was reassigned to a navy escort group in the English Channel to protect the western flank of the invasion force. At his duty watch on the starboard side of the bridge, Whitten remembered the June 6 operation as an anxious one.

"All we knew about D-Day was what we could see and hear. We could see the sky was full of aircraft, but there was radio silence at sea," Whitten said. "We reported everything, even bird sightings. . . . At times, I'd wonder, 'Which way will I jump when the torpedo hits us?'"

AB Whitten saw no enemy ships at all on June 6. In fact, he only learned the full story of D-Day later during the fall of 1944, when *Prince Rupert* sailed into Liverpool, Nova Scotia, for a refit. His connection with the D-Day invasion might even have ended there. He was honourably discharged a year later and returned to civvy street, eventually working and raising a family in Toronto.

Fifty-nine years later, however, he found himself crossing the Atlantic aboard a charter airline en route to France for a once-in-a-lifetime veterans' reunion. His local Royal Canadian Legion, Branch 606, in Pickering, Ontario, had learned that a Pickering councillor, Dave Ryan, and members of the army and navy cadets had raised enough money to send two veterans on a return trip to Normandy. Although he hesitated at first to accept the offer, his three daughters quickly persuaded him that they all should go.

Normandy has beckoned to Richard Rohmer more than once since June 1944. Initially, as a pilot with the RCAF, Flying Officer Rohmer had eagerly taken to the skies with other members of his No. 430 Squadron of photo-reconnaissance Mustangs on D-Day morning. He and his fellow pilots criss-crossed in the skies above Juno Beach as the first troops dashed from their landing craft. Years after the war, while researching various historical records for several of his books of fiction and non-fiction, he had occasion to return to some of those same historic Battle of Normandy locations. More recently, he has attended D-Day anniversaries at war memorials in France, and while revisiting the invasion beaches area he stayed at an eighteenth-century manor house-turned-bed and breakfast, the Manoir du petit Magny near Bayeux.

For Rohmer, returning to Normandy was a bit like coming home. The modern-day vacation hotel, it turned out, had been the wartime home of his No. 430 Squadron when the 2nd Tactical Air Force (TAF) transferred its operations from southern England to the Continent right after D-Day. Then known simply as "airstrip B8," the location next to the manor house had always held special significance for the former RCAF pilot.

"The first landing was really quite an emotional moment," Rohmer said. "We were in France. We were on their turf and this was the objective that we had clearly in our minds to be part of the liberation of the country. It was an exciting moment."

From then until the first week of August 1944, the pilots of No. 430 Squadron lived under canvas and occasionally in slit trenches. They used the kitchen in the manor house to prepare food for the officers' mess. On the upper level of the house's north wing, pilots waited for their daily call to operation briefings. Several hundred yards from the stone complex had sat the squadron's briefing van, where the pilots received their ops orders. Just steps from the van were the flight line and the lengthy east-west airstrip, with its Mustangs ready to launch into action each day.

In June 2003, however, both the history and a sense of loss drew Richard Rohmer back to the 2nd TAF invasion area of Normandy yet again.

Signaller Don Kerr readily admits he was "scared stiff . . . my life flashing in front of me" during the D-Day landings. After training scores of Royal Canadian Corps of Signals crewmen for the assault on Juno Beach, he and a small section of Canadian signallers had received last-minute orders to join the British Force G group landing at Arromanches instead. During his first moments ashore on Gold Beach, Kerr saw men die and the landscape erupt with explosions and gunfire. Somehow he came through it all without a scratch. Then, despite the risks of stringing and maintaining the telephone wires near frontline combat, Lieutenant Kerr's good fortune continued.

"This one day I was looking for forward locations to set up a divisional headquarters communications spot," Kerr recalled. "Suddenly I saw a swastika flag draped over a dead horse in a farmer's yard. I had to have the flag."

On countless other occasions he had reminded his own signals crews to resist souvenir-collecting, since retreating German troops booby-trapped everything from doorways to vehicles to bodies. He himself had taken extra field training in defusing mines, however, so he felt confident that he could remove the flag safely. He had just begun slipping it carefully off the dead animal when the door of the nearby farmhouse burst open and out ran dozens of German soldiers.

"I thought, 'Well, you fell into the trap, you silly ass!' But no. The [Canadian] infantry had already passed this location, so the Germans were giving themselves up. They all ran out and threw their rifles on the ground and surrendered to me. . . . So I marched them down the road and turned them over to some other Canadian troops. . . . I never did get the flag."

Kerr managed to stay out of harm's way across Normandy, into Belgium and Holland, and even through the last days of the war in Germany. Many of the signals crewmen he had trained survived as well. Some received medals for their meritorious service. Kerr was mentioned in despatches. And yet, while he travelled back to Europe on business numerous times after the war, he could never return to the Normandy beaches.

"I could deal with just about anything on D-Day," he said. "You had to survive. You had to make sure you saw the sun rise tomorrow, so you did everything you could to ensure that happening. So you weren't worried."

The thought of facing his emotions, his memories of surviving June 6, 1944, kept him away for years. It kept him away for the rest of the century.

One day, in June 2003, D-Day veteran Don Kerr did come back to Normandy. So did Penny and Beverly, the adult daughters of Royal Winnipeg Rifles' veteran Don James. As well, Hal Whitten, a former RCNVR seaman, returned to the invasion beaches he had helped protect. RCAF pilot Richard Rohmer did too. They all returned to the Norman coast, to Juno Beach, on the same day. They came back because some of their peers, some of their fellow veterans, had given them a powerful reason to come back.

Another survivor of the Second World War, Lise Cooper, was responsible for giving Don Kerr and a thousand other veterans a reason to gather in France on the fifty-ninth anniversary of D-Day. As a teenager during the war, Lise had served on Canada's home front, knitting socks, collecting used items, and selling them to raise money for wartime service groups. In September 1941, one of her fundraisers had even elicited a response from the Quebec branch of the Red Cross for her "bazaar held in the memory of Sgt. Pilot Ian Beaton, netting the large sum of $85. . . . We appreciate this fine effort," the letter's writer stated and then concluded, "Keep up the good work and we shall surely win this dreadful war."

At a roller-skating party in 1946, Lise fell in love with and later married a veteran of the Royal Canadian Artillery. It turned out that George Cooper, the son of a First World War veteran and the eldest of five brothers, had joined the 14th Field Regiment and had landed on Juno Beach on D-Day. Not a professional soldier, Cooper had spent most of the war armed with engine-mechanics' tools rather than rifles and grenades. But in the eyes of his more patriotic wife, Lise, what "that generation of young men" accomplished overseas was simply a miracle.

In 1969, on the twenty-fifth anniversary of D-Day, the couple returned to several of the areas in Europe that Canadians had liberated in 1944 and 1945, including Normandy. They had been planning to do the same on the fiftieth anniversary, but George died in 1992. Mother and daughter made the pilgrimage instead and visited several liberation sites in Holland. In one town, Dutch children showered the visiting veterans with flowers, embraced them, and sang songs of freedom in their honour. At the end of the tribute, another 14th Field Regiment veteran had thanked the children and made a spur-of-the-moment offer.

"We'd like you to come to Canada," Garth Webb told them.

Somehow the veterans raised the funds and brought those children to Canada for three weeks. A return visit of Canadian children to Europe seemed the appropriate next step.

"But what are we going to show them in Normandy?" Lise Cooper had wondered. "Beautiful sandy beaches, markers, streets called 'Liberation' or 'Bienvenue aux Canadiens.' But what else? We have the Vimy memorial [and museum] for the First World War. But we have nothing for the Second World War."

The dream of preserving the memory of "that generation of young men" with a permanent memorial/museum and interpretive centre in Normandy was born in that moment. Lise Cooper and Garth Webb joined another D-Day vet, Don Jamieson, and formed a non-profit association in 1995 to establish a facility in Normandy to pay tribute to all the Canadian veterans of the 1939–1945 war. At first, the association had considered a modest plan, renting an existing building, perhaps even the famous Tudor-style beach house that so many Canadian D-Day veterans saw during their first moments coming ashore in the Nan White sector of Juno Beach. The rental evolved into a hope that the town of Bernières might donate land on which the vets would design and construct their own building. The land proposal fell through. And the plan might have withered and died there if not for Normandy resident Roger Alexandre.

Five days after D-Day, troops of the Queen's Own Rifles of Canada and tanks from the 6th Armoured Regiment (1st Hussars) had advanced over the high ground near the village of Le Mesnil-Patry. The Alexandre family farmed that area under the German occupation. Roger and his parents had watched the Canadians suddenly meet strong machine-gun and mortar fire in the grain fields outside their village. The German defenders threw back the Canadians' attempt to liberate the Alexandres' community.

"Members of my family were down in trenches as the Canadians fought," said Roger Alexandre, who was fourteen at the time of the battle. "More than a hundred Canadians were killed."

Actually, D Company of the Queen's Own lost ninety-nine men, including fifty-five killed. B Squadron of the 1st Hussars lost men in the engagement, too, eighty officers and other ranks, including fifty-nine killed. Only two of its tanks returned. The attack on Le Mesnil-Patry would be the last large Canadian operation in the month of June. While the Allies did manage to liberate the village a few days later, Roger Alexandre and his family were not liberated until August when they returned to their virtually obliterated village. Years later, when Roger Alexandre was mayor of Le Mesnil-Patry, the village of 120 unveiled its own monument to the fallen Canadians.

"Many Canadians came to the memorial," he said. "We made many friends and we became more and more attached to Canada."

When Alexandre met the Juno Beach Centre group in 1996, the Canadians still hoped the Bernières land deal would materialize. Then, in February 2000, the veterans approached the neighbouring village of Courseulles-sur-Mer. The mayor and council suggested they might provide an old seaside campground as the site for a memorial facility. Regular users of the campground opposed the idea until Alexandre and a Normandy historian named Jean-Pierre Bénamou organized a petition and a demonstration to bring together hundreds of veterans, politicians, and other patriotic supporters of a Canadian war memorial in the region. The mayor, Jean-Louis de Mourgues, campaigned just as vigorously within the municipal government, and by 2001 his council proudly presented the former campground to the newly formed non-profit Juno Beach Centre Association. Don Cooper, Lise's son, became project manager.

For Cooper, taking on the managing role of the Centre made sense. He was an engineering graduate of the Royal Military College in Kingston, Ontario, had served in the military during some of the Cold War years, and understood Canada's commitment to its allies. His grandfather had served in France during the First World War, and his father had landed in Normandy on D-Day with the 14th Field Regiment. The idea of joining the Juno Beach Centre project had appealed to him for other reasons as well.

"We would have a very different existence today if people like my dad hadn't stepped up and done what needed to be done at the time," he said. "My dad wasn't a patriot. He was a typical Canadian citizen soldier. The Canadian Army was an army of amateurs. They weren't people who had dedicated their careers, their lives to fighting, or to war. It makes what they accomplished all the more remarkable."

That same sense of commitment that Canadians exhibited between 1939 and 1945 motivated the Juno Beach Centre Association half a century later. In Canada the veterans and the volunteers organized themselves into an executive, a board, and various specialized committees and then set out to build something unique. In 2001, the group put out a call for content proposals and building designs. It commissioned a sculpture for the entrance to the building, an eight-foot bronze memorial called *Remembrance and Renewal* by Colin Gibson, a Canadian sculptor. It chose an exterior design by architect Brian Chamberlain, one that accommodated both the neighbouring environment and the exhibits inside. The association also invited virtually all of the Normandy trades that would make up the construction team to participate in the planning for the centre. For example, the builders suggested steel studs, rather than concrete, for the facility walls, which reduced construction time, the quantity of necessary materials, and ultimately the cost.

"With each step we kept setting our sights higher," Cooper said. "Courseulles from a commercial and visitors' point of view was a step up for us, so we said we have to put up a facility that suits this great site. . . . The architect didn't come up with a square building [but] with a series of pods all hooked to a pentagon or maple-leaf design."

Within the walls of the centre, Don Cooper and his project team worked with exhibit specialists to create the five permanent multimedia display areas that would illustrate Canada's worldwide role in the Second World War. They aimed to pay tribute to Canadians who had participated in every theatre of the war and to dispel what Cooper called "a Steven Spielberg perception among French young people . . . that the Americans won the war."

As the project grew, however, so did its overall price tag. Original estimates of several hundred thousand dollars in 1995 climbed to a budget of $11 million by 2003.

Awareness-raising and fundraising became top priorities. Association members canvassed every level of Canadian government, expecting automatic support from the provinces and Ottawa. They made their pitches in the classrooms of every school board that would hear them and in the boardrooms of corporate Canada, where they hoped major contributors would step forward eagerly. The centre was a tougher sell than they had expected. At the same time, the association began to appeal directly to the veterans themselves. Unsure it would help their cause, the executive hesitantly consented to construct a Web site, inviting Canadians to purchase Juno Beach Centre bricks ranging in price from $250 for individuals to $2,500 for corporations, each to be inscribed with a veteran's name and to be incorporated into a series of outdoor kiosks. Suddenly, the trickle of donations became a steady stream.

"The responses in the mail made me cry," Lise Cooper said. "We'd receive a ten-dollar cheque from Newfoundland or B.C. and a note saying 'I lost my brother there' or 'Bless you for doing this. It's something that should have been done ages ago.' I had some very difficult days."

Along the way, the Juno Beach Centre found other allies in unexpected places. In addition to the 11,000 Canadians—and some Americans—who purchased commemorative bricks, the association suddenly found itself welcome at the executive level of one of the biggest retailers in the country. Garth Webb had written a letter to Mario Pilozzi, who had grown up in Montreal, to congratulate him on becoming CEO of Wal-Mart Canada. Webb had received a response and an audience, and best of all Pilozzi's promise to help. Wal-Mart Canada agreed to raise $1.5 million for the centre. It invited Canadian veterans into their 213 retail stores across the country to promote and sell the commemorative bricks. Wal-Mart eventually contributed another $2 million worth of publicity, including television ads shot on location in Normandy.

Veterans and dignitaries turned first sod at Courseulles in February of 2002. Excavation began in March. That June, as the 15,000-square-foot concrete foundation cured in the Norman sunshine, Canadian and French representatives dedicated the cornerstone. Back in Canada, work began on the five permanent interior displays—"Courseulles, June 6, 1944"; "Canada in the 1930s"; "Canada Goes to War"; "Roads to Victory"; and "Some Came Back, Others Did Not." In Toronto, Ted Davie of the centre's board of directors met with CBC TV producers to acquaint them with the story of "Canada, the forgotten ally." He unveiled schematic drawings of the site in Courseulles and walked them through plans for the opening ceremonies.

Meanwhile, other members of the Juno Beach Centre's board of directors and its working committees fanned out across the country to raise funds and public awareness for their project.

D-Day paratrooper Jan de Vries and others attended ceremonies in city halls, town councils, and school assemblies to receive brick donations. Another veteran and the Royal Canadian Legion liaison, Bruce Melanson, led scores of fellow veterans into corporate centres, malls, and plazas to plead their case and gather cash. D-Day signaller Don Kerr wrote to provincial politicians, some of whom he knew personally, reminding them of the regiments that had come from their regions during the war and appealing for their financial support. Ultimately, in the spring of 2003, as the titanium-and-glass exterior of the facility took shape on the beach at Courseulles-sur-Mer, the association's coffers were building too: more than $2 million from various levels of the government in France, $1 million each from Ontario and British Columbia, nearly $200,000 from the other provinces combined, and $3.5 million from individual citizens and private corporations.

There was also welcome news from Ottawa; the Department of Veterans Affairs' contribution would bring the federal government's total investment to $3 million. Meanwhile, contacts both in Ottawa and Paris began the delicate process of coaxing the Canadian and French prime ministers to attend the opening of the centre. John Clemes, the Juno Beach Centre's board representative in Paris, was resolute about the project and the board's intentions.

"Right from the beginning," he said, "we all expressed an innocent faith that what should be done, would be done."

D-Day 2003 dawned much brighter and more certain for the Juno Beach Centre than had the D-Day of 1944. Like the first D-Day, however, the same day fifty-nine years later presented numerous challenges.

Paint was still drying on the walls inside the centre as the facility's director, Natalie Worthington, juggled staff assignments, tour guides, souvenir-shop supplies, and media requests right down to the wire. In front of the centre, Colin Gibson worked well into the evening of June 5 to ensure that the night-time lighting of his *Remembrance and Renewal* sculpture was just right. Ted Davie barely stood still as he worked out the endless logistics for the centre's two-hour opening ceremonies, the television coverage, the arrival and departure of the prime ministers, Jean Chrétien and Jean-Pierre Raffarin, the wreath-laying, the veterans' parade, and the various aerial events, including the arrival of a team of skydivers, a display of aerobatics by a vintage RAF Spitfire, and a symbolic drop of poppies to honour Canada's Second World War dead.

Project manager Don Cooper coped with his share of snafus. The centre's air-conditioning system would not work on opening day. Because veterans had been touring through the museum days before the official opening, the souvenir-shop shelves were nearly bare. At the last minute, French public-service strikers announced they would picket the event to publicize a pension dispute with the French government; consequently, the French police demanded that the centre's staff erect and anchor restraining fences around the facility and beef up the centre's admission security. As well, the planned poppy-pin drop suddenly presented a unique challenge.

"Veterans Affairs had offered us the poppies," Cooper said, "because they had thousands of the old ones with the green centres left over [from Remembrance Day]. . . . Problem was we thought we could kill somebody with all those pins falling from the sky. . . . So we had army cadets removing the pins from 43,000 poppies the day before the event."

Like D-Day 1944, the Juno Beach Centre launch enjoyed much success. In mid morning, about a thousand veterans and several thousand invited guests began filing through the police checkpoints at the eastern edge of Courseulles-sur-Mer and moving toward the sun-baked apron in front of the Centre. Another thousand spectators moved to the slightly elevated beach area beyond the fences to watch the proceedings. An encampment of tents and canopies along the entrance way slowly filled with ceremony participants, band instruments, wreaths, media correspondents, and hospitality staff preparing post-ceremony refreshments. About noon, the centre's staff conducted microphone checks and staged a hasty rehearsal of the opening ceremony at the main podium, while media crews from Canada and France interviewed scores of veterans in front of the commemorative kiosks and the *Remembrance and Renewal* sculpture. As H-Hour for the start of the ceremony approached, a number of helicopters landed and delivered the dignitaries. Soon after that, the Canadian Forces Parachute Teams, the Sky Hawks, made a pinpoint drop, delivering a Canadian flag to officially launch the ceremonies and initiate the first of the dignitaries' speeches.

The two prime ministers paid eloquent tribute to the veterans. "You were more than a million Canadians fighting in Europe," Prime Minister Jean Chrétien said. "More than forty thousand of your comrades, including eight thousand in France, would never see their country again.... At the Juno Beach Centre, visitors will learn about the contributions of that generation."

Jean-Pierre Raffarin, the prime minister of France, picked up on the same theme: "In the evening of the longest day, more than nine hundred and sixty Canadians had fallen in the line of duty. They were strong because they were aware of their mission for liberty. Veterans, we thank you for our freedom."

Those words of gratitude moved Hal Whitten greatly. The RCNVR veteran had always minimized his own role aboard the Canadian frigate HMCS *Prince Rupert* on D-Day, as "just floating around out in the Channel." Indeed, the former able seaman needed to be convinced by his family that the trip to Juno Beach

Centre was worthwhile. Ultimately, he felt it would be educational for members of his family to attend. So there he sat on the Juno Beach Centre guest benches with his three adult daughters, two sons-in-law, and two grandchildren.

"I shed a few tears more than once," Whitten said. "To think that the French prime minister still feels that way about Canadians all these years later. I was blown away."

During the contemplative section of the ceremony the Juno Beach Centre plaque was unveiled, and the sculpture *Remembrance and Renewal* and the memorial brick kiosks were dedicated. Those present joined in prayers for the fallen and buglers played The Last Post and Reveille. All observed minutes of silence. Then wreaths were laid and young people recited, "They shall not grow old as we who are left grow old. Age shall not weary them, nor the years condemn. At the going down of the sun and in the morning, we will remember them."

This act of remembrance humbled one veteran as much as it expressed homage. On D-Day morning, Flying Officer Richard Rohmer had piloted his Mustang across the Channel as a member of No. 430 (RCAF) Squadron in a photo-reconnaissance mission over the beachhead. Though he had nearly run out of fuel during the morning operation, he had survived it as well as the rest of his tour, for which he was awarded the Distinguished Flying Cross. Standing next to the French ambassador during the ceremony, Major-General Rohmer thought about his good fortune.

"I had been able to grow old," Rohmer said. Not all the pilots attached to his wing had been so lucky. "Flying Officer Jack Cox was part of our Mustang squadron. His section was doing reconnaissance over the beach and they were attacked by Focke-Wulf 190s. Jack was our only casualty on D-Day."

Of the politicians participating in the Juno Beach Centre ceremony, Jean-Louis de Mourgues, mayor of Courseulles, received the veterans' warmest welcome. He returned their recognition with an impassioned tribute.

"Any war of deliverance is sacred . . . and Canada has always been present in our hearts." He pointed out that each June 6 the people of Courseulles honour the memory of tank crewman Sgt. Leo Gariepy of the 6th Armoured Regiment (1st Hussars), who, ten years after D-Day, returned to Courseulles to live out his life in France. The mayor concluded: "The 1st Hussars, the Royal Winnipeg Rifles, the Regina Rifles are forever engraved in our memory. We will never forget you."

The mayor's words particularly touched Beverly Vasey and Penny Adair, the daughters of the Royal Winnipeg Rifles' Capt. Don James, whose diaries described his near fatal wounding and narrow escape from execution by his German captors at the Château d'Audrieu on June 8, 1944.

"He never talked about the war," Penny Adair said, "but he never threw anything away, the newspaper clippings, the diaries, pictures. . . . We brought them with us. We thought we should bring his story here." During their pilgrimage they donated copies of Don James's D-Day story to the centre's library.

D-Day valour was at the heart of the speech the premier of Ontario delivered. "The soldiers, the sailors, and the airmen who set out on D-Day didn't set out to be heroes," Premier Ernie Eves said. "They were simply ordinary young men from all over Canada. But by the end of the day, heroes they had become, immortalized in the eyes of Canadians and the entire free world."

The premier's words struck a chord with Don Kerr. The eighty-two-year-old D-Day signaller admitted he got a little teary-eyed looking at some of the pictures in the centre and listening to some of the speeches. Generally, he had been comfortable with getting emotional about raising money for the centre; since 2000, he had written a blizzard of passionate and patriotic letters coaxing money from corporate executives and provincial politicians, and he was proud of the results. However, until a few months before the opening ceremonies, he had even doubted whether he would attend.

"I fought with it," he said. "I thought I would get too emotional when I got to Normandy. But I sat back and said, 'So what. So you're going to get emotional. It's part of life.' And there aren't many of us left. This gathering at Juno Beach is probably the largest gathering of D-Day veterans left."

The originator of the Juno Beach Centre, Garth Webb, recognized the highly charged atmosphere of the occasion too. A gun-position lieutenant with the 14th Field Regiment on D-Day, he had often described his experience that day in 1944 as "the Grey Cup, the Stanley Cup, and the World Series all played on the same day, and I'm not only there, but I'm playing." Then, on the anniversary in 2003, the opening day of the only Canadian war memorial and interpretive centre in Europe, Webb approached the microphone with his fellow Juno Beach Centre director, Lise Cooper, and tried to sum up his emotions again.

"I was on this beach fifty-nine years ago," Webb explained to the veterans and spectators. "And it's just as big a thrill to be here today."

For the next few moments, Garth Webb and Lise Cooper, co-creators of the dream-come-true facility, congratulated many of their partners, the people of Courseulles-sur-Mer, three levels of government in two countries, the unpaid volunteers and board of directors, corporate Canada, and the 13,000 Canadians and French civilians who had made cash donations towards its construction. Webb concluded his thank-yous by declaring the Juno Beach Centre "a partnership between Canada and France that will last forever." Then he led the veterans and other spectators in three cheers for France.

A helicopter flew low over the proceedings and released the 43,000 poppies, one for each Canadian who died in the Second World War as the pipes played "Amazing Grace." The breezes scattered the fluttering scarlet display over the podium, the spectators, the centre, and the beaches.

Tony Burns bent down to pick up some of the poppies. He had crossed this same beach as part of No. 1 Canadian Mobile Neuro-Surgical Unit shortly after D-Day. As a private and an operating room assistant, he had been part of the medical team repairing the damage that D-Day fighting had inflicted on hundreds of Canadian soldiers. In one of those operating sessions when a German shell struck the trailer where he worked, Private Burns too had become a casualty. He had been in a coma for days. On June 6, 2003, he celebrated his survival and gathered up twelve of the poppies for his fellow veterans back home in Halifax.

"I knew the trip to the Juno Beach memorial would be my last," Burns wrote. During the trip he also visited the grave of his brother, Lt. Dan Burns of the Royal Canadian Regiment, at the Argenta Gap War Cemetery in Italy. "The war was hell. . . . Peace—so many millions never experienced it. What a pity."

The emotional outpouring at the inauguration was not over. As the last of the poppies drifted inland from the skies above the beach toward the town of Courseulles, Garth Webb called on his fellow veterans to join him in a final march past. Many of those who had stormed those same beaches half a lifetime earlier crowded the square in front of the centre. Without the military precision that marked the rest of the ceremony, the march past took some time to organize. Eventually, Webb shouted, "World War Two veterans, by the right, quick march! . . ." With medals and ribbons up, backs straight, and marching steps that connected them to their youth, the veterans, one thousand of them, paraded past the entrance to their new Juno Beach Centre. The spectators stood and applauded and shouted their gratitude in French and English until the last of the old soldiers had passed.

Two generations descended from veteran Mark Lockyer applauded the seventy-nine-year-old D-Day paratrooper as he marched with his comrades that afternoon. His middle-aged children, Bill Lockyer and Roberta Sommerville, and her twenty-seven-year-old daughter, Serenity Corlett-Lockyer, clapped proudly and snapped pictures. Grandfather Lockyer, early on D-Day morning, had dropped with the 1st Canadian Parachute Battalion into territory the Germans had flooded by damming the River Dives to the east of the D-Day invasion beaches. Though the family knew he had reached his objective, the bridge over the River Dives near Robehomme, and had helped blow it up with explosives, Roberta and Bill knew little more.

"I was always pulled along to the cenotaph each Remembrance Day and most often Dad led the parade," Bill Lockyer said. "The first [Canadian Parachute Battalion] reunion was held at our house. The brigadier slept in my bed. They all talked about the good times, never the bad."

Mark Lockyer had travelled to Europe once earlier, in 1969, to mark the twenty-fifth anniversary of D-Day and the liberation of Holland. His daughter Roberta had also accompanied him on the trip and at one point into a cemetery of war dead.

"He found a couple of headstones and he sat right down and started to cry," she said. "I was in shock. I had never seen my father cry before."

To his family's surprise, around Christmas 2002, Mark Lockyer had announced he was withdrawing enough of his savings to pay for a family trip to Normandy in June of the following year. It was time to share some of his war story with his family. On their way to Courseulles-sur-Mer and the Juno Beach Centre opening ceremony, Lockyer made the time to lead his son, daughter, and granddaughter to the Robehomme bridge. There it stood, still one lane wide, still made of wood, and for Lockyer still full of memories. By coincidence, as the Canadians drove up, two Frenchmen arrived to install a plaque acknowledging the British and Canadian paratroopers who had destroyed the structure on D-Day.

"In our broken French, Bill and I tried to explain to the French workers why we were there," Roberta Sommerville said. "We pointed to the bridge and kept saying 'Kaboom' and they finally understood. They gave my father the plaque to hold for a while."

As emotional as the moment had become, Mark Lockyer carefully explained his D-Day story to his granddaughter then and there. It was as if he were passing the experience on, like a gift, to the next generation. Serenity stood attentively at the railing of the Robehomme bridge. She said she felt thankful and proud to be there.

"I got choked up," her grandfather said. "People often say young people today don't take responsibility seriously. Well, during the war we were all young, too. The oldest guy in our platoon was twenty-three. . . . I wanted my family to understand what it was all about. We had a job to do and got it done."

Notes

PRELUDE

page

1 "having bugs . . .": John Marteinson and Michael R. McNorgan, *The Royal Canadian Armoured Corps: An Illustrated History*, p. 105.

2 "halfway across . . .": Stephen Bell, interview, Uxbridge, Ont., 1993.

2 4,963 . . . French: Denis and Shelagh Whitaker, *Dieppe*.

2 commando-type raid: Copp, *Battlefields of Northwest Europe*, p. 34.

2 "We had a foreboding . . .": Archie Anderson, *The Journal*, CBC TV, August 1992.

5 Altogether 3,367 . . . : Granatstein and Morton, *Bloody Victory*, p. 11.

8 Canadian shock troops: Ross Munro, *Winnipeg Tribune*, Aug. 20, 1942.

8 Looking out . . . : Ross Munro, *Gauntlet to Overlord*.

9 "the magnificent fiasco": Ralph Allen, *Ordeal by Fire*, pp. 397, 407.

CHAPTER ONE

page

11 "Nervous? No . . .": Charley Fox, interview, Toronto, Ont., March 6, 2003.

14 "Meteorological . . .": Robert Dale, interview, Toronto, Ont., May 13, 2003.

17 "Isn't there . . .": Quoted in Hilary St. George Saunders and Denis Richards, *Royal Air Force, 1939–1945*, Vol. III, *The Fight Is Won*, p. 104.

18 "Rip cord plus 24": Rohmer, *Patton's Gap: Mustangs Over Normandy*, p. 59.

20 "The question . . .": Joseph Stalin, letter to Winston Churchill, July 23, 1942, quoted in *The Second World War*, Vol. 4, *Hinge of Fate*, p. 271.

20 "the Russians . . .": Franklin D. Roosevelt, letter to Winston Churchill, April 3, 1942; also Vol. 4, p. 314.

21 "a full-scale assault . . .": Stephen E. Ambrose, *D-Day, June 6, 1944: The Climactic Battle of World War II*, p. 71.

21 "lodgement area": Col. C. P. Stacey, *The Victory Campaign*, p. 17.

26 "that no attack . . .": Field-Marshal Gerd Von Rundstedt, quoted in Stacey, p. 49.

26 "856,000 men": Granatstein and Morton, *Bloody Victory*, p. 49.

28 remained upbeat: Lillian Turnbull, quoted in "Govan, The Home of Heroes," in Regina *Leader-Post*, April 26, 1944.

28 Wartime records: Les Allison, "Three Brothers, Three DFCs," *Airforce* magazine, Winter 1998/99.

28 highest casualties: Barris, *Behind the Glory*, p. 176.

28 "tweaking the nose . . .": John Turnbull, interview, Toronto, March 4, 2003.

29 "an awful . . .": John Turnbull, quoted in *So Many . . .* , p. 235.

31 "but we returned . . .": Ron Gillett, quoted in *So Many . . .* , p. 135.

32 "It is better . . .": Jacques Martin, interview, Bernières-sur-Mer, June 3, 2003.

33 system of 15,000: Le Memorial de Caen, data compiled at the museum archives.

35 "We went . . .": Murray Peden, quoted in *So Many . . .* , p. 196.

36 "the theory . . .": R. V. Jones, *Most Secret War*, p. 369.

36 German controller: Murray Peden, *A Thousand Shall Fall*, p. 367.

37 accurate defence: Ibid.

37 Operation Taxable: Saunders and Richards, *The Fight Is Won*, p. 109.

38 "Seal off . . .": Murray Peden, e-mail, Sept. 9, 2003.

38 "Our orders . . .": Peden, *A Thousand Shall Fall*, p. 382.

38 "We were . . .": Charley Fox, interview, Toronto, Ont., March 6, 2003.

39 "calling cards . . .": Barris, *Behind the Glory*, p. 4.

42 thirty-two enemy: McCaffery, *Air Aces*, p. 133.

42 "We took off . . .": Charley Fox, interview, London, Ont., May 9, 1991.

45 "In the middle . . .": Laurette (Parsons) Hilborn, interview, Waterloo, Ont., March 3, 2003.

47 "Eileen is married . . .": Wallechinsky and Wallace, *The People's Almanac*, p. 56.

CHAPTER TWO

page

49 "To assist them . . .": Eisenhower quoted in Saunders and Richards, *The Fight Is Won*, p. 106.

50 "There's no doubt . . .": Leigh-Mallory quoted in ibid.

51 "He ain't gonna": Jan de Vries, correspondence August 7, 2003

51 "We always sang . . .": Jan de Vries, interview, Pickering, Ont., January 26, 2003.

52 July 1, 1942: Willes, *Out of the Clouds*, p. 11.

52 Fallschirmjager: Lt./Col. Bernd Horn and Michel Wyczynski, *Tip of the Spear*, p. 15.

56 eleven Albemarles: Hartigan, *A Rising of Courage*, p. 63.

58 "There she goes . . .": Richard Dimbleby, from BBC "Radio Newsreel" broadcast, June 6, 1944.

59 made an error: Willes, *Out of the Clouds*, p. 71.

60 "Ham and Jam": Ellis Plaice, "Securing the Left Flank, Seizing the Bridges: Red Berets '44," *The Illustrated London News*, London, 1994, p. 32.

60 Drop Zone V: Dept. of National Defence, Directorate of History records.

65 "As I approached . . .": Graeme Metcalf, transcribed conversation, Dec. 7, 1986.

65 "It happened . . .": Richard Hilborn, interview, Waterloo, Ont., March 3, 2003.

67 "I was never . . .": Mark Lockyer, interview, Oshawa, Ont., July 7, 2003.

72 "Here we've come . . .": Ernie Jeans, interview, Toronto March 4, 2003

73 "The room was . . .": Hartigan, p. 127.

76 264 aircraft: Saunders and Richards, *The Fight Is Won*, p. 108.

76 "The planes in . . .": Ralph Campbell, *We Flew by Moonlight*, p. 57.

CHAPTER THREE

page

80   "(We) figure . . .": Ray Mecoy, interview, Toronto, Ont., May 25, 2003.

80   crew of eighty-three: Ken Macpherson, *Minesweepers of the Royal Canadian Navy, 1938–1945*, p. 70.

81   "Pious dream": Joseph Schull, *The Far Distant Ships*, p. 233.

82   Piccadilly Circus: Cdr. Anthony Storrs, quoted in Jean Portugal (ed.), *We Were There: The Navy*, RCMI, 1998, p. 21.

83   "Up until that . . .": Reg Weeks, interview, Ottawa, Ont., April 18, 2003.

86   Bristling with: C. Anthony Law, *White Plumes Astern*, p. 14.

86   "We got the . . .": Jack Foote, interview, Toronto, May 14, 2003.

87   Park merchant ships: Law, *White Plumes Astern*, p. 69.

88   "craft-buzzed . . .": Ibid., p. 62.

89   "Initial Joint Plan": Stacey, *The Victory Campaign*, p. 69.

89   The prototype was . . . : Col. C. P. Stacey, *The Canadian Army*, p. 171.

90   Eastern Task Force: Schull, *The Far Distant Ships*, p. 239.

90   "like a vulture . . .": Winston Churchill, quoted in Schull, pp. 243–44.

90   230 surface ships: Schull, *The Far Distant Ships*, p. 244.

94   X-Craft: David Howarth, *Dawn of D-Day*, p. 197.

96   Nine war correspondents: A. E. Powley, *Broadcast from the Front*, pp. 87–88.

97   "The wardroom is . . .": Marcel Ouimet, CBC Radio Archives, June 6, 1944.

99   senior war correspondent: Powley, *Broadcast from the Front*, pp. 37–38.

99   "In the lounge . . .": Matthew Halton, CBC Radio Archives, June 6, 1944.

101   "God damn air . . .": Schull, *The Far Distant Ships*, p. 275.

101   "I could sense . . .": Desmond Piers, interview, Toronto, May 17, 1997.

102   "I respected the . . .": John H. Gorsline, interview, Don Mills, Ont., July 16, 2003.

104   "All during the night . . .": Gorsline, courtesy Dominion Institute, Memory Project, Toronto.

105   "We had been told . . .": Fred Turnbull, quoted in Jean Portugal (ed.), *We Were There: The Navy*, Vol. 1, p. 60.

106   "There were so many . . .": Phil Marchildon, *Ace: Canada's Pitching Sensation and Wartime Hero*, p. 117.

107   "We wound up . . .": Sam Levine, quoted in Ted Barris and Alex Barris, *Days of Victory*, pp. 159–60.

107 9,989 vehicles: Lt. Peter Ward, *Crowsnest Magazine*, Vol. 16, No. 5 (May 1964).

108 57,500 troops: Granatstein and Morton, *Bloody Victory*, p. 62.

CHAPTER FOUR

page

109 "If there was . . .": George Meakin, to his mother, Jennie Meakin, and sister Ellen, May 24, 1944, courtesy Cecil Pittman, Neepawa, Manitoba, 2003.

110 "The (Allied naval . . .": War Diary, Royal Winnipeg Rifles, June 6, 1944.

111 "None of you . . .": Frank Godon, quoted in Bill Redekop, "Mission: To conquer Hitler," *Winnipeg Free Press*, June 7, 2002.

111 "Belgian Gates": C. P. Stacey, *The Victory Campaign*, p. 69.

113 "I looked through . . .": Charles Belton, quoted in Jean Portugal (ed.), *We Were There: The Army*, Vol. 6, RCMI, p. 3042.

113 "Seven dead Canadian . . .": William Stewart, interview, Montreal, March 8, 2003.

114 The courage . . . : William Stewart, transcript of submission to Jean Portugal, *We Were There: The RCAF and Others*, Vol. 7, p. 3415.

114 "Imagine. They are . . .": Stewart, interview.

115 "I wondered if . . .": Stanley Todd, quoted in Portugal (ed.), *We Were There: The Army*, Vol. 4, p. 1810.

118 "to encounter and . . .": Ibid., p. 1804.

120 German aircraft: G. W. L. Nicholson, *The Gunners of Canada*, p. 272.

122 "There was no . . .": Wesley M. Alkenbrack, unpublished memoirs, with permission, September 2003.

123 earned Holtzman: Nicholson, *The Gunners of Canada*, p. 278.

124 "As we watched . . .": Stuart Tubb, quoted in Portugal (ed.), *We Were There: The Army*, Vol. 2, p. 905–6.

125 "Two young German . . .": Bernard Martin, interview, Courseulles-sur-Mer, June 5, 2003.

128 "The dirt track . . .": Stewart, transcription.

CHAPTER FIVE

page

131 "My tank went . . .": Bill Little, interview, Ottawa, April 18, 2003.

131 DD for Duplex Drive: John Marteinson, written presentations to Royal Military College, Kingston, Ont., Dec. 1999.

133 "Hobart's funnies": Howarth, *Dawn of D-Day*, pp. 169–70.

136 "I knelt for a second . . .": Hickey, *The Scarlet Dawn*, p. 164.

141 "I had done three . . .": Bob Cameron, interview, Thornhill, Ont., May 24, 2003.

143 "friendly fire": Stacey, p. 223.

144 The Dieppe hold: Bill Ross, unpublished memoirs, with permission Kirkland, Que., Dec. 28, 2002, p. 2.

144 An RAF Spitfire: Alex Kuppers, quoted in Jean Portugal (ed.), *We Were There: The Army*, Vol. 6, p. 3097.

145 "As we were going down . . .": Fred Barnard, interview, Uxbridge, Ont., July 20, 2003.

146 "You've got fifteen . . .": Joe Oggy, interview, Scarborough, Ont., Aug. 23, 1993.

147 Hodie non cras: A. Brandon Conron, *A History of the First Hussars 1856–1980*, p. 174.

147 "In the beginning . . .": Bruce Evans, interview, Etobicoke, Ont. Jan. 4, 2003.

149 "After launching . . .": Leo Gariepy, quoted in *A History of the First Hussars*, p. 55.

151 "We scored a . . .": Richard S. Malone, quoted in *A World in Flames*, p. 32.

151 CFPU cameraman: Lionel Shapiro, *Maclean's*, April 15, 1945.

152 "The commanding . . .": Chuck Ross, CFPU cameraman/driver interview, Edmonton, July 27, 2003.

153 "I picked up . . .": Brian O'Regan, quoted in letter from O'Regan to Carol Phillips, with permission, August 13, 1992.

153 "The first thing . . .": Ken Ewart, CFPU editor, interview, Fort Saskatchewan, Alta., July 27, 2003.

154 "The London papers . . .": Malone, *A World in Flames*, p. 32.

CHAPTER SIX

page

156 "Old Blood and Guts": Rohmer, *Patton's Gap*, p. 23.

157 500 serviceable: Saunders and Richards, *The Fight Is Won*, pp. 112–13.

158 "It was euphoric . . .": Rohmer, interview, Richmond Hill, Ont., July 29, 2003.

159 "You're not concerned . . .": Pierre Gauthier, interview, Chambly, Que., Aug. 4, 2003.

160 "these men seemed . . .": René Lévesque, *Memoirs*, p. 89.

163 Speed would be essential: Stacey, *The Victory Campaign*, Vol. III, p. 77.

163 "We trained for . . .": John Angus McDonald, interview, Cornwall, Ont., Dec. 14, 2002.

164 "to test the speed . . .": Lt.-Col. W. Boss, *The Stormont, Dundas and Glengarry Highlanders, 1783–1951*, p. 180.

165 "When the LCA": Charles Cline, interview, Toronto, May 21, 2003.

165 "Some of the guys . . .": Jimmy Wilson, interview, Toronto, July 22, 1993.

167 "demoralized": John Angus McDonald, correspondence, Cornwall, Ont., Jan. 17, 2003.

167 Resistance fighters: Jacques Vico and Jean Quellien, *Massacres Nazis en Normandie: Les fusillés de la prison de Caen*, 1994.

168 etched into the stone: Le Mémorial de Caen, archives/exhibits, June 2003.

168 "Suddenly we heard . . .": Jacques Martin, interview, Bernières-sur-Mer, France, June 3, 2003.

170 "From a Norman . . .": Marcel Ouimet, CBC Radio broadcast from June 6, 1944, courtesy CBC Radio Archives.

171 "first job . . .": Osborne Perry, interview, Courseulles-sur-Mer, France, June 6, 2003.

172 "The thing I remember . . .": Reg Weeks, interview, Ottawa, Ont., April 18, 2003.

174 just fifty miles: Granatstein and Morton, *Bloody Victory*, p. 20.

175 "Our regiment . . .": Gordon Drodge, interviewed by Alex Barris, Ottawa, Ont., Aug. 13, 1993.

CHAPTER SEVEN

page

177 prickly ego: Granatstein, and Morton, *Bloody Victory*, p. 35.

177 "We all went to . . .": Garth Webb, interview, Toronto, Ont., Mar. 4, 2003.

178 "you would not see . . .": Gen. Sir Bernard Montgomery, quoted in Stacey, *The Victory Campaign*, p. 47.

179 "The first vehicle . . .": Bill Warshick, correspondence, St. Catharines, Ont., Dec. 11, 1993.

180 "In the desperate . . .": Wesley M. Alkenbrack, unpublished memoirs with permission.

183 Their original eighteen: Nicholson, *The Gunners of Canada*, p. 279.

184 "You're pretty experienced": Garth Webb, quoted in Jean Portugal, *We Were There: The Army*, Vol. 4, pp. 1898–99.

185 "The saddest . . .": Tony Burns, unpublished memoirs with permission, March 10, 2003.

188 "The [British] . . .": Don Kerr, interview, Port Perry, Ont., Jan. 25, 2003.

190 Yellow smoke: Stacey, *The Victory Campaign*, p. 244.

191 fifty-six aboard: Schull, *The Far Distant Ships*, p. 283.

191 "Around noon . . .": Dr. Paul G. Schwager, unpublished memoirs with permission, 1994.

192 "There was a hell . . .": John Gorsline, interview, Toronto, Ont., July 16, 2003.

193 "Okay if my sergeant . . .": Mary Lea Bell, interview, Gibsons Landing, B.C., July 27, 2003.

194 "The experience of . . .": Bell, *Not in Vain*, p. 7.

196 invasion front: Ambrose, *D-Day June 6, 1944*, p. 577.

CHAPTER EIGHT

page

197 Operation CA: Schull, *The Far Distant Ships*, pp. 260–61.

198 "The submarine . . .": George Devonshire, correspondence, Picton, Ont., Aug. 24, 1993.

199 "This was no ordinary . . .": Russell McKay, *One of Many*, p. 82.

200 "code-named Mallard: Saunders and Richards, *The Fight Is Won*, Vol. III, pp. 113–14.

200 "I was coming back . . .": Walter Schierer, interview, Port Hope, Ont., Feb. 19, 2003.

202 "We met in a briefing . . .": Fred Sampson, interview, Port Hope, Ont., Dec. 30, 2002.

208 240 glider pilots: Ellis Plaice, *Red Berets, '44* (Official Publication of the Airborne Forces), *The Illustrated London News*, London, 1994, p. 98.

208 "singularly successful": Saunders and Richards, *The Fight Is Won*, p. 114.

211 fifty E-boats: Schull, *The Far Distant Ships*, p. 244.

211 "It was our job . . .": Fred Walden, interview, Scarborough, Ont., May 14, 2003.

213 "We would be directed . . .": Jack Foote, interview, Scarborough, Ont., May 14, 2003.

213 3,000 yards: J. B. Borthwick, *History of the 29th Canadian Motor Torpedo Boat Flotilla*, p. 22.

213 "Maximum speed . . .": Tony Law, Halifax, *White Plumes Astern*, p. 75.

215 "a congestion of cement": Ibid, p. 62.

217 "On the way over . . .": Scott Young, interview conducted by Alex Barris, Peterborough, Ont., July 12, 1993.

219 "History is standing . . .": Shapiro, *Canada at War*, p. 170.

220 "A seasoned correspondent": K. Napier-Moore, "In the Editor's Confidence," *Maclean's*, Feb. 1, 1944.

220 "burning Canadianism": Ross Munro, quoted in Carl Mollins, "Giant of the Times," *Maclean's*, June 4, 2001, p. 26.

220 "Darkness was falling . . .": Shapiro, *Canada at War*, p. 176.

CHAPTER NINE

page

221 "This is a national . . .": Earl Cameron, CBC news, excerpted in film *Canada at War: The Norman Summer*, National Film Board of Canada, Canadian War Museum.

222 their D-Day final objective: John Marteinson, discussion paper, "The Battle of Normandy: The Landings and Break-in," Dec. 1999, p. 6.

222 "the longest day": Cornelius Ryan, *The Longest Day*, p. 224.

224 "As we were moving . . .": Hubert Thistle, interview, St. John's, Nfld., Aug. 24, 1993.

225 degree of barbarity: Stacey, *The Victory Campaign*, p. 129.

227 beyond recognition: Campbell, *Murder at the Abbaye*, p. 105.

229 "Two Bren gun units . . .": Mark Lockyer, interview, Oshawa, Ont., March 3, 2003.

231 "Anything you see . . .": E. J. Aveling, quoted in passage of *Critical Moments: Profiles of Members of the Greater Vancouver Branch of the Aircrew Association*, Aircrew Association, 1989, p. 299.

234 "Most people in . . .": Monty Berger, quoted in *Invasions Without Tears*, p. xi.

234 "We tried . . .": Brown, editor, *Invasion Diary*, p. 7.

235 "We worked hard . . .": Cliff Robb, interview by Bill McNeil, *Fresh Air*, CBC Radio, May 5, 1974.

236 "When we lowered . . .": Charley Fox, interview, Toronto, Ont., March 6, 2003.

237 22,373 sorties: Berger, pp. 215–16.

237 "I remember when . . .": John More, interview, York, Maine, Aug. 27, 2003.

238 "Where there were . . .": W. Ray Stephens, *The Canadian Entertainers of World War II*, 1993.

239 "We'd go on leave . . .": Gene More, interview, Peterborough, Ont., Aug. 28, 2003.

240 "While I sat . . .": Ruth Carmichael, quoted in *Days of Victory*, Dec. 1943, p. 158.

240 "At approximately 0045 . . .": War Diary, No. 3 Detachment, 15th Canadian Auxiliary Service Section, Aug. 5, 1944.

241 "at all times . . .": Lt. J. B. Hay, letter to Mary Beatrice More, Uxbridge, Ont., Aug. 23, 1944.

243 "Doesn't sound . . .": King of Norway, quoted in Powley, *Broadcast from the Front*, p. 95.

243 "A half-hour . . .": Stewart, transcript of submission to Jean Portugal (ed.) with permission, *We Were There: The RCAF and Others*, Vol. 7, p. 3420.

244 "Send us some paper . . .": Powley, *Broadcast from the Front*, p. 92.

244 "By the night of . . .": Matthew Halton, CBC Radio, June 20, 1944.

245 non-commissioned outlook: Trent Frayne, Ralph Allen profile, *Liberty* magazine, March 10, 1945, p. 19.

245 "I never see . . .": Ralph Allen, quoted in Ibid.

245 "In God's good . . .": Winston Churchill, quoted in Schull, *The Far Distant Ships*, p. 359.

246 "How far away . . .": Churchill, *The Second World War: Triumph and Tragedy*, p. 12.

246 "service guys": Bénamou, *10 Million Tons for Victory*, p. 20.

247 "Our vessel was tied . . .": Walter Filbrandt, telephone interview, St. Lucia, West Indies, Sept. 21, 2003.

249 road to nationhood: Berton, *Marching as to War*, p. 180.

249 place in the world: Granatstein and Desmond Morton, "The Great Crusade," *Toronto Star*, June 6, 1994.

250 "we've been paying . . .": Bob Cameron, letter to Betty Beaton, Normandy, June 9, 1944.

251 "an astonishing feat . . .": Jack Granatstein and Desmond Morton, *Bloody Victory*, p. 58.

251 "set a standard . . .": Maj-Gen Meade Dennis, quoted in Portugal, p. 1801.

251 "one of the most . . .": Copp, *Fields of Fire*, 2003, p. 13.

CHAPTER TEN

page

254 "A cart came along . . .": Donald James, interview on ferry from Calais to Folkestone, June 17, 1994, with permission from daughters Penny Adair and Beverly Vasey.

255 "I remember in . . .": Beverly (James) Vasey, interview, Courseulles-sur-Mer, France, June 4, 2003.

255 "Every night . . .": Penny (James) Adair, interview, Courseulles-sur-Mer, France, June 4, 2003.

255 "the Battle of . . .": German, *The Sea Is at Our Gates*, p. 98.

255 cost the Allies: Dunmore, *In Great Waters*, 1999.

256 "All we knew . . .": Hall Whitten, interview, Toronto, Oct. 3, 2003.

257 "The first landing . . .": Richard Rohmer, interview, Toronto, July 29, 2003.

258 "This one day . . .": Don Kerr, interview, Port Perry, Ont., Jan. 25, 2003.

260 "bazaar held in . . .": Lise Cooper, interview, Toronto, Mar. 4, 2003.

261 "Members of my family . . .": Roger Alexandre, interview, Le Mesnil-Patry, France, June 5, 2003.

263 "We would have . . .": Don Cooper, interview, Toronto, Mar. 4, 2003.

264 "The responses in . . .": Lise Cooper, Mar. 4, 2003.

265 "Canada, the forgotten . . .": Ted Davie, at CBC meeting in Toronto, Mar. 2003.

266 "Right from the . . .": John Clemes, interview, Courseulles-sur-Mer, France, June 6, 2003.

268 "You were more . . .": Jean Chrétien at Juno Beach Centre, France, June 6, 2003.

268 "In the evening . . .": Jean-Pierre Raffarin at Juno Beach Centre, France, June 6, 2003.

269 "I shed a few . . .": Hal Whitten, interview, Toronto, Oct. 3, 2003.

269 "I had been . . .": Richard Rohmer interview, July 29, 2003.

270 "Any war of . . .": Jean-Louis de Mourgues at Juno Beach Centre, France, June 6, 2003.

271 "I fought . . .": Don Kerr, interview, Jan. 25, 2003.

271 "The Grey Cup . . .": Garth Webb, interview, Toronto, Mar. 4, 2003.

272 "I knew the trip . . .": Tony Burns, unpublished memoirs with permission, Halifax, Mar. 10, 2003.

273 "I was always . . .": Bill Lockyer, interview, Nestleton, Ont., Sept. 17, 2003.

273 "He found a couple . . .": Roberta Sommerville, interview, Nestleton, Ont., Sept. 17, 2003.

274 Thankful and proud: Serenity Corlett-Lockyer, correspondence, Sept. 2003.

274 "I got choked up . . .": Mark Lockyer, interview, Oshawa, Ont., July 7, 2003.

Glossary

AB	Able Seaman
ABC	Airborne Cigar radio jamming device
ack-ack	anti-aircraft gunfire
ACM	Air Chief Marshal
AG	airgunner
AOC	Air Officer Commanding
ASDIC	underwater locator device derived from acronym for Anti-Submarine Detection Investigation Committee
AVM	Air Vice-Marshal
AVRE	assault vehicle, Royal Engineers
BBC	British Broadcasting Corporation
Belgian Gates	obstacles like those erected at the Belgium–Germany border
bobbin	steel mesh matting to cover unstable ground
Bofors gun	anti-aircraft gun used by British and Canadian troops
Bren gun	light weight .303 calibre machine gun (blend of *Br*no, the Czech city where it was originally made, and *En*field, town in southern England where it was made under licence)
Bn.	battalion
Brig.	Brigadier
Calvados	Normandy region and fruit-based liqueur
Capt.	Captain
carley	life raft
casualty	killed, wounded, or missing in action

CB	confined to barracks
CBC	Canadian Broadcasting Corporation
CBs	confidential books (navy) containing top secret D-Day instructions
CFPU	Canadian Film and Photo Unit
Cmdr.	Commander
CMNSU	Canadian Mobile Neuro-Surgical Unit
CO	Commanding Officer
Col.	Colonel
coned	caught in a concentration of searchlight beams
corncob	ship scuttled as a breakwater for Mulberry harbour
COSSAC	Chief of Staff to the Supreme Allied Commander
COTC	Canadian Officers Training Corps
Cpl.	Corporal
crab	Sherman tank with a revolving flail attached in front
crocodile	flame-throwing tank
Dan buoy	temporary buoy
DD	Duplex Drive tanks (amphibious)
D-Day	"D" is the military symbol meaning the day "it" happens; the *Dictionary of Military and Associated Terms* defines D-Day as "an unannounced day on which a particular operation commences or is to commence"
dead-reckoning	air navigation by use of predetermined vectors of wind and true airspeed and pre-calculated heading, ground speed, and estimated time of arrival, i.e. a calculated guess
DFC	Distinguished Flying Cross
DFM	Distinguished Flying Medal
Div.	division
DZ	drop zone for paratroopers
E-boat	*Raumboote* and *Schnellboote*, euphemistically lumped together as "enemy" boat
Element C	beach obstacles
Enigma	German encoding device
ESNA	Entertainments National Service Association
fascine	bundle of logs used to fill anti-tank ditches
Fd.	field
Firefly	Sherman tank with 17-pounder gun
fishpond	airborne radar
F/L	Flight Lieutenant

F/O	Flying Officer
FW	Focke-Wulf, German aircraft
fo'c'sle	forecastle, the upper deck of a ship in front of the foremast
FOO	Forward Observation Officer
Freya	long-range German radar

G/C	Group Captain
Gen.	General
gooseberry	ship scuttled as a breakwater for Mulberry harbour
Gp.	Group
GPO	Gun Position Officer
Gnr.	Gunner

Hamilcar	glider
Happy Valley	Ruhr Valley
HMCS	His Majesty's Canadian Ship
Hitlerjugend	Hitler youth soldiers
HMS	His Majesty's Ship
Horsa	glider
Hotspur	glider
HQ	headquarters

Inf.	infantry
IO	Intelligence Officer

jostle	radio jamming device
Ju	Junkers, German aircraft

KRAI	King's Rules and Admiralty Instruction
Kriegsmarine	German Navy

LAC	Leading Aircraftman
LCA	landing craft, assault
LCI	landing craft, infantry
L/Cpl.	Lance Corporal
LCT	landing craft, tanks
L/Sgt.	Lance Sergeant
Lee Enfield	army issue .303 bolt-action rifle
Lieut. or Lt.	Lieutenant
LSI	landing ship, infantry
L/Stkr.	leading stoker
Lt.-Col.	Lieutenant-Colonel

Luftwaffe	German Air Force
LZ	landing zone for gliders
Mae West	lifejacket
Maj.	Major
Mandrel	radar interference device
MC	Military Cross
Me.	Messerschmitt, German aircraft
MID	Mentioned in Despatches
Mike	Juno Beach sector
mm	millimetre
MM	Military Medal
Moaning Mini	German mortar bomb
MTB	motor torpedo boat
NAAFI	Navy, Army, and Air Force Institutes
Nan	Juno Beach sector
NCO	non-commissioned officer
NET	Non-Effective Transfer or shell-shocked troop area
OC	Officer Commanding
oerlikon	20-mm naval guns
Op(s)	Operation(s) against the enemy
Operation CA	naval protective patrols in English Channel
Operation Fortitude	deception plan in Dover area
Operation Gambit	X-Craft mini-subs to ships to invasion beaches
Operation Jubilee	raid on Dieppe Aug. 21, 1942
Operation Mallard	paratroop drop in Normandy evening of D-Day
Operation Neptune	D-Day invasion phase of Overlord
Operation Overlord	overall invasion plan for German-occupied Europe
Operation Taxable	spoofing operations over English Channel
Operation Tractable	advance to capture Falaise
Oropesa	float tethered to stern of minesweeper
ORA	operating room assistant
Panzer	German tank regiment
para	paratrooper
petard	bomb-throwing tanks
PHE	plastic high explosive
phoenix	concrete caisson for Mulberry harbour
PIAT	Projector, Infantry, Anti-Tank
Piccadilly Circus	Operation Neptune assembly area off English south coast

Pioneer	explosives expert in Royal Canadian Engineers
P/O	Petty Officer *or* Pilot Officer
pom-pom	single or multi-barrelled automatic gun firing two-pound shell
POW	prisoner of war
Priest	self-propelled artillery vehicle
Pte.	Private
RAF	Royal Air Force
RAP	Regimental Aid Post
Rating	any non-commissioned sailor
Raumboote	German minesweeper equivalent of motor launch
RCA	Royal Canadian Artillery
RCAF	Royal Canadian Air Force
RCAMC	Royal Canadian Army Medical Corps
RCCS	Royal Canadian Corps of Signals
RCE	Royal Canadian Engineers
recce.	reconnaissance flight
Rfn.	Rifleman
RMC	Royal Military College (Kingston)
roly-poly	steel mesh matting to cover unstable ground
Rommel's asparagus	anti-glider poles erected in Normandy
RSM	Regimental Sergeant Major
Sapper	explosive and engineering soldier in Royal Canadian Engineers
Satan's Quadrangle	drop zone flooded by German
Schnellboote	German gunboat
Sgt.	Sergeant
SHAEF	Supreme Headquarters, Allied Expeditionary Force
S/L	Squadron Leader
S/L	Sub-lieutenant
SP	self-propelled artillery vehicle
Spud	pierhead for Mulberry harbour
Sqn.	Squadron
S.S.	Schutzstaffel (Nazi party organization including military formations)
Staff Sgt.	Staff Sergeant
Standartenfurher	S.S. Col. Kurt Meyer
starshell	shell designed to explode and illuminate in the air
Sten gun	light weight 9-mm caliber sub-machine gun (named for *S*heppard and *T*urpin, the inventors and *En*gland)
stick	a group of about 10 to 20 paratroopers

TAF	Tactical Air Force of Allies once in France
tinsel	noise transmission device
TRE	British Telecommunications Research Establishment
Tpr.	Trooper
U-boat	German submarine
ULTRA	British counter-intelligence file on German wartime activities
USO	United Service Organization
Vergeltungswaffen-1	V-1 flying bomb
W/C	Wing Commander
Wehrmacht	German Army
Widerstandsnester	resistance nests
Winco	Wing Commander
window	tinfoil strips released in air to confuse German radar
Würzburgs	short-range German radar

Bibliography

Allen, Ralph. *Ordeal by Fire*. Toronto: Doubleday Canada, 1961.

Ambrose, Stephen E. *D-Day, June 6, 1944: The Climactic Battle of World War II*. New York: Simon and Schuster, 1994.

Barris, Ted. *Behind the Glory: The Plan that Won the Allied Air War*. Toronto: Macmillan Canada, 1992.

Barris, Ted, and Alex Barris. *Days of Victory: Canadians Remember 1939–1945*. Toronto: Macmillan Canada, 1995.

Bell, Ken. *Not in Vain*. Toronto: University of Toronto Press, 1973.

Bénamou, Jean-Pierre. *10 Million Tons for Victory*. Cully, France: OREP Editions, 2003.

Benedict, Michael, ed. *Canada at War*. Toronto, Penguin, 1998.

Benedict, Michael, ed. *Canada at War: Volume II*. Toronto: Penguin, 2002.

Berger, Monty, and Brian Jeffrey Street. *Invasions Without Tears*. Toronto: Random House of Canada, 1994.

Berton, Pierre. *Marching as to War: Canada's Turbulent Years, 1899–1953*. Toronto: Doubleday, 2001.

Borthwick, J. B. *History of the 29th Canadian Motor Torpedo Boat Flotilla*. Winnipeg: The Naval Museum of Manitoba, n.d.

Boss, Lt.-Col. W. *The Stormont, Dundas and Glengarry Highlanders, 1783–1951*. Ottawa: Runge Press, 1952.

Broadfoot, Barry. *Six War Years: 1939-1945*. Toronto: Doubleday, 1974.

Brown, Gordon and Terry Copp. *Look to Your Front . . . Regina Rifles, A Regiment at War: 1944–45*. Waterloo: Laurier Centre for Military Strategic and Disarmament Studies, 2001.

Brown, Mary L. ed. *Invasion Diary: The Diary of Richard W. Brown with RCAF's 127th Wing, 1944–1945*. Toronto: Pro Familia Publishing, 1994.

Campbell, Ian J. *Murder at the Abbaye*. Ottawa: Golden Dog Press, 1996.

Campbell, Ralph. *We Flew by Moonlight*. Orillia: Kerry Hill Publications, 1988.

Churchill, Winston. *The Second World War: Hinge of Fate* (vol. IV): Boston: Houghton Mifflin, 1950.

Churchill, Winston. *The Second World War: Closing the Ring* (vol. V). Boston: Houghton Mifflin, 1950.

Churchill, Winston. *The Second World War: Triumph and Tragedy* (vol. VI). Boston: Houghton Mifflin, 1950.

Copp, Terry. *Battlefields of Northwest Europe*. Waterloo, Ontario: Laurier Centre for Military Strategic and Disarmament Studies, 1995.

Copp, Terry. *Fields of Fire: The Canadians in Normandy*. Toronto: University of Toronto Press, 2003.

Conron, A. Brandon. *A History of the First Hussars 1856–1980*. London, Ontario: First Hussars Regiment, 1981.

Dunmore, Spencer. *In Great Waters: The Epic Story of the Battle of the Atlantic*. Toronto: McClelland & Stewart, 1999.

German, Tony. *The Sea Is at Our Gates: The History of the Canadian Navy*. Toronto: McClelland & Stewart, 1990.

Golley, John. *So Many: A Folio Dedicated to All Who Served with RAF Bomber Command, 1939–45*. Toronto: Macmillan Canada, 1995.

Granatstein, J. L., and Desmond Morton. *Bloody Victory: Canadians and the D-Day Campaign, 1944*. Toronto: Lester & Orpen Dennys, 1984.

Hartigan, Dan. *A Rising of Courage*. Calgary: Drop Zone Publishers, 2000.

Hickey, Rev. R. M. *The Scarlet Dawn*. Fredericton, New Brunswick: Unipress, 1980.

Horn, Lt.-Col. Bernd, and Michel Wyczynski. *Tip of the Spear: An Intimate Account of 1 Canadian Parachute Battalion, 1942–1945*. Toronto: Dundurn, 2002.

Howarth, David. *Dawn of D-Day*. London: William Collins, 1959.

Jones, R. V. *Most Secret War*. London: Hamish Hamilton, 1978.

Keegan, John. *Six Armies in Normandy*. London: Jonathan Cape, 1982.

Kemp, Anthony. *D-Day: The Normandy Landings and the Liberation of Europe*, London: Thames and Hudson, 1994.

Law, C. Anthony. *White Plumes Astern*. Halifax: Nimbus Publishing, 1989.

Lévesque, René. *Memoirs*. Toronto: McClelland and Stewart, 1986.

Lynn, Vera. *We'll Meet Again: A Personal and Social History of World War Two*. London: Sidgwick & Jackson, 1989.

Macpherson, Ken. *Minesweepers of the Royal Canadian Navy, 1938–1945*. St. Catharines, Ontario: Vanwell Publishing, 1990.

Malone, Richard S. *A World in Flames, 1944–45*. Toronto: Collins, 1984.

Marchildon, Phil. *Ace: Canada's Pitching Sensation and Wartime Hero*. Toronto: Penguin Books, 1993.

Marteinson, John, and Michael R. McNorgan. *The Royal Canadian Armoured Corps: An Illustrated History*. Toronto: Robin Brass Studio, 2000.

Messenger, Charles. *World War Two Chronological Atlas*. London: Bloomsbury, 1989.

Middlebrook, Martin, and Chris Everitt. *The Bomber Command War Diaries: An Operational Reference Book, 1939–1945*. London: Penguin, 1985.

McCaffery, Dan. *Air Aces: The Lives and Times of Twelve Canadian Fighter Pilots*. Toronto: James Lorimer, 1990.

McKay, Russell. *One of Many*. Burnstown, Ontario: General Store Publishing, 1989.

Munro, Ross. *Gauntlet to Overlord*. Vancouver: Macmillan of Canada, 1945.

Nicholson, Col. G. W. L. *The Gunners of Canada: The History of the Royal Regiment of Canadian Artillery*. Toronto: McClelland and Stewart, 1972.

Nijboer, Donald. *Cockpit: An Illustrated History of World War II Aircraft Interiors*. Erin, Ontario: Boston Mills Press, 1998.

Peden, Murray. *A Thousand Shall Fall*. Toronto: Stoddart, 1988.

Portugal, Jean, ed. *We Were There: A Record for Canada*. 7 vols. Toronto: Royal Canadian Military Institute Heritage Society, 1998.

Powley, A. E. *Broadcast from the Front: Canadian Radio Overseas in the Second World War*. Toronto: Hakkert, 1975.

The RCAF Overseas: The First Four Years (vol. I). Toronto: Oxford University Press, 1944.

The RCAF Overseas: The Fifth Year (vol. II). Toronto: Oxford University Press, 1944.

The RCAF Overseas: The Sixth Year (vol. III). Toronto: Oxford University Press, 1944.

Richards, Denis, and Hilary St. George Saunders. *Royal Air Force, 1939–1945*, Vol. III, *The Fight Is Won*. London: Her Majesty's Stationery, 1954.

Rohmer, Richard. *Patton's Gap: Mustangs Over Normandy*. Toronto: Stoddart, 1998.

Ryan, Cornelius. *The Longest Day*. New York: Simon and Shuster, 1959.

Saunders, Hilary St. George, and Denis Richards. *Royal Air Force 1939–45: The Fight Is Won* (vol. III). London: Her Majesty's Stationery Office, 1954.

Schull, Joseph. *The Far Distant Ships: An Official Account of Canadian Naval Operations in the Second World War*. Ottawa: Queen's Printer, 1961.

Shapiro, Lionel. *Canada at War*. Toronto: Penguin, 1997.

Stacey, Col. C. P. *The Canadian Army, 1939–1945: An Official Historical Summary*. Ottawa: DND/King's Printer, 1948.

Stacey, Col. C. P., *The Victory Campaign: The Operations in North-West Europe, 1944–1945*, Vol. III, *Official History of the Canadian Army in the Second World War*. Ottawa: Department of National Defence, 1960.

Stephens, W. Ray. *The Canadian Entertainers of World War II*. Oakville, Ontario: Mosaic Press, 1993.

Various. *Critical Moments: Profiles of Members of the Greater Vancouver Branch of the Aircrew Association*, Aircrew Association, 1989.

Vico, Jacques, and Jean Quellien. *Massacres Nazis en Normandie: Les fusillés de la prison de Caen*. Editions Charles Corlet, 1994.

Wallechinsky, David, and Irving Wallace. *The People's Almanac*. Toronto: Bantam, 1982.

Whitaker, Denis, and Shelagh Whitaker. *Dieppe: Tragedy to Triumph*. Toronto: McGraw-Hill Ryerson, 1992.

Willes, John A. *Out of the Clouds*. Port Perry, Ontario: Port Perry Printing, 1981.

Photograph Credits

12 DD tank Library and Archives Canada PA-132897; Little courtesy Fort Garry Horse Museum and Archives; Hobart's Funnies Library and Archives Canada PA-116523

SECOND SECTION

page

1 Munro Library and Archives Canada PA-136206; Cameron courtesy Bob Cameron; Shapiro, Stewart, Munro Library and Archives Canada PA-167541

2 Grant and film still courtesy the Ken Bell collection; Ross courtesy Chuck Ross

3 all courtesy Fred Barnard

4 McDonald brothers courtesy John Angus McDonald; wading ashore Library and Archives Canada PA-122765

5 1st Hussars Library and Archives Canada PA-128791; Welcoming French civilians Library and Archives Canada PA-133748; "Up the Glens" Library and Archives Canada PA-138272

6 Priest tank Library and Archives Canada PA-132886; Webb and Bell courtesy Mary Lea Bell

7 ambulance Library and Archives Canada PA-129031; Burns courtesy Tony Burns; hospital Library and Archives Canada PA-132723

8 "Shytot" courtesy Fred Sampson; Schierer courtesy Walter Schierer; gliders courtesy 1st Canadian Parachute Battalion Association Archives

9 MTB Library and Archives Canada PA-144587; MTB *459* Library and Archives Canada PA-108024; MTB skirmish Library and Archives Canada PA-127038

10 marching prisoners Library and Archives Canada PA-133742; mines Library and Archives Canada PA-131441; strategy room PA-131438

11 Tin Hats D HIST DND 5043; Thistle courtesy Hubert Thistle; Mulberry Harbours Library and Archives Canada PA-143801

12 Webb and Kerr from the author's collection; Juno Beach Centre courtesy Bochsler PhotoImaging

Index of Formations, Units, and Corps

General Index

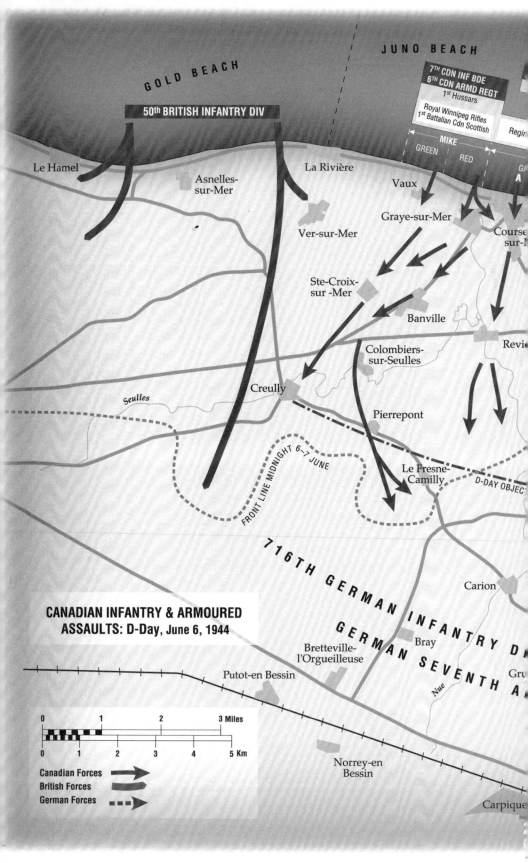

GOLD BEACH

JUNO BEACH

50th BRITISH INFANTRY DIV

7TH CDN INF BDE
6TH CDN ARMD REGT
1st Hussars

Royal Winnipeg Rifles
1st Battalion Cdn Scottish

Regir

MIKE

GREEN | RED

G
A

Le Hamel

Asnelles-
sur-Mer

La Rivière

Vaux

Ver-sur-Mer

Graye-sur-Mer

Cours
sur-

Ste-Croix-
sur -Mer

Banville

Revi

Colombiers-
sur-Seulles

Seulles

Creully

Pierrepont

Le Fresne-
Camilly

D-DAY OBJEC

FRONT LINE MIDNIGHT 6–7 JUNE

7 1 6 T H   G E R M A N   I N F A N T R Y

Carion

G E R M A N   I N F A N T R Y   D

CANADIAN INFANTRY & ARMOURED
ASSAULTS: D-Day, June 6, 1944

Bretteville-
l'Orgueilleuse

Bray

G E R M A N   S E V E N T H   A

Gr

Putot-en Bessin

Nue

0   1   2   3 Miles

0   1   2   3   4   5 Km

Canadian Forces
British Forces
German Forces

Norrey-en
Bessin

Carpique